Syntactic Change in Akkadian

Syntactic Change in Akkadian

The Evolution of Sentential Complementation

GUY DEUTSCHER

St John's College, Cambridge

OXFORD
UNIVERSITY PRESS

OXFORD
UNIVERSITY PRESS

Great Clarendon Street, Oxford OX2 6DP
Oxford University Press is a department of the University of Oxford.
It furthers the University's objective of excellence in research, scholarship,
and education by publishing worldwide in

Oxford New York

Athens Auckland Bangkok Bogotá Buenos Aires Calcutta Cape Town
Chennai Dar es Salaam Delhi Florence Hong Kong Istanbul Karachi
Kuala Lumpur Madrid Melbourne Mexico City Mumbai Nairobi
Paris São Paulo Shanghai Singapore Taipei Tokyo Toronto Warsaw

with associated companies in Berlin Ibadan

Oxford is a registered trade mark of Oxford University Press
in the UK and in certain other countries

Published in the United States
by Oxford University Press Inc., New York

First published 2000

British Library Cataloguing in Publication Data
Data available

Library of Congress Cataloging in Publication Data
Deutscher, Guy, Dr.
Syntactic change in Akkadian: the evolution of sentential complementation / Guy Deutscher.
p. cm.
Includes bibliographical references and index.
1. Akkadian language—Grammar, Historical. 2. Akkadian language—Complement.
3. Akkadian language—Syntax. I. Title.
PJ3241.D48 2000 492′.15—dc21

ISBN 0–19–829988–5

10 9 8 7 6 5 4 3 2 1

Typeset in Minion
by Peter Kahrel, Lancaster
Printed in Great Britain
on acid-free paper by
Biddles Ltd., Guildford and King's Lynn

לאמי ולאבי זכרונו לברכה

כִּי הָיִיתָ מַחְסֶה לִי מִגְדַּל עֹז מִפְּנֵי אוֹיֵב

Contents

Part III Functional History: The Changes in the Functional Domain of Complementation from 2500 BC to 500 BC

Part IV The Development of Complementation as an Adaptive Process

Preface

Akkadian has rarely been the object of diachronic linguistic investigation, although it is one of the earliest and longest attested languages. In fact, Akkadian is rarely examined from a general linguistic perspective at all. This study offers a slightly unusual combination of concrete philological analysis and broader theoretical debate. These two areas, however, are clearly separated. The detailed presentation of the diachronic developments does not depend on the theoretical interpretation offered for them.

I hope that this book will be of interest both to specialists in the language, and to a general linguistic audience. As a case study, this book makes a contribution to a historical grammar of the Akkadian language. The Assyriological literature often preaches the need for such a grammar, but seldom follows such preaching in practice. Assyriologists may therefore find some parts of this study useful, even if its agenda is primarily linguistic, and the presentation correspondingly unfamiliar. (A glossary of some linguistic terms is provided at the end of the book. Assyriologists will also have to be patient with my attempts to present Akkadian texts in normalization. These attempts are necessary in order to make the examples comprehensible to those who are not familiar with the peculiarities of the writing system.) On the other hand, I hope that linguists may find interest not only in the theoretical discussion of the nature of complementation and its development, but also in the case study itself. Akkadian is not often presented to a non-specialist audience, probably because of the impenetrability of its writing system. The case study may therefore open a window on an unfamiliar language that has enormous potential for linguistic investigation.

It is my pleasure to thank the many people from whom I received help and advice. This book is based on my doctoral dissertation, submitted to Cambridge University in 1998. I am indebted to my supervisor, Dr April McMahon, for all her generous help and support during the writing of the dissertation. I am especially grateful to Professors Nicholas Postgate and Peter Matthews. Nicholas Postgate not only taught me Akkadian, but also gave up much of his precious time to offer vital insights and advice. I owe to him countless improved readings and corrections of interpretation, too many to be acknowledged in the text. Peter Matthews gave invaluable guidance in the linguistic issues at hand throughout all stages of my research. I greatly profited from many helpful comments, corrections, and excellent suggestions for improvement from Dr Jeremy Black, Professor J. Huehnergard, and especially from Professor D. O. Edzard.

I would like to thank Professor S. Parpola, for permission to use the computerized Corpus of Neo-Assyrian in the University of Helsinki; Dr R. Whiting, for teaching me how to use the search mechanisms of the Corpus during my visit to Helsinki in January 1997; Professor K. R. Veenhof, for allowing me to use the Old Babylonian material in Leiden, and L. Sassmannshausen, for permission to use his unpublished edition of the Middle Babylonian letters from Nippur.

I am also grateful to Professor Bob Dixon, Professor K. R. Veenhof, Dr Bill Croft, Dr Geoffrey Khan, Professor John Emerton, Matthias Müller, Kim Schulte, and Jo Willmott, for valuable and constructive comments, Professor M. Stol, for help with dating some Old Babylonian letters, and especially Janie Steen, for correcting some of the more severe lapses of grammar and style. A research fellowship in St John's College, Cambridge, provided an ideal environment in which to complete this manuscript, and for this I am indebted to the Master and Fellows of St John's.

Last but not least, I want to thank my native Akkadian informants: Bēlšunu, Sin-iddinam, Etel-pī-Marduk, Šamaš-nāṣir, and all the others, without whose domestic quarrels, commercial hagglings, and political intrigues such a study would not have been possible.

G.D.

Abbreviations

1	1st person
2	2nd person
3	3rd person
AbB	Old Babylonian letters (Kraus 1964–94, vols. I–XIII)
ABL	Neo-Babylonian letters from Nineveh (see Sources, Text Editions)
ACC	accusative
BE	*Babylonian Expedition of the University of Pennsylvania, Series A: Cuneiform Texts* (Philadelphia: Dept. of Archaeology, University of Pennsylvania) (BE 17=Radau 1908)
BIN	Babylonian Inscriptions in the Collection of J. B. Nies (New Haven: Yale University Press, 1917–)
CAD	*The Assyrian Dictionary of the Oriental Institute of the University of Chicago*, editorial board John A. Brinkman et al.; editor-in-charge Erica Reiner (Chicago: Oriental Institute, 1956–)
CH	Code of Hammurabi (from Roth 1997)
Cole	Early Neo-Babylonian letters (Cole 1996)
COMP	complementizer
CT	*Cuneiform Texts from Babylonian Tablets in the British Museum* (London: British Museum) (CT 54: Neo-Babylonian letters from Nineveh; see Sources, Text Editions)
EA	Middle Babylonian El-Amarna letters (Knudtzon 1915)
EMPH	emphatic particle (see §3.5.5)
F	feminine
FDC	Functional Domain of Complementation (see §2.2)
GEN	genitive
GN	geographical name
IMP	imperative
INF	infinitive
KTU	Dietrich, Loretz, and Sanmartín 1976
Laws of Ešnunna	from Roth (1997)
M	masculine
MB	Middle Babylonian
NB	Neo-Babylonian
NG	Neo-Sumerian legal texts (Falkenstein 1956–7)
NOM	nominative
O	object

OAkk	Old Akkadian
OB	Old Babylonian
OED	Oxford English Dictionary
.of	construct state (see §3.5.2)
P	particle, usually the coordination or emphatic particle *-ma* (see §3.5.6)
PBS 1/2	Lutz 1919
PL	plural
PN	personal name
PN+	personal name + some title (e.g. Šamaš-hāzir the registrar)
QUOT	quotative
RA	*Revue d'assyriologie et d'archéologie orientale*
REL	relative
S	subject
SAB	Old Akkadian letters (Kienast and Volk 1995)
SG	singular
SUB	subordinative form of the verb (see §3.5.8)
SUBORD	the subordination/nominalization morpheme *-a* in Sumerian
TCL	*Textes cuneiformes* (Musée du Louvre: Département des antiquités orientales; Paris: P. Geuthner, 1910–)
UET	*Ur Excavations, Texts* (The Trustees of the British Museum and of the University of Pennsylvania Museum; London, 1928–)
UM	Tablets in the collection of the University Museum of the University of Pennsylvania, Philadelphia
V	verb
YOS	*Yale Oriental Series, Babylonian Texts* (New Haven: Yale University Press)

The following signs are used in textual transcription:

[text]	suggested restoration of broken signs
⸢text⸣	suggested restoration of partially broken signs
<text>	omission by the scribe
«text»	mistaken insertion by scribe
?	translation is uncertain
!	reading which does not agree with the copy

Sources, Text Editions

The Old Akkadian letters are quoted from Kienast and Volk (1995). Many of these letters are also edited in Michalowski (1993). A few other letters are from Foster (1990). Since material from this period is sparse, I also examine other texts, mainly royal inscriptions (Gelb and Kienast 1990).

Old Babylonian is attested in various dialects. My enquiry is limited to the dialect of Babylonia proper. I do not include examples from what are commonly known as 'peripheral' dialects. The very large corpus of texts from Mari is not included in this study either. The main edition for the Old Babylonian letters is the series *Altbabylonische Briefe in Umschrift und Übersetzung*, which contains thirteen volumes so far (see under Kraus 1964–94). Further letters used are from Al-A'dami (1967), Finkelstein (1965), Goetze (1958), Kienast (1978), Leemans (1960), Walters (1970), Whiting (1987). The legal documents are mainly from Schorr (1913).

Middle Babylonian letters in transliteration appear in Waschow (1936), Bernhardt and Aro (1958), Biggs (1965), Cornwall (1952), Gurney (1949), Lutz (1919) and Radau (1908). I was also able to use the unpublished edition of Middle Babylonian letters from Nippur by Leonhard Sassmannshausen. Knudtzon (1964) was used for the Babylonian Amarna letters, with improvements from von Soden (1952), and Moran (1992).

There are three main groups of Neo-Babylonian letters used here. The earliest group is from Nippur, dating from around 755–725 BC, published by Cole (1996). The second group is the Babylonian letters from the royal library in Nineveh, covering roughly a century from around 725 to 625 BC. They are abbreviated ABL and CT54, according to the cuneiform editions. The ABL letters are edited in the badly outdated edition of Waterman (1930). I was allowed to consult the improved computerized transliteration of these letters in the Corpus of Neo-Assyrian in the University of Helsinki. Some of these letters are also edited by Dietrich (1970), Parpola (1993), Cole and Machinist (1998), and de Vaan (1995). The latest group of letters is edited by Ebeling (1930–4, and 1949). These date mainly from the second half of the sixth century. Further texts consulted are from Moore (1935), and Cocquerillat (1968). Treatments of the grammar of Neo-Babylonian appear in Dietrich (1969), Woodington (1982), de Vaan (1995), and Hueter (1996).

Part I

Preliminary Chapters

1

Introduction

This book is both a study in the history of one particular area of one particular language, and a general investigation of the motivation for language change. The case study traces the development of some subordinate structures in the Babylonian dialect of Akkadian, one of the earliest written languages (*c.*2500 to 500 BC). The theoretical part of the study tries to interpret aspects of this development as an adaptation to the increased complexity of patterns of communication.

The richly attested history of Akkadian provides an opportunity to observe diachronic changes over a period of two thousand years. It also allows us to view syntactic change from both a structural and a functional perspective. This study examines the development of one class of subordinate structures, sentential complements, from these two perspectives. On the one hand, this study describes the emergence of new structures. It examines how finite sentential complements emerged for the first time from adverbial clauses during the historical period. It also describes the emergence of another structure, a quotative construction, through a long process of grammaticalization. On the other hand, this study traces the changes in the functional roles of different existing structures over time. The study thus attempts to describe the diachronic changes in the functional organization of the language system. We shall see that during the history of Akkadian, some structures, such as finite complements, gain in functional load, whereas other structures, such as infinitival complements, recede.

The theoretical part of this study attempts to view the changes in the functional organization of Akkadian in a general and comparative light. The developments in Akkadian are shown to have parallels in many other languages. I claim that finite complementation (and finite subordination in general) can deal more effectively with complex and elaborate propositions than alternative structures, and that this fact may be the motivation for the rise of finite complementation at the expense of other structures. The historical changes that we can observe in Akkadian and in other languages may thus be related to the development of more complex patterns of communication in more complex societies.

The structure of the book and its main arguments are outlined below.

Part I Preliminary Chapters

Chapter 2 lays out the linguistic foundations for the discussion, by tackling some problems in the prevailing interpretation of complementation. Sentential complements are often defined as clauses which function as subjects or objects of verbs. I argue, however, that this need not always be the case, and that some complements in fact function as 'oblique' arguments. Complements should therefore be understood in terms of the semantic category 'argument' rather than the surface categories 'object' and 'subject'. This interpretation of complementation will then help to explain various issues in the behaviour of finite complements which would otherwise seem perplexing, and in particular it will clarify how adverbial clauses can develop into finite complements.

I also point out the difficulties in examining 'complementation' from a cross-linguistic perspective. Different languages (or different diachronic stages of the same language) can use different structures to perform similar functions. For this reason, a valid comparison between languages needs to examine the role not only of complements, but also of other structures (such as parataxis), which can perform similar functions. This study differentiates between two concepts: 'complementation' (the embedding of a clause as an argument of a predicate), and the 'Functional Domain of Complementation', which includes complements as well as other strategies that perform similar functions. The study is not only concerned with complementation, but also with the historical development of the Functional Domain of Complementation as a whole.

Chapter 3 is a brief introduction to Akkadian, for the benefit of linguists who are not familiar with the language. The chapter outlines the history of Akkadian, and the role of the Babylonian dialect in particular. This diachronic study is based mainly on a large corpus of letters. The chapter describes this genre of texts, and explains why the letters are ideally suited for a diachronic linguistic investigation. It also outlines a few general points of Akkadian grammar.

Part II Structural History: The Emergence of Complementizers and Quotatives

The two chapters in Part II examine the emergence of new structures.

Chapter 4 describes how finite complements developed from adverbial clauses, only during the historical period. At the heart of this development was a process of semantic change, in which the adverbial conjunction *kīma* was 'bleached' of its causal meaning and emerged as a 'factive' complementizer.[1] That adverbial clauses should develop into complements may appear problematic from a structural point of view, especially if one makes the (unjustified) assumption that sentential complements have to function as objects. I try to show,

[1] Some linguists use the term 'complementizer' for conjunctions which introduce any subordinate clause. In this book, however, the term 'complementizer' is reserved for conjunctions which introduce a complement clause. Relative particles and adverbial subordinators will not be called complementizers.

however, that with a better understanding of the nature of sentential complements, this development in fact seems natural and unproblematic. Moreover, there are parallels to such developments in other languages. The chapter also examines another path through which finite complements emerged, with two specific verbs which I call the 'proving' verbs. This path involves the merging of two distinct arguments of the verb into one complement clause, and passes through intermediary stages that display close similarity to 'raising' (or 'proleptic') constructions.

Chapter 5 describes the development of the quotative construction in Babylonian, which can serve as a 'model textbook example' of a process of grammaticalization. The chapter follows the quotative construction through a long time span, and describes how it undergoes a process of reduction over a period of two thousand years. What had started as a whole independent clause (meaning roughly '(this is what) X said') was then gradually reduced in both form and meaning. It first became a direct quotation marker, and finally developed into a more general complementizer. The chapter also explores some of the many parallels to this development in other languages.

Part III Functional History: The Changes in the Functional Domain of Complementation from 2500 BC to 500 BC

The functional history in Part III is not concerned with the emergence or grammaticalization of new structures, but rather with the diachronic changes in the relative roles of different structures within the Functional Domain of Complementation.

Chapter 6 is a general introduction to the Functional Domain of Complementation in Babylonian. It presents the major semantic categories of verbs in this domain, and the main structures which are used with these verbs (including finite and non-finite complements, and different types of paratactic constructions).

Chapter 7 starts the diachronic survey of the Functional Domain of Complementation. It describes the structures used with verbs of knowledge and perception, as well as with other semantic groups (including verbs of speech, proving, and fearing). The most important development in the Functional Domain of Complementation is the emergence of finite complements. In the earliest stage of Akkadian, finite complements are not attested. During the historical period, finite complements emerge, and start taking over functions which were earlier performed by alternative structures (parataxis and non-finite complements). The chapter also describes the other important developments in the Functional Domain of Complementation: the rise and then dramatic decline in the use of infinitive complements, and the functional realignment which followed the emergence of the originally quotative construction as an alternative complementation strategy.

Chapter 8 continues the diachronic survey of the Functional Domain of Complementation, by examining the structures used with verbs of manipulation. Two main structures are used to express manipulation in Babylonian, which appear consistently in complementary distribution. Coordination is used to express manipulation in the present and future, whereas infinitival complements are used to report manipulation in the past. This system remains quite stable, until the latest period of the language, when infinitive complements almost disappear, and are replaced by the quotative construction.

Chapter 9 examines the '*wh*-functional domain' (the range of structures used to perform the function of *wh*-complements and indirect questions). The development of the *wh*-functional domain is similar to that of the Functional Domain of Complementation. Embedded indirect questions appear in Babylonian even later than finite complements, and achieve currency only in the latest period of the language. In earlier stages, direct questions and nominal strategies (based on relativization) are used instead.

Part IV The Development of Complementation as an Adaptive Process

The final part of the study explores the motivation for the diachronic developments in Babylonian.

Chapter 10 suggests first that the functional development which was sketched in Part III is not unique to Babylonian, but is in fact mirrored in various other languages. Neither the absence of finite complements from the earliest stages, nor the expansion in their use during the historical period is a Babylonian idiosyncrasy. Rather, both seem to be instances of a general trend.

Chapter 11 suggests a motivation for the emergence of finite complements and the extension in their use. It shows that finite complementation is a more powerful structural mechanism than both parataxis and non-finite complementation, because it can cope better with more complex and elaborate propositions. I then suggest that the development of finite complementation may be seen as an adaptation to the increased complexity of the communicative environment. I also interpret this development as a part of the more general shift in the strategies used to achieve inter-clausal cohesion, from a greater reliance on iconicity to an increased reliance on subordination.

2

What is Sentential Complementation?

The elementary question, 'what is complementation?', may seem a strange way to start this study. Sentential complements, as is well known, are clauses embedded as subjects or objects of verbs, like the italicized clause in the sentence 'he believes *that the world is round*'. A closer look, however, will quickly reveal that the issue is much less simple than it may appear at first sight. Although the aim of this study is not a theoretical examination of the nature of complementation, even the practical concerns of a diachronic study soon lead to serious difficulties. In the following sections, therefore, I highlight the main problems with the traditional concept of sentential complementation, and suggest how they can be resolved.

2.1. Complements and objects

Two definitions for complementation are current in linguistics. The first defines complements as 'clauses which are arguments of a predicate'. The second defines complements as 'clauses which function as the subject or object of a verb'. These two definitions are often explicitly considered to be equivalent. For example, in the beginning of Noonan's much quoted survey of complementation (1985: 42), we read:

> By complementation we mean the syntactic situation which arises when a notional sentence or a predication is an argument of a predicate. For our purposes, a predication can be viewed as an argument of a predicate, if it functions as the subject or object of that predicate.

Givón (1990: 515) makes a similar equation: 'sentential complements are propositions functioning in the role of either subject or object argument of the verb'. In more traditional philological circles, complement clauses are often simply called 'subject and object clauses'. There is a strong implication, moreover, that object complements should function as direct objects of verbs. Noonan, for example, demonstrates the concept of object complements with example (1) below, which he explains as follows (1985: 42): '*Nell*, the object of remember . . . can be replaced by a predication that also functions as the object of remember'.

(1) Zeke remembered *Nell.*
Zeke remembered *that Nell left.*
Zeke remembered *Nell's leaving.*
Zeke remembered *to leave.*

But is the relation between complements and objects always so obvious? Do complements always have to function as objects? In chapter 4, we shall see that finite complements in Akkadian developed from adverbial clauses. This historical development places considerable strain on the interpretation that finite complements always have to function as objects. We do not need to wander as far away as Akkadian, however, to encounter the problems in the equation between objects and sentential complements. Even if we consider English for a moment, it is far from clear that finite complements always have to 'function as' objects. Let us assume that 'function as' means 'have the same distribution as', or in other words, that finite complements 'function as' objects if they appear in the same 'slots' as objects. We then see that even if some finite complements (like the clause 'that Nell left' in (1) above) may function as nominal objects, not all finite complements have to do so. Consider, for example, the distribution in (2) below:

(2) *direct objects*	*finite complements*
*I pray his failure	I pray that he fails
*I hope his failure	I hope that he fails
*I complain his failure	I complain that he failed
*I warned him his failure	I warned him that he failed
*I informed him his failure	I informed him that he failed
*I convinced him his failure	I convinced him that he failed
*I said his failure	I said that he failed
*I am surprised his failure	I am surprised that he failed
*I am angry his failure	I am angry that he failed
*I am afraid his failure	I am afraid that he failed
*The news/hope/fact his failure	The news/hope/fact that he failed

Here, finite complements and direct objects stand in complementary distribution. The predicates above do not take nominal direct objects, but they all take finite complements. At least in the sense of distribution, therefore, we cannot say that the finite complements above 'function as' direct objects. These finite complements in fact appear in the 'slots' of oblique arguments, not of direct objects. For example, in 'I informed him *that he failed*', the finite complement stands for an oblique nominal argument, introduced by 'of' or 'about': 'I informed him *of/about* his failure'. Similarly, 'I pray *that he fails*' stands for 'I pray *for* his failure'.

The situation is even worse with some other predicates in (2) above. What is the status, for example, of the finite complement in the sentence 'I am angry *that he failed*'? When we replace the complement with a noun phrase, we find that the complement stands in the 'slot' of an element which would normally be considered an adverbial: 'I am angry *because of/about* his failure'. Similarly, the complement in 'I was surprised *that he failed*' stands for 'I was surprised *by* his failure'. Unless one denies that the 'that clauses' in (2) above are finite complements (which is not a reasonable position), then one must reach the conclusion that finite complements do not always have to 'function as' objects. Various intransitive predicates which do not take nominal direct objects, or objects at all, nevertheless appear with finite complements.

But if finite complements do not have to 'function as' objects, how should we interpret them instead? It seems to me that our problems derive from the mistaken equation between the two definitions of complements which were mentioned above (the first defines them as arguments, and the second as objects and subjects). Many problems will be solved if we discard the assumption that finite complements have to 'function as' objects, and only define them as clauses which are arguments of predicates.

An object is a syntactic surface category, recognizable (with varying degrees of confidence across languages) by factors such as case marking, word order, or passivization. An argument is a category which denotes the intimacy in the relation between an element and a predicate. An argument (as opposed to an adjunct, or a peripheral element) is a central element, which is required by the predicate, and which in some sense 'completes' a missing part in the interpretation of the predicate. Although all objects may be arguments, not all arguments are considered objects. For example, the locative 'on the table' is an argument of the verb 'put' in 'he put the box on the table'. But 'on the table' is not considered an object, and is definitely not a direct object.

On the surface, perhaps the most important manifestation of the distinction between arguments and peripheral elements is that an argument either has to be overtly present in the clause, or if it is not overtly present, must be 'latent'. (That is, there must be a definite and immediately accessible argument in the context; cf. Matthews 1981: 123.) This is not to say, however, that a simple binary distinction between arguments and peripheral elements is easy to draw. In fact, since the difference between argument and non-argument is based on semantic criteria, this difference (that is, the difference between argument and peripheral elements) is a matter of degree (Langacker 1987: 300 ff., Croft 1998: 108).

Nevertheless, the distinction between arguments and peripheral elements can be drawn on a prototypical level, and this distinction should serve as the basis for defining sentential complements. Sentential complementation is a form of clause linkage, in which a clause is embedded as an argument of a predicate. What is common to finite complements is not that they function as objects. (Some may do, but others do not.) What characterizes finite complements is that they are arguments of a predicate, rather than peripheral elements in the clause.

Since the difference between arguments and peripheral elements is a matter of degree rather than a binary distinction, there is also no clearly marked borderline between finite complements (which are clausal arguments), and adverbial clauses (which are peripheral elements). As we shall see in chapter 4, it is precisely for this reason that adverbial clauses could develop seamlessly into complements in the history of Akkadian.

What are the implications of such an interpretation of sentential complementation? It seems to me that when we discard the (mistaken) requirement that sentential complements always have to function as objects, many problems resolve themselves. First, we can see why finite complementation does not entail any particular semantic role relation between the complement and the predicate. It is well known that predicates take arguments in different semantic roles. A patient (such as 'the table' in 'he kicked the table') may well be a prototypical argument, but not every argument has to be a patient. I mentioned above the example of the locative 'on the table', which is an argument of the verb 'put'.

Just as nominal arguments can appear in various semantic roles in relation to the predicate, so can sentential arguments. The examples in (2) above demonstrate various roles that sentential complements can take with respect to the predicate. With nominal arguments, these semantic roles would need to be explicitly marked ('pray *for*', 'complain *about*' etc.). But with finite complements, the semantic roles are not explicitly marked. Finite complementation with 'that' only marks the intimate link between the predicate and its clausal argument. It does not mark explicitly the semantic role that this argument takes. Thus, one 'prays *for* peace', but one 'prays *that* peace will come'; one 'decides *on* a plan of action', but one 'decides *that* a plan of action should be pursued'; one 'complains *of*/*about* the weather', but one 'complains *that* the weather is awful'.

Moreover, as the examples in (2) show, some predicates require sentential arguments in semantic roles which are usually associated with adverbs, not objects. In 'I am angry *that he failed*', the 'that' clause is an argument of 'angry', because it expresses a central element in the interpretation of the predicate 'angry'. But in terms of its semantic role, the 'that' clause has the same relation to the predicate as the 'because' clause in 'I am angry *because he failed*'. Both the 'that' clause and the 'because' clause denote the reason for anger. The predicate 'be angry', therefore, requires an argument in a reason (or causal) semantic role.

The fact that sentential complements can appear in a causal (or reason) semantic role will make their historical development in Akkadian much easier to understand. As we shall see in chapter 4, finite complements in Akkadian developed from (mainly causal) adverbial clauses. On the basis of the discussion in this section, the development of complements from adverbial clauses will appear a natural and gradual semantic change, rather than an abrupt and rather problematic reanalysis.

Finally, the interpretation of finite complements which was suggested above makes clear that it is not only verbs which can take sentential complements. According to this interpretation, there is no fundamental difference between verb-complements, adjective-complements, and noun-complements. Noun-complements, such as 'the news *that he failed*', are often treated as a syntactic category distinct from verb-complements. The only reason for this separate treatment is that nouns do not take objects, and so noun-complements obviously cannot 'function as' objects. But the intimate link between the 'that' clause and the predicate noun in 'I conveyed to him the news *that he failed*' is similar to the link between the 'that' clause and the verb in 'I informed him *that he failed*'. In both cases, the 'that' clause completes a central missing part in the interpretation of the predicate. Since we do not have to insist that finite complements should function as objects, there is no justification for treating noun-complements as distinct from verb-complements, just because nouns do not take objects. We can regard verb-complementation, adjective-complementation, and noun-complementation as one category of clause linkage.

It could even be argued that whole clauses can sometimes be complement-taking predicates. In §7.7, we shall meet a rarely discussed construction which (for lack of a better term) I call the 'what have I done that . . .' construction. This construction consists of variations on the theme 'what have I done that you (should) treat me like this?' What role does the 'that' clause play in this construction? One could dismiss it as an adverbial clause of result: 'what have I done *so that* you treat me like this?'. Yet in many languages (including English), this construction has the surface form of finite complements, not of adverbial clauses. Why is this the case?

The 'that' clause in the sentence 'what have I done *that you* (*should*) *treat me like this*?' may indeed denote the result of the action. Nevertheless, the 'that' clause is not a peripheral or circumstantial element, but rather a central element for the interpretation of the sentence, an element without which the meaning of the sentence remains incomplete. The clause 'that you treat me like this' should therefore be regarded as an argument, not as a peripheral (adverbial) element. But an argument of what? It is not an argument of any particular element inside the clause 'what have I done?' Rather, the whole clause 'what have I done?' acts as a predicate, since it is incomplete on its own, and needs to be complemented by a sentential argument. For this reason, the clause 'that you treat me like this' in this construction should be regarded as a clause-complement. 'That you treat me like this' is a finite complement, but it does not complement a noun or a verb. It complements a whole clause which acts as a predicate.

In this section, I have claimed that the core defining feature of finite complements is their status as arguments, not their identification with objects. Some sentential complements may function as objects (for example with the verb 'remember' in (1) above), but this need not always be the case. Many predicates ('complain', 'angry', 'news') take sentential complements but not objects. Moreover, some sentential complements appear in semantic roles (such as cause/reason or result) which are normally associated with adverbial elements, not objects. We shall see in chapter 4 that this last point was crucial in the development of finite complements in Akkadian. We shall also see that a similarity between finite complements and nominal objects did develop, but that this similarity is only partial, and diachronically secondary.

2.2. Function and structure I: the 'Functional Domain of Complementation'

In addition to the structural difficulty in defining complementation, a cross-linguistic investigation of complementation quickly stumbles across another serious problem: the relation between form and meaning (that is, between structure and function). The definition of sentential complements requires that they be structurally subordinate or 'embedded'. Consider, however, the three examples in (3) below. The clause 'I did favours for you' is embedded within a higher clause only in (3*a*). But all three examples have a similar meaning:

(3) (*a*) You know that I did favours for you.
 (*b*) I did favours for you, and you know it.
 (*c*) As you know, I did favours for you.

Different structures can thus be used to achieve a similar functional effect. This fact becomes more significant when we try to examine 'complementation' across different languages, or in different historical stages of the same language. We soon find that where one language can use real complements like (3*a*), other languages can use other constructions in the same context, like (3*b*) and (3*c*). Noonan's survey of 'complementation' in fact discusses some structures that are not complements in any strict structural sense. Consider (4) below, which Noonan calls a 'paratactic complement'. Here the second clause is an entirely independent clause, and is not embedded in the first:

(4) *ìcó òdìá àcégò dógólá*
 man he.pressed.me I.closed door
 'the man pressed me, I closed the door'
 (~ the man forced me to close the door) (Lango. Noonan 1985: 77)

A structure like (4) is certainly not a complement by Noonan's own definition (which was quoted above). Why then does Noonan include it in a survey of 'complementation', and why does he call it a complement? The reason for including it must be that this structure performs the same function as a genuine (infinitival) complement in languages like English. Although Noonan does not state it explicitly, his cross-linguistic survey is not concerned only with 'complementation' in various languages, but rather with the range of structures which perform similar functions to those performed by complementation.

Nevertheless, it can be very misleading to call structures like (4) above 'complements'. We must be able to distinguish between the structural properties of embedded sentential complements, and the functions that they perform, especially if we want to compare the use of different structures that perform similar functions. Therefore, in order to avoid confusion, I propose to define two distinct concepts: 'complementation' on the one hand, and the 'Functional Domain of Complementation' on the other.

Complementation will be used in the narrow sense which includes structural embedding. A sentential complement is a clause which is embedded in another clause as an argument of a higher predicate. According to this definition, the clause 'I closed the door' in (4) above would not be regarded as a complement, because it is not embedded in another clause as an argument of a predicate. The *Functional Domain of Complementation* (FDC), on the other hand, consists of the range of structures which are used to perform similar functions to those performed by complementation. In examining the FDC, we shall look at the range of predicates that take sentential complements in languages like English, and examine all the different structures which are used with these verbs to achieve similar functions.

According to the definitions above, I shall refer to the construction in (4) as a 'paratactic structure belonging to the FDC'. The term 'paratactic complement' is a contradiction in terms. Similarly, the examples in (3*b*) and (3*c*) contain structures belonging to the FDC, but these structures are not complements.[2] Complementation is thus one structure which belongs to the FDC, but there are other structures in the FDC, for example parataxis. Noonan's and Givón's surveys are in fact not only on 'complementation', but on the 'Functional Domain of Complementation'. Similarly, this study is not only concerned with complementation, but also with the historical development of the FDC as a whole.

2.3. Function and structure II: subordination, hypotaxis, parataxis, coordination

A further potential minefield for a study of the development of subordinate structures is the abundance of (sometimes conflicting) definitions which have been given to the terms 'subordination', 'hypotaxis', 'parataxis', and 'coordination'. It seems that much of the confusion again stems from the relation between structure and function. Subordination is traditionally understood as a purely structural, hierarchical phenomenon, which involves the embedding of a clause in a larger clause (Matthews 1997: 360). A subordinate clause is a constituent of a larger clause, whereas an independent clause is not.

[2] This distinction is equivalent to Dixon's (1995) distinction between 'complement clauses' on the one hand, and 'strategies of complementation' on the other. His 'strategies of complementation' are other structures which are not complements, but which perform similar functions to complements. I think that the term 'strategies of complementation' may be misleading for structures which are not real complements. I therefore prefer to use the less confusing term 'structures belonging to the FDC'.

A different approach to the question of structure and function is taken by Cristofaro (1998*b*). She sets out to give a purely functional definition for subordination in general, in order to facilitate cross-linguistic comparisons. Her definition for complementation accordingly does not require structural embedding. The functional approach may be the only truly consistent method of conducting cross-linguistic comparisons. But since the term 'complementation' is normally used to indicate structural embedding, I prefer to reserve the term 'complementation' for this more traditional meaning, and refer to the functional entity as the 'Functional Domain of Complementation'.

Structural embedding, however, is not the only relevant factor in clause linkage. A clause can be semantically dependent on another clause, without being a constituent of a higher clause. For example, in the sentence 'he does that and I'll scream' (which in some registers is equivalent to 'if he does that, I'll scream), there is a clear semantic dependence between the two clauses, but neither is a constituent of the other. The attempts to capture both the semantic notion of dependence and the hierarchical notion of embedding, especially in a cross-linguistic perspective, have resulted in a variety of sometimes conflicting definitions. Some authors use the terms 'hypotaxis' and 'subordination' for distinct phenomena (C. Lehmann 1988, Matthiessen and Thompson 1988, Cristofaro 1998*b*), but each draws the distinction along different lines.

In this study, I shall avoid the term 'hypotaxis' altogether. The term 'subordination' will be used in the traditional, purely hierarchical sense, as a synonym for 'embedding'. The term 'parataxis' will also be used in a purely hierarchical sense, to denote clauses which are not structurally embedded in other clauses. Thus, when referring to two clauses in paratactic relation, I do not mean that there is no semantic dependence between them, only that neither of the clauses is syntactically subordinate. I shall differentiate between two types of paratactic structures. 'Asyndetic parataxis' will denote paratactic juxtaposition without any coordinating particle, whereas 'coordination' will denote paratactic structures that are linked by a coordinating particle. The notion of semantic dependence will be subsumed under the term 'Functional Domain of Complementation'. Structures belonging to the FDC will automatically be assumed to involve semantic dependence.

2.4. Function and structure III: structural change and functional replacement

The last issue which needs to be addressed at the outset is the difference between two distinct perspectives on diachronic change. A clear distinction between function and structure is necessary here as well, in order to avoid confusions which have arisen, especially in discussions of the development of subordination. The first perspective from which one can view diachronic change is local and structural. We can follow a certain construction through time, and observe the change in its form or its meaning. For example, we can follow the history of the phrase 'going to', on the path from the verbal phrase meaning 'walk (in order) to', to the reduced future marker 'gonna'. In this case, we follow the *structural change* of the phrase 'going to'.

But we can also look at diachronic change from a global functional perspective. We can observe that at one point in time, one structure X performs a certain function in the language, whereas at a later point, a different structure Y may replace X in that function. For example, suppose that at some future stage, the modal verb 'will' will fall into disuse, and futurity in English will be marked exclusively by 'going to' or 'gonna'. If this change occurs in the future (whether or not it does is irrelevant), we will then be able to say that although 'going to' did not develop *from* 'will', 'going to' nevertheless replaced 'will' as the future marker. We can call this type of change *functional replacement*. (The term 'renewal' is also sometimes used in this context.) The often quoted chain of changes in the evolution of the Romance future markers (for example in Hopper and Traugott 1993: 10) can serve as a demonstration of the two perspectives. In sketching this development from pre-Latin to colloquial French, we can use the arrow to represent structural change, and begin a new line to represent functional replacement:

(5) **kanta b^humos* → *cantabimus*
cantare habemus → *chanterons*
allons chanter

That structural change and functional replacement are two distinct issues is of course a trivial point. Nevertheless, at least when it comes to the development of subordination, the two types of change have sometimes been confused in the past. The question of whether subordination was 'less developed in earlier languages' has aroused controversy in the past, partly because it was vaguely formulated, and in particular because it did not clearly distinguish between functional replacement and structural change. Similarly, debates on whether 'subordination has developed historically from parataxis' frequently confuse the structural question (what is the structural source of subordinate clauses?) and the question of functional replacement (whether older languages used paratactic structures to perform functions for which modern languages use subordinate structures).

This study makes a clear distinction between structural change and functional replacement. Part II describes structural changes, whereas Part III describes functional replacement. In Part II we shall see that finite complements did not develop from any paratactic structures, but rather from other subordinate structures (adverbial clauses). On the other hand, Part III will demonstrate that during the history of Babylonian, the use of subordinate complements was extended at the expense of paratactic structures (amongst others). Thus, although parataxis was not the structural source of finite complements, finite complements nevertheless took over some functions which parataxis performed in earlier periods.

In light of the discussion above, it is now possible to recapitulate the aim and scope of this study more succinctly. Part II is concerned with the development of structures (structural change). It describes the history of two particular structures in the FDC, finite sentential complements, and the quotative construction (which itself develops into a more general complement construction in the latest historical stages). Part III describes functional replacement, and is concerned with the Functional Domain of Complementation as a whole. It follows the history of the FDC over two thousand years, and examines how the relative roles of the different structures in the FDC change over time. In particular, we shall see that finite complements take over some functions which were earlier performed by other structures in the FDC (parataxis and non-finite complements). The final part of the study surveys parallels from other languages for the direction of change in the FDC, and suggests an 'adaptive' motivation for the growing reliance on finite complementation in the FDC.

3

Akkadian

Akkadian is the earliest known Semitic language. It was spoken in ancient Mesopotamia, the 'land between the rivers' (the Tigris and the Euphrates), an area which roughly corresponds to today's Iraq. Akkadian is one of the earliest and longest attested languages, with a history spanning more than two thousand years. The first written attestations of Akkadian are from around 2500 BC, and the language was spoken until around 500 BC, when it was displaced by Aramaic. Nevertheless, texts in Akkadian continued to be written even until the time of Christ.

The ancient name of the language, *Akkadûm*, derives from the city of Akkad, founded by King Sargon as his capital around 2300 BC. From the second millennium BC, two distinct dialects of Akkadian emerged, Babylonian and Assyrian. Babylonian was spoken in the southern part of Mesopotamia, an area which was dominated by the city of Babylon (*Bābili*). Assyrian was spoken in the northern part of Mesopotamia, which was likewise dominated by the city of Assur (or *Aššur*).

For almost two millennia, Akkadian speakers were the dominant political and cultural power of the Near East. Their political star waxed and waned, but for a good part of two thousand years, from Sargon in the third millennium to the Neo-Assyrian and Neo-Babylonian emperors of the first millennium, many Mesopotamian rulers called themselves the 'king of the universe'. They ruled over 'the four corners (of the world)', 'from the lower sea to the upper sea' (from the Gulf to the Mediterranean). The names and exploits of some Neo-Assyrian and Neo-Babylonian kings, most notably Sennacherib and Nebuchadnezzar,[3] are of course familiar from the Bible.

More stable than the power of the sword was the cultural hegemony of Mesopotamia over the region. Mesopotamian civilization shaped the dominant cultural canon for much of the Near East, in religion, literature, science, and law. Most well known, perhaps, is the legacy of Babylonian religion and legal practices in the Hebrew Bible. The Akkadian language was used as a lingua franca throughout the Near East (even by Hittite kings to write to Egyptian pharaohs). From (today's) Iran to Syria, and from Turkey to Egypt, local scribes learnt to read and write Akkadian.

[3] This form is a corrupted version of Nebuchadrezzar, from Akkadian *Nabû-kudurrī-uṣur.*

Nevertheless, a few centuries after the demise of Assyria and then Babylon as political powers in the middle of the first millennium BC, both the Akkadian language and its complex writing system fell into oblivion. The language was rediscovered only in the nineteenth century, when the cuneiform writing was (gradually) deciphered. The Assyrian dialect was discovered first, and this gave rise to the misleading term 'Assyriology' for the study of Akkadian in general.

Today, hundreds of thousands of Akkadian texts are known. These encompass many different genres, including poetry (such as the epic of Gilgamesh), religious compositions, royal and monumental inscriptions, histories, monolingual and multilingual dictionaries (word-lists), grammatical texts, astronomical and mathematical texts, legal documents (most famously the Code of Hammurabi), private and diplomatic correspondence, and an endless quantity of economic and administrative documents.

The reason for such abundance is clay. Akkadian scribes wrote on damp clay tablets, using a sharpened reed to make marks in the clay. Clay, once dried, is highly durable, and so hundreds of thousands of tablets have been recovered from the soil of Iraq and neighbouring countries, and thousands more still patiently wait to be discovered. (For general introductions to the history and culture of Babylon and ancient Mesopotamia see, for example, Oppenheim 1964, Oates 1986, Roaf 1990, and for the legacy of this culture, Dalley 1998. For an introduction to the cuneiform script, see Walker 1987.)

This study is concerned specifically with the Babylonian dialect of Akkadian. The following section gives an outline of the historical stages of Babylonian within the Akkadian language. Section 3.2 then explains the relation between the Akkadian and the Sumerian languages. Section 3.3 gives a brief account of orthography. Section 3.4 is an introduction to the particular genre of texts which formed the basis of this study, the Babylonian letters. Finally, section 3.5 explains a few basic points about Akkadian grammar, to make it easier for readers unfamiliar with the language to follow the glosses.

3.1. Historical periods

During the two thousand years in which Akkadian was both spoken and written (*c.*2500 to 500 BC), considerable linguistic changes took place. The history of the Akkadian language is conventionally divided into four main chronological periods, which are represented in (6) below. The exact determination of boundaries between the periods and the dialects is sometimes a matter of disagreement between scholars, but it is of no overriding importance for this study.

(6)

Old Akkadian		(2500–2000 BC)
Old Babylonian	Old Assyrian	(2000–1500 BC)
Middle Babylonian	Middle Assyrian	(1500–1000 BC)
Neo-Babylonian	Neo-Assyrian	(1000–500 BC)

Old Akkadian is the earliest period attested in writing. The language is known to us mainly from letters, and from the royal inscriptions of the Sargonic dynasty of Akkad. Sargon, the founder of the dynasty, was the first Semitic ruler to dominate Mesopotamia. The conventional name 'Old Akkadian' was given to this stage of the language because it was assumed initially that no dialectal variation between the Babylonian and Assyrian idioms existed in this period. In reality, the situation is more complex, and there must have already been a dialect continuum in the region by this time. In particular, texts from more northern regions show various features closer to later Old Assyrian than to later Old Babylonian (Kienast and Volk 1995: 4, Westenholz 1999: 33). In this study, I consider Old Akkadian as a part of the history of Babylonian, but this is not meant to be a statement about the precise dialectal relation between Old Akkadian, Old Assyrian, and Old Babylonian. For the purpose of the syntactic issues examined in this study, the exact determination of lineage between very close dialects is not of crucial importance.

The Old Babylonian period generally coincides with the rule of the first dynasty of Babylon, the city which rose to unrivalled prominence mainly through the achievements of the famous king Hammurabi (1792–1750 BC). Old Babylonian is the best attested dialect of Akkadian. It was considered the classical stage of the language by later generations of Babylonians (and Assyrians), and it was the language towards which later poetic idiom aspired. For modern ears also, the Old Babylonian language shares many of the characteristics that we associate with 'classical languages', such as rich synthetic morphology, an intact case system, and extensive use of non-finite verbal structures. There are many Old Babylonian texts in all genres, including literary and scientific works, but mainly administrative and legal texts, and thousands of royal and private letters.

The Middle Babylonian period is very poorly attested compared to previous and later stages. Babylon was sacked by the Hittites around 1595 BC, and a dark age which lasted for more than two centuries ensued. There is thus a fairly long gap between the last Old Babylonian texts and the first extant Middle Babylonian documents.[4] Our knowledge of Middle Babylonian derives mostly from legal documents, economic texts, inscribed boundary stones, and letters from the city of Nippur (and a few from elsewhere). The quantity of extant Middle Babylonian texts, however, is only a fraction of the amount of documents from Old Babylonian. Akkadian was the language of most of the diplomatic correspondence

[4] The gap between Old Babylonian and the first Middle Babylonian texts means that we cannot trace in detail the changes which took place during this dark age. Mainly because of a few phonological peculiarities in Middle Babylonian, scholars have posed the question whether the dialect of the Middle Babylonian texts is a precise descendant of the dialect represented by the Old Babylonian texts, or whether it is the descendant of a slightly different dialect. In any case (as I explained above), for the purpose of this study, the determination of lineage among very close dialects is not very important. In particular, there is nothing in the (very modest) syntactic changes from Old Babylonian to Middle Babylonian which does not look like a perfectly natural diachronic development.

from the fourteenth century BC that was found in the archive of El-Amarna in Egypt. But only twelve of the letters come from Babylon itself, and so faithfully represent the Middle Babylonian dialect. The rest were written by non-native speakers (Egyptians, Canaanites, Hittites) using Akkadian as a foreign language, to various degrees of competence.

The Neo-Babylonian period was the time of the mighty Assyrian and Babylonian empires. This era was mostly dominated by the power of Assyria, but towards its end, Babylon rose to unrivalled political power and architectural splendour (including, reputedly, Nebuchadnezzar's 'hanging gardens'). The Neo-Babylonian period is very well attested with all genres of texts. The idiom of the literary texts of this period hearkens back to the Old Babylonian standard, and is at a great distance from the colloquial language of the time. (This literary language is considered to be a distinct 'dialect', called Standard Babylonian.) The colloquial language of the period is manifested in letters and legal documents. There are many private letters from Babylonia, and a large number of letters to and from the kings of Assyria, which were found in the royal library of Nineveh. (Most of these were written in the Assyrian dialect, but about five hundred also in Babylonian.)

Considerable linguistic changes took place in the Neo-Babylonian period, including the disintegration of the case system, and the loss of other morphological distinctions. During the first millennium, Aramaic (a North-west Semitic language) gradually ousted Babylonian as the spoken language of the region. Babylonian ceased to be spoken sometime around 500 BC, but the exact time of its death is a matter of dispute (Streck 1998: 322).

3.2. Sumerian and Akkadian

No introduction to Akkadian should omit to mention Sumerian, although the two languages are genetically unrelated. The Sumerians were the earlier inhabitants of the southern part of Mesopotamia, and were settled there before the infiltration of the Semitic population. The Sumerians were the first inventors of many things, but most importantly, they invented writing. They developed the cuneiform writing system towards the end of the fourth millennium BC, and it was from them that the Akkadians later borrowed the cuneiform script, and adapted it to write their own language.

Sumerian is an agglutinating, ergative, verb-final language. It is entirely unrelated to the Semitic languages, and is in fact a language isolate, since no relative of Sumerian is known. Nevertheless, during the third millennium, there developed a very intimate cultural symbiosis between the Sumerians and the Akkadians, which included widespread bilingualism. (On the nature of this symbiosis see most recently Westenholz 1999: 25 ff.) The influence of Sumerian on Akkadian (and vice versa) is evident in all areas, from lexical borrowing on a massive scale, to syntactic, morphological, and phonological convergence.

This has prompted scholars to refer to Sumerian and Akkadian in the third millennium as a 'Sprachbund' (Edzard 1977, Pedersén 1989). For example, Akkadian lost many of the Semitic pharyngeal and emphatic consonants, in all probability because of Sumerian influence. Akkadian also acquired a very 'un-Semitic' verb-final word order.

Sumerian was spoken in southern Mesopotamia until some time before or after 2000 BC. The precise time of its death is a matter of disagreement (Edzard 1990: 37). But for centuries after it ceased to be spoken, Sumerian continued to be used as a literary and scholarly language. Sumerian was taught in the scribal schools, and Sumerian literary compositions were learnt and copied by Akkadian scribes. (For general introductions to the Sumerian language see Thomsen 1984, Römer 1994.)

3.3. Orthography

The writing system of Akkadian uses both syllabic and logographic signs (see further below). Akkadian has four vowels, *a*, *e*, *i*, *u*, with phonemic length distinction. In the cuneiform texts themselves, vowel length was only rarely distinguished. In modern transcriptions, long vowels are marked with a macron (*ā*, *ē*, *ī*, *ū*), and long vowels resulting from a contraction of a diphthong are marked with a circumflex (*â*, *ê*, *î*, *û*). The signs *q*, *ṣ*, *ṭ* denote the 'emphatic' stops (velar, alveolar, and dental respectively). The sign ' is used for glottal stop, *š* is used for 'sh', and *j* is used for the semivowel 'y'. In editions of Akkadian texts, the sign *ḫ* is used for the velar fricative, but for convenience, I use the normal *h* instead. Since there is only one 'h' sound in Akkadian, this should not create any confusion.

The Akkadians borrowed their writing system from the Sumerians. The most obvious mark of this fact is the use of Sumerian 'logograms' in Akkadian texts, especially for nouns. These logograms are signs for Sumerian words, which are treated in the Akkadian texts as invariable word-signs, rather than syllabic signs. When Sumerian logograms are used in the Akkadian texts, the Akkadian case ending is often not marked. For example, the Sumerian logogram A.ŠÀ ('field') would be used for the Akkadian word *eqlum*, and the same logogram can stand for *eqlum*, *eqlam*, *eqlim*, or *eqel* (respectively: 'field.NOM', 'field.ACC', 'field.GEN', 'field.of').

Akkadian cuneiform texts can be transcribed in two ways. They can be *transliterated*, sign by sign, in a system which retains a one-to-one correspondence between the original syllabic or logographic cuneiform signs and the modern conventional equivalents. Hyphens are used between signs belonging to the same Akkadian word. These hyphens of course do not exist in the original, which is just a continuous list of signs without breaks between words. In transliteration, a graphic distinction is made between phonetic (syllabic) signs, logograms, and determinatives. Signs with phonetic value are printed in italics. The accents and subscript numbers in transliteration are used to indicate different cuneiform signs with the same phonetic value. For example, *na*, *ná* (= na_2), *nà* (= na_3), na_4 represent different cuneiform signs with the phonetic value 'na'. Logograms are signs that are used to represent whole words. They are printed in capitals, according to the Sumerian rather than the Akkadian pronunciation of the word. For example, in the letter quoted below, the logogram for 'man' is printed in capitals, according to the Sumerian reading LÚ, not the Akkadian *awīl*(*um*). Determinatives are logograms which indicate the class of object to which some nouns belong. They do not have a phonetic realization, and are printed in superscript. For example, in the word ^{uru}*ku-ta-al-la*^{ki} below, the determinatives ^{uru} ('town') and ^{ki} ('land') indicate that the word *Kutalla* represents a town's name.

Normalization is an attempt to render the language in an alphabetic phonemic system, including vowel length. In this book, almost all examples are normalized, for the benefit of linguists who are not familiar with the peculiarities of the cuneiform writing system. Some words, however, are left in transliteration, if they are not clear, or if normalization would add uncertain information which is not contained in the text. As an example for the different renderings of the texts, the following short letter is given in transliteration, normalization, gloss, and translation.

Translit: *a-na* ^{d}EN.ZU-*i-di-nam qí-bí-ma um-ma ha-am-mu-ra-bi-ma*
Norm:[5] *ana Sin-iddinam qibi-ma umma Hammurabi-ma*
Gloss: to Sin-iddinam say.IMP-P QUOT Hammurabi-P
Trans: 'Tell Sin-iddinam, this is what Hammurabi said:

Translit: DUB-*pí an-ni-a-am i-na a-ma-ri-im*
Norm: *ṭupp-ī anni'-am ina amār-im*
Gloss: letter-my this-ACC on see.INF-GEN
Trans: on seeing this letter of mine

Translit: ^{P}*a-bi-i-din-nam* LÚ ^{uru}*ku-ta-al-la*^{ki} *a-na* KÁ.DINGIR.RA^{ki} *šu-ri-a-am*
Norm: *Abī-iddinam awīl Kutalla ana Bābili šūri'-am*
Gloss: Abī-iddinam man.of Kutalla to Babylon send.IMP-to me
Trans: send Abī-iddinam, the man of Kutalla, to me to Babylon

Translit: *ù* ^{lú}*ma-aṣ-ṣa-ru li-iṣ-ṣú-ru-ni-iš-šu*
Norm: *u maṣṣarū liṣṣurūniš-šu*
Gloss: and guards.NOM they.should.guard-him
Trans: and guards should escort him' (AbB 13: 40)

[5] In this book, I use the hyphen in normalized texts to indicate morpheme boundaries in order to make the glosses more transparent. This use should not be confused with the function of the hyphen in transliterated texts. In transliteration, the hyphen simply binds different signs belonging to the same Akkadian word. For example, if we take a word which appears in transliteration as *i-pu-šu*, and in normalization as *īpuš-u* (he.did-SUB), the hyphen in the normalization marks the boundary between the verb *īpuš* (he.did) and the subordinative morpheme *-u*. But this does not correspond to the division made in the cuneiform signs themselves.

3.4. The language and style of the letters

dub-sar šu ka-ta sá-a e-ne-àm dub-sar-ra-àm
'a scribe whose hand rivals his mouth (in speed), he is indeed a scribe'
(Sumerian proverb from the Old Babylonian schools)

The corpus of texts used for this diachronic study consists mainly of one genre, namely letters. Legal documents are also considered, but I do not examine the language of poetry, as it is highly stylized, and at a remove from the spoken language. Like other Akkadian documents, letters were written with a stylus on tablets of damp clay. The letters were mostly dictated by illiterate clients to quick and able scribes, and were then read aloud to the recipient.

Letters are available from the earliest to the latest period of the language, and they form a very stable genre spanning a period of two millennia. They are ideally suited for linguistic study, because (unlike much of the material available to us from ancient languages) they give a very close idea of what the spoken language must have actually been like. As F. R. Kraus, the doyen of Old Babylonian letters, has explained, the letters dealt with everyday topics, in a spontaneous, colloquial, and idiomatic language:

Soweit es sich beurteilen läßt, behandeln die . . . altbabylonischen Briefe ohne viel Umschweif normale, meist triviale Vorfälle und typische Themen des babylonischen Alltags in einfacher Sprache, wenn auch nicht immer kühlen Tones, mit simplen Worten und zahlreichen stereotypen Wendungen. (AbB 1: xiii)

In order to give an idea of the tone and style of the letters, as well as their subject matter, a few examples are transcribed below. The first letter is from the earliest period of the language, Old Akkadian, and is probably the first ever attested endeavour to solve petty domestic quarrels. It was written around the twenty-third century BC, and it shows that on some issues little has changed in more than four thousand years:

enma Babi ana Šārtim aṣehham-mi ana mīnim atti u Ibbi'ilum
QUOT Babi to Šārtim I.'laugh'-P why you(FSG) and Ibbi'ilum
in bīt-im taṣa''alā ištēniš šibā
in house-GEN you(PL).quarrel with each other live.IMP(PL)
šamn-am šūbilī-m
oil-ACC send.IMP(FSG)-to me
'This is what Babi says to Šārtum: I am angry![6] Why do you and Ibbi'ilum quarrel at home? Live with one another! Send me (sesame) oil!' (SAB: Di 1)

[6] The normal sense of the verb *ṣiāhum* is 'laugh', not 'be angry'. The editors of SAB (following K. R. Veenhof) suggest that this verb is a 'Wort mit Gegensinn', and is used not only to express joy, but also to express anger. D. O. Edzard (in *Nabu* (*Nouvelles Assyriologiques Brèves et Utilitaires*) 1996/52), however, claims that this interpretation is unnecessary, and that the verb does mean 'laugh', but is used here in a sarcastic sense: 'da kann ich, wie man so sagt, nur lachen'.

An Old Babylonian letter with its envelope (AbB 7: 52). ©Trustees of the British Museum.

The rest of the examples are all from the Old Babylonian period (2000–1500 BC). The following letter is one of many hundreds dealing with common financial transactions. What is revealing about this particular letter is its somewhat confused style, which illustrates the spontaneous nature of the medium. A certain Ibqatum writes to his superior to request a cow. Ibqatum starts his letter by claiming that he has never 'written' (sent a written document) to his lord before. From his style, it would not be unreasonable to assume that he has never written to anyone else either. His tangled style could perhaps be explained by the unfamiliar experience of having every word he utters recorded by a scribe. The result is reminiscent of someone who has had to leave a message on an automatic answering machine for the first time.

> [1] *ana bēlija qibima umma Ibqatum waradkama* [4] *kīma bēlī atta tešmû alpī nakrum itbal matīma ana bēlija kâta ul ašpuram inanna ṭuppī ana bēlija kâta uštābilam* [10] *1 arham būrtam bēlī atta šūbilamma* 5 GÍN *kaspam luṣmidamma ana bēlija kâta lušābilam* [14] *bēlī atta ina qibīt Marduk bānika ašar taqabbû tammaggar mamman ana bēlija kâta ul ikalla* [18] *bēlī atta kīmuša ina* 5 GÍN *kaspim ša ana bēlija kâta aṣammidamma ušabbalam kīmuša šu-zi-iz* [23] *bēlī atta ina annītim kaqqadī kubbitma ina birīt ahhīja kaqqadī lā iqallil* [27] *ana ša ana bēlija kâta ašpuram bēlī lā uštāwâm anāku waradka ṣibût bēlija kâta epēšam ele"i* [31] *u arhum būrtum ša bēlī atta tušabbalam lū taklatma ina āli Baṣu lū šumum damqu ša bēlija kâta* [35] *šumma bēlī atta tudammaqamma tušabbalam itti Ili-iqīšam ahīja arhum būrtum šī lillikam* [38] *u anāku ana ša bēlī arhiš udammaqamma arham būrta ušabbalam* 15 GÍN *kaspam aṣammidamma arhiš ana bēlija kâta ušabbalam* (AbB 2: 86)

> [1] Tell my lord, this is what Ibqatum your servant said: [4] As you my lord know, the enemy has taken away the cattle. I have never written to my lord, but now I am sending my letter to my lord. [10] Let you, my lord, bring me a cow, and I will prepare 5 shekels of silver and send (them) to you, my lord. [14] You my lord, on the command of Marduk, who made you, wherever you command, you will be obeyed. No one will deny you anything. [18] You, my lord, replace it for 5 shekels of silver, which I will prepare for my lord and send you – replace it! [23] You my lord treat me respectfully in this matter, so that I will not be treated disrespectfully among my 'brothers'. [27] About what I wrote to my lord, my lord should not be negligent towards me. I, your servant, can fulfil the request of my lord. [31] Also the cow, which you, my lord, will send, let it be of the best quality, so that in the town Baṣu my lord will have a good name. [35] If my lord kindly sends it to me, let it come with Ili-iqīšam, my brother. [38] And for that my lord kindly sends me a cow quickly, I will prepare 15 [mistake for 5?] shekels of silver and will send them quickly to my lord. (Superscript numbers are line numbers)

The next letter also deals with a simple financial matter, the non-payment of rent. It shows again that 'there is no new thing under the sun'. With a few terms renamed, it would be difficult to guess that this letter was written almost four thousand years ago.

> [1]*ištu* MU.3.KAM *aššum bilāt eqlija u kiṣir bītija aštanapparakkumma ul še'am ul kaspam tušabbalam* [7] *u atta ana Bābili tēli'amma mimma ul taddinam u kīma tattalku ul īdema šāpirka šandabakkum ul iqbi'akkum* [14] *inanna Šumun-libši ana mahrīka aṭṭardam še'am kaspam idiššumma ana Bābili liblam* [18] *šumma še'am u kaspam lā tuštabbalam ana šandabakkim ša ina āli wašbu lušpuramma bilāt eqlija ša* MU.4.KAM *lišaddinūnim* [22] *ūlūma ana awīlim Siniqīšam šandabakkim luqbima ṭuppašu u našparum lillikamma bilat eqlija lilqûnim* [26] *Šumun-libši ša aṭrudam rīqūssu lā iturram še'am u kaspam šūbilam* (AbB 7: 155)

> [1] For 3 years I have kept writing to you about the rental payments for my field and the rent for my house, and you send me neither barley nor silver. [7] Moreover, you came up to Babylon, but you haven't given me anything. I also didn't know that you went away, your superior, the Šandabakkum (high ranking official), didn't order you (to do so?). [14] Now, I have sent Šumun-libši to you. Give him barley or silver, so that he will bring it to me to Babylon. [18] If you don't send me barley or silver I will write to the Šandabakkum who serves in the city so that they will collect for me the rental payments of 4 years for my field.[22] Or else I will ask the gentleman Sin-iqīšam, the Šandabakkum, that his letter or an envoy will come and they will take for me the rental payment for my field. [26] Šumun-libši whom I sent should not return empty handed! Send me barley or silver!

As Kraus remarks, the letters are not always written in tranquil tones. The following is an extreme example, which again shows the spontaneity of the medium:

> [1] *ana Duga-Šara qibima umma Marduk-nāṣirma ul Marduk il ālija ul Šamaš ilum nûm* [6] *eqelka u bītka uhallaq ana bītijama ana šitarruqim qātam taštakan* [11] *u awīlam wardī tanaššima ina muhhi eqlika tušzaz* [15] *ul Marduk il ālija Warhum-nawir anummeam ana Asarluhi-mansum aqabbima ina Edurugida ul ušeššebšu* [21] *u itarrûniššuma mahar dajjānī ušakmassuma ušpāssu* [25] *ūmam uqqama šumma libbi urram awīlam lā tušarri'am ša ina mātim lā ibaššû eppuška* [31] *awīlamma wardī šūri'am imarraṣakkum* (AbB 10: 178)

> [1] Tell Duga-Šara, this is what Marduk-nāṣir said: Is Marduk not the God of my town? Is Šamaš not our God? [6] I will destroy your field and your house! You have started stealing repeatedly from my house (of all houses)! [11] And you take a man who is my servant and put him in charge of your field! [15] Is Marduk not the God of my town? This Warhum-nawir – I will tell Asarluhi-mansum not to let him live in Edurugida, [21] and they will bring him to me, and I will make him kneel before the judges and get him locked up! [25] I shall

wait one day, then if you don't let the man be brought here by tomorrow, I will do to you what doesn't happen in the land! [31] Let the man, my 'servant' be brought here, (or else?) it will be unpleasant for you!

Not all letters are written in such confusion or rage. In particular, letters from the royal chancellery are often written in a factual and authoritative style, sometimes with constructions which would not put any modern bureaucrat to shame. So for example, King Hammurabi (1792–1750 BC) starts a letter to his governor in Larsa, Sin-iddinam, in this way:

> [1] *ana Sin-iddinam qibima umma Hammurabima* [3] *aššum Šēp-Sin wakil tamkārī qadum 1800* ŠE.GUR *ša šamaššammī u 19* MA.NA *kaspim labirtišu* [5] *u Sin-muštāl wakil tamkārī qadum 1800* ŠE.GUR *ša šamaššammī u 7* MA.NA *kaspim labirtišu ana Bābili ṭarādimma šīpātim mahārim u* UGULA.N[AM.]5.TA.X *ittīšunu ṭarādim* [11] *ša ašpurakkumma umma attama umma waklū tamkārīma* [14] *ina kīma inanna ebūrum warki ebūrim i nillik* [17] *kīam iqbûkumma tašpuram* [19] *inanna ebūrum ittalak ṭuppī anni'am ina amārim* [21] *kīma ašpurakkum Šēp-Sin wakil tamkārī qadum 1800* ŠE.GUR-*šu u 19* MA.NA *kaspim labirtišu u Sin-muštāl wakil tamkārī qadum 1800* ŠE.GUR-*šu u 7* MA.NA *kaspim labirtišu ana Bābili ṭurdam . . .* (AbB 2: 33: 1–27)
>
> [1] Tell Sin-iddinam, this is what Hammurabi said: [3] Concerning the sending to Babylon of Šēp-Sin, overseer of the merchants, with 1800 kor of sesame and 19 minas of silver, his old debt, [5] and Sin-muštāl, overseer of the merchants, with 1800 kor of sesame, and 7 minas of silver, his old debt, and the receiving of wool, and the sending of the overseer of [something] with them, [11] about which I wrote to you, and (about which) you said as follows: 'the overseers of the merchants said as follows: [14] "as it is right now harvest time, let us go after the harvest"' [17] thus they said to you and you wrote to me. [19] Now the harvest is over. [21] On seeing this tablet of mine, just as I wrote you, send to me to Babylon Šēp-Sin, overseer of the merchants, with his 1800 kor and 19 minas of silver, his old debt, and Sin-muštāl, overseer of the merchants, with his 1800 kor, and 7 minas of silver, his old debt . . .

Another royal letter, a touching note from king Rīm-Sin of Larsa, demonstrates the efficacy of the penal system at the time:

> *ana Lu-Ninurta Balmu-Namhe Ipqu-Erra u Mannum-kīma-Sin qibima umma Rīm-Sin bēlkunuma aššum ṣuhāram ana tinūrim iddû attunu wardam ana utūnim idiā* (AbB 9: 197)
>
> Tell Lu-Ninurta, Balmu-Namhe, Ipqu-Erra, and Mannum-kīma-Sin, this is what Rīm-Sin your lord said: Because he cast the boy into the oven, you, throw the slave into the kiln.

The sender of the following letter (from the early Old Babylonian period) reports of an epidemic in town, and tries to organize public prayers to appease the responsible God:

> [1] *ana Lipit-Ištar u Lu-Baba qibima umma Ahum-ma* [5] *mūtānu anumma ina ālim ibaššû* [9] *mūtānu ula ša Nergal mūtānu ša Asaru . . .* [13] *nāgirum lissima taphūrī ina išrim ana Asaru šuknāma* [19] *ilam sullima ilum linūh adi taphūrīšu* (AbB 2: 118)
>
> [1] Tell Lipit-Ištar and Lu-Baba, this is what Ahum said: [5] There is now an epidemic in town. [9] The epidemic is not (because) of (the god) Nergal, the epidemic is (because) of (the god) Asaru.[13] The herald should announce, organize assemblies (of supplicants) in the village for Asaru, pray to the god so that he may be appeased before his assemblies.

In fact, gods could also be the recipients of letters. The following example is a letter from a certain Apil-Adad to his personal god, written in an hour of need. He begs his god to intercede with Marduk, a higher god, on his behalf:

> *ana ilim abīja qibima umma Apil-Adad waradkama ammīni tušta''i'am ša kīma jâti ana kâšim mannum liddin ana Marduk rā'imika šupramma i'iltī lipṭur pānīka lūmur šēpīka luššiq u qinnī ṣeher rabi amur aššumišunu rēmanni na'rārka likšudanni* (AbB 9: 141)
>
> Tell the God, my father, this is what Apil-Adad, your servant said: Why have you become indifferent to me? Who could give you one like me? Write to Marduk, who loves you, so that he may break my bondage. May I see your face, may I kiss your feet. Also, look after my family, old and young; have mercy on me for their sake. May your help reach me.

The following letter demonstrates some Babylonian draft-dodging techniques:

> *ana Lipit-Adad qibima umma X-ma Šamaš* [. . .] [6] *inanna* [*ṭuppi šarrim*][line broken] *Sippar-liwwir Erība-Sin Ilšu-bāni* [*ana B*]*ābili ṭarādim ittalkam* [13] *kīma ālam lā wašbāta aqbi* [15] *pīqat ša ṭuppi šarrim ublam isahhurka lā tanakkud* [19] *mimma ṭuppum aššumika ul illik* [21] *ramānka i-ta-ba-al-ma našparum lā immarka* [23] *šūhizma kīma ālam lā wašbāta lidbubū* [26] *ana pīqat našparum ištene''ika . . . annītam ašpurak*<*kum*> (AbB 7: 42)
>
> Tell Lipit-Adad, this is what X (name illegible) said: May Šamaš [keep you well]. [6] Now a letter from the king has arrived [about] sending Sippar-liwwir, Erība-Sin and Ilšu-bāni to Babylon. [13] I said that you were not staying in town. [15] Perhaps (the messenger) who brought the letter will look for you, (but) don't be frightened. [19] No letter about you has arrived. [21] Get yourself off, so that the messenger doesn't see you. [23] Instruct (the people) so that they say that you are not staying in town. [26] If perhaps the messenger keeps searching for you [do something]. This is what I have written to you.

Information and requests for information on the well-being (or otherwise) of relatives are very common. The following letter is from a man to his (not necessarily biological) 'mother', to tell her about the whereabouts of a relative who apparently has not written for a long time.

[1] *ana ummija qibima umma Šamaš-bani mārukima Ilabrat u Lugalnamtarra* MU.ŠÁR.KAM *liballiṭūki* [6] *aššum Sin-gāmil ša tašpurī ištu ūmim ša tašpurī ana hissatiki rūq ina bīti tappišti wašib* [12] *paršīgum u ṣubātū turrūšu kīma ša ina bītišu wašbu pānūšu daglū* [16] *ina waṣîšu tašâlīšu kīma libbiki lā marāṣi adi awīlum illakamma ú-ši-ṣú-uš pānīšu adaggal* [22] *anāku ana ša tašapparī ahī anaddi* (AbB 9: 230)

[1] Tell my mother, this is what Šamaš-bani your son said: May Ilabrat and Lugalnamtarra keep you well for 3600 years. [6] Concerning Sin-gāmil, about whom you wrote, since the day when you wrote, he is (too) far away to remember you. He is living in a home of relaxation[?]. [12] The head-dress and the garments have been returned to him. He is being waited upon, as if he was living in his own house. [16] You can ask him (about it) when he goes out. In order not to annoy you I will attend to him until the gentleman comes to take him out. [22] Would I be negligent about what you write?

The next letter is a greeting sent from a merchant on a business trip to his mother and his wife (?) at home.

[1] *ana Šunutum ummija u bēltija u Ahatum qibima umma Šamaš-iddinamma* [6] *šalmāku ina Awal anāku ana Aššur pānūja arhiš allakam* [10] *kurbīma ibbê limaṭṭi atti aššumija lū šalmāti anāku aššumiki lū šalmāku mahar bēliki kurbīm* (AbB 3: 60)

[1] Tell Šunutum my mother and lady, and Ahatum, this is what Šamaš-iddinam said: [6] I am well, I am in Awal. My destination is Aššur, I am coming to you soon. [10] Pray so that he (the god) will decrease the losses. May you be well for my sake, may I be well for your sake. Pray for me to your lord.

The following letter is a distressed message from a woman to an ill relative:

[1]*ana Rīš-Šubula qibima umma Bēlessunuma* [4] *bēlī Šamaš u bēltī Ṣarpānītum aššumija dāriš ūmī liballiṭūka* [7] *ištu silihtaka ešmû mādiš attaziq* [9] *u kala ūmi u kala mūšim abtanakki* [11] *ana šulmika ašpuram šulumka šupram* (AbB 7: 62)

[1] Tell Rīš-Šubula, this is what Bēlessunu said: [4] May my lord Šamaš and my lady Ṣarpānītum keep you well for ever for my sake. [7] Since I have heard about your illness, I have become very worried. [9] I have been crying all day and all night. [11] I am writing to ask how you are, write to me how you are!

The last example is a letter from a nanny (?), who is sending a shopping list to her employer. This again demonstrates the everyday nature of the medium, even if the choice of ingredients for dinner may not whet the appetite of modern readers:

> *ana bēlija qibima umma Tatūr-mātum amatkama Šamaš u Aja kallātum aššumija dāriš ūmī liballiṭūka bītum šalim u ṣuhārū šalmū aššum enkētim u erbī ša una''iduka lā tamašši leqe'am* . . . (AbB 2: 141)

> Tell my lord, this is what your maid Tatūr-mātum said: May Šamaš and the bride Aja keep you well for ever for my sake. The house is well and the children are well. Don't forget the fish and the locusts that I told you about. Get them for me . . .

The spontaneous and colloquial nature of many of the letters can be seen in their language as well as in their content. The style and grammar of the letters show various noticeable differences not only from the language of poetry, but also from more formal prose genres such as legal documents. For example, in all periods, the use of discourse particles such as 'now then' is common in the letters. (In Old Babylonian we find *gana* or *magana*, 'now then' or 'come on', and in Neo-Babylonian we find *amur* 'look', 'now then'.) The register of Old Babylonian letters is also set apart from more formal texts by their use of anaphora (Aro 1955: 156). Letters also use many idiomatic expressions which do not appear in other genres.

There are undoubtedly formulaic expressions in the letters, but they are mostly confined to the opening and the greetings. The text itself is often very free. In this respect, the Babylonian letters are not different from modern ones, where even in the most informal contexts some formulaic expressions are used (for example, the date, 'dear X', 'yours') but the content itself can be more spontaneous.

3.5. Some points of Akkadian grammar

The following sundry points are not meant to present a general introduction to Akkadian or Babylonian grammar. They only serve to highlight a few specific grammatical issues, mainly to make it easier for readers who are not familiar with the language to follow the glosses. For general introductions to Akkadian grammar see von Soden (1995) (the standard reference grammar), Buccellati (1996), and Huehnergard (1997).

3.5.1. *Nouns*

Akkadian nouns have three cases: nominative, accusative, and genitive. All prepositions take the genitive case. Pronouns also show a dative case. Akkadian distinguishes between singular, plural, and in the earlier periods also dual. There are two genders, masculine and feminine. In this book, the Akkadian object suffixes *-šu* ('him') and *-ša* ('her') are sometimes glossed as 'it' when they refer to inanimate objects, in order for the gloss to make sense in English.

3.5.2. *Possessive*

There are two possessive constructions, which are demonstrated in (7) and (8) below. The construction in (7) is periphrastic, with the particle *ša* (which is also the relative particle). The 'possessed' noun ('king') receives the case ending according to its place in the clause, whereas the 'possessor' is in the genitive case. In the second construction (8), the 'possessor' is still in the genitive case, but the 'possessed' noun is in a special nominal form called the 'construct state'. I gloss a noun X in the construct state as 'X.of'.

(7) *šarr-um ša māt-im imūt*
king-NOM of land-GEN he.died
'the king of the land died'

(8) *šar māt-im imūt*
king.of land-GEN he.died
'the king of the land died'

3.5.3. *Verbal system*

The verbal system of Akkadian, like that of other Semitic languages, is very complex. The system is based on (mainly) tri-consonantal roots, which are completed by prefixes, infixes, suffixes, and gemination, to express person agreement, tense/aspect, and other distinctions. Categories such as passive, causative, reflexive, iterative, or stative are all marked synthetically using this system. (A general introduction to the verbal system and to the concept of the root is given in Buccellati 1996.) The intricacies of the verbal system, however, are not directly relevant to this study. Accordingly, the internal structure of the verbal forms is not indicated in the glosses. I simply try to provide the nearest English equivalent. For example, the form *ušapšiṭ* of the root *pšṭ* ('erase') will be glossed as 'he.caused to erase', and the form *ittanarradā* of the root *wrd* 'go down' will appear as 'they.keep going down'.

A few words should nonetheless be said about the tense/aspect system. Akkadian has three main 'tenses' which are traditionally called present, preterite, and perfect. The present form (*iparras*), which should more accurately be called 'non-past', is used for present, future, durative, and habitual actions, as well as for a range of modal meanings such as 'may', 'can', 'should' (von Soden 1997: 127, Streck 1995: 88 ff.). The examples in this book are glossed so as to make sense in the context, and future or modal nuances appear in brackets. The Akkadian phrase in (9) will be glossed and translated as one of the options below, depending on the context:

(9) *šarr-um iparras*
king-NOM he.decides/he.(will)decide/he.(can)decide
'the king decides'/'the king will decide'/'the king can decide'

The preterite form (*iprus*) is mainly used for past actions or events, and is demonstrated in (10) below. The third form (*iptaras*) is traditionally called 'perfect'. In broad outline, this form also denotes past activities, but the actual use of this form is complex. (Detailed analysis is offered by Streck 1995.) The difference in use between the 'preterite' and the 'perfect' forms depends on discourse and stylistic issues, and since the distinction is entirely irrelevant for the purpose of this study, I do not differentiate between the two forms in the glosses. Both the *iprus* and *iptaras* forms will be glossed as simple English past, and translated so as to make sense in the context.

(10) *šarr-um iprus*
king-NOM he.decided
'the king decided'

3.5.4. *Infinitive*

The Akkadian infinitive is a more nominal form than its English counterpart. The infinitive verb itself takes case endings, like nouns. In terms of argument structure, the infinitive can take nominative or accusative arguments (like a verb), and the structure of the phrase is then verbal, as in (11) below. On the other hand, the infinitive can take a genitive argument (like a noun), and the structure of the phrase is then nominal, as in (12). Infinitives in nominal constructions are often most easily translated with an English gerund (*-ing*).

(11) Verbal construction:
šipr-am epēš-am iqbi'-am
task-ACC perform.INF-ACC he.said-to me
'he told me to perform the task'

(12) Nominal construction:
epēš šipr-im ušaddi
perform.INF.of task-GEN he.prevented
'he prevented the performing of the task' (based on AbB 11: 10: 11)

3.5.5. *The precative, imperative, emphatic particle* lū

The imperative form *purus*, which exists only for the second person, is similar in use to the imperative in English, and is glossed accordingly, as in (13ii). Akkadian has a verbal form called 'precative', which is used for the first person (13i), and third person (13iii). The precative expresses a wish ('let me go' or 'let him go') or command ('he should go'), and is formed by the prefixing of the particle *l(ū)*. (On the morphological details of the process see Testen 1998: 118 and Streck 1995: 210, n. 480.) I gloss the precative using 'let.me/him' or 'he.should', so as to make sense in context.

(13) (i) *luprus* let.me.decide/I.should.decide/I.want to.decide
(ii) *purus* decide.IMP(MSG)
(iii) *šarr-um liprus* king-NOM let.him.decide/he.should.decide

The particle *lū* can also appear as an independent word, to express a wish, or in the meaning 'indeed', in which case it is glossed as EMPH (for EMPHATIC). We shall meet it often with the verb 'know' in the phrase *lū tīde* (EMPH you.know) 'you should know' (or 'beware!').

3.5.6. *Coordination, the particle* -ma

The particle -*ma* (glossed -P) is used for a variety of purposes. It is a coordinating particle, and can also have an emphatic and a predicative function. In this study, we shall only be interested in the coordinating function of -*ma*. As a coordination particle, -*ma* joins clauses which are intimately linked. The nature of the relation is not explicitly specified, so the choice of translation for -*ma* ('and then', 'so that', 'but', 'therefore') must depend on the context, as the examples below show:

(14) 1 *bā'er-am* *takl-am* . . . *lirdi'ak-kum-ma*
1 fisherman-ACC trusty-ACC he.should.lead-to you-P
bā'er-am *šuāti* *ana Bābili* *šūri'am-ma*
fisherman-ACC that.ACC to Babylon send.IMP-P
ana bīt *šipr-im* *linnadin*
to house.of work-GEN he.should.be.given
'he should lead to you one trusty fisherman and (= and then) send that fisherman to Babylon and (= so that) he should be given to the "workhouse"' (AbB 13: 7: 20)

(15) *aššum* *aqbû-kum-ma* *lā* *tamguran-ni*
because I.spoke-to you-P not you.agreed-to me
'because I spoke to you and (= but) you didn't agree with me' (AbB 13: 62: 17)

(16) *gerr-um* *paris-ma* *adi* *inanna* *ul* *ašpurak-kim*
road-NOM blocked.STATIVE-P until now not I.wrote-to you(FSG)
'The road was blocked and (= therefore) I haven't written to you until now' (AbB 6: 64: 10)

There is another coordination particle, an independent word *u*, which I gloss 'and'. This particle serves to coordinate intra-clausal elements ('send me barley *and* oil'), and to join clauses more loosely (in which case it can often be translated by 'and also', 'another thing', or 'moreover').

3.5.7. *Verbless clauses, 'stative'*

There is no verbal copula in Akkadian. Sentences of the form 'A is B' can simply be expressed as 'A B', as in (17). Sometimes the particle -*ma* can be used in verbless clauses in a predicative function, as in (18).

(17) *ul ab-ī atta*
not father-my you(MSG).NOM
'you are not my father'

(18) *napišti māt-im eql-um-**ma***
soul.of land-GEN field-NOM-P
'the soul of the land is the field'

There is also a verbal adjective, traditionally called 'stative', which is used in a predicative function in verbless clauses, as in (19):

(19) *nār-um sekrat*
canal-NOM blocked.STATIVE(3FSG)
'the canal is/was/will be blocked'

3.5.8. *The 'subordinative' form of the verb*

Akkadian has a special verbal form called here 'subordinative', which appears in finite subordinate constructions: relative clauses, adverbial clauses, and complements. The subordinative is obligatory in subordinate clauses, and marks their dependence.[7] The subordinative is mostly formed by suffixing *-u* to a verb, provided the verb does not have other suffixes already. It is glossed as -SUB. The subordinative form of the verb is largely responsible for the clear syntactic distinction between subordinate and independent clauses in Akkadian. This distinction is discussed in more detail in §6.3.

[7] For forms with a similar function in other languages (e.g. Irish, Abkhaz, and West Greenlandic) cf. Noonan (1984: 50), Cristofaro (1998*b*: 14).

Part II

The Emergence of Complementizers and Quotatives

4

The Emergence of Finite Complements

Finite complements in Akkadian developed from adverbial clauses. This process may appear unusual, since adverbial clauses are not often reported as sources of finite complements, and since adverbial conjunctions are not often reported as sources of complementizers.[8] Moreover, according to the common interpretation of finite complements as object clauses (an interpretation which I tried to discredit in §2.1 above), the structural aspect of the change from adverbial clauses to complements may seem very problematic.

This chapter examines the emergence of finite complements by tracing the development of the conjunction *kīma* from an adverbial subordinator to a complementizer. I argue that the change from an adverbial to a complement can, in fact, be smooth and very natural, and that it does not present any genuine problems on either the semantic level or the structural level. Section 4.2 describes the core part of this process, the 'bleaching' of *kīma*, from the causal meaning ('because') to the factive meaning ('that'). The following section then examines the structural consequences of this process of semantic change. Section 4.4 suggests another path through which finite complements emerged (slightly later), with two specific verbs used in legal contexts (the 'proving' verbs). Finally, section 4.5 surveys some parallels from other languages for the development of adverbial conjunctions to complementizers. The chapter starts with a brief sketch of the early life of the conjunction *kīma*.

4.1. The early life of *kīma*

The development of the adverbial conjunction *kīma* into a complementizer is the main object of inquiry in this chapter. This development, however, is only the last stage in the long life of the particle *kīma*. In order to put the emergence of the complementizer *kīma* in its historical context, it is worthwhile to cast a quick look at the early life of *kīma*, which lies mainly in prehistoric times. The adverbial conjunction *kīma* must have derived from the preposition *kīma*, which

[8] The best known sources for complementizers are demonstrative, interrogative, and relative particles. Other well-known sources are case markers (Heine and Reh 1988, Harris and Campbell 1995: 291 ff.) and quotative particles (Lord 1993, cf. also chapter 5).

is composed of the preposition *kī* and the emphatic particle *-ma*. In the earliest attested period of Akkadian, the semantic range of *kīma* is already very wide. There are three basic meanings of the conjunction/preposition *kīma*: comparative/manner ('like', 'as', 'according to', 'instead of', 'in the manner of'), temporal ('when', 'as soon as'), and causal/purpose ('because', 'on account of', 'so that'). These three basic meanings are attested already in the earliest period, Old Akkadian.[9]

Such a semantic range must be the result of a historical process whereby an original more restricted range·is extended, without suppletion. But since the three basic uses of *kīma* are attested from the earliest period, we cannot determine directly which of them is original and which derived. Nevertheless, the evidence suggests that *kī*/*kīma* was originally a comparative preposition, and that the temporal and causal meanings developed later. The direct evidence for the primacy of the comparative meaning comes from the fact that *kīma* has cognates in all Semitic languages in this meaning. (For example, Ugaritic *k*, *km*, Hebrew *k*, *kî*, *kmô*, Arabic *ka*, *kamā*, *kay*, Ethiopic *kama*. Moscati et al. 1964: 121.) The comparative meaning is not the only one attested in other Semitic languages, but it is the only one attested as a preposition across Semitic. Since the preposition must be taken to be earlier than the conjunction, this suggests that the comparative meaning was the original one. Moreover, the comparative meaning tends to be the most phonetically reduced.

There is also strong cross-linguistic evidence that the route of semantic extension usually proceeds from comparative (and other modal meanings) to temporal and causal meanings, and not vice versa. Basing himself on a study of adverbial subordinators in Europe, Kortmann (1998: 5) states that 'adverbial subordinators generally acquire temporal senses later than locative or modal senses, and causal, conditional or concessive senses later than the three other types of senses'. For example, consider the English conjunction 'as', which has a semantic range similar to that of *kīma*. 'As' started as a worn down form of 'all so', Old English *ealswā* ('wholly so, quite so, just so'). From this comparative meaning, the temporal and causal uses of 'as' later developed. The first recorded examples in the OED for each of the three basic meanings of 'as' are given below:

(20) Comparative (*c*.1000):
seo beorhtnys is ealswā *eald* swā *þæt fyr*
'the brightness is *just as* old *as* that fire'

(21) Temporal (1220):
he strahte forþ his riht earm ase [*he*] *stode o rode*
'he stretched forth his right arm *as* he stood on the cross'

[9] The three different meanings can be found in Old Akkadian royal inscriptions (Gelb and Kienast 1990). Comparative: Varia 13: 62, temporal: Elam 2: 112, causal: *Nar C 20: 17.

(22) Causal (1400):
lete me fro this deth fle, as *I dede nevyr no trespace*
'let me flee from this death, *as* I never did any wrong'

Fisher (1992: 359) explains this development as follows:

The conjunction *as* could develop into a temporal subordinator when it was used to compare the duration of an activity in the main and subclause: 'Thus pleyneth John as he gooth by the way' (Canterbury Tales I. 4114). *As* does not yet have a clear causal meaning in Middle English but many instances can be given where the beginning of such a development are seen: 'help, god, in this nede!/As thou art stere-man good' (help, God, in this need, like the good helmsman you are/because you are a good helmsman).

The same development can be seen with German *als*, which has an identical origin to 'as'. *Als* is a weakened form of *alse* which in turn is a weakened form of *also* (parallel to Old English *ealswā*). The historical development is given from Grimm's *Deutsches Wörterbuch*:

(23) Comparative (1070):
ich gluobo daz der haltente Christus an dîrre werlte lebeta als *ein ander mennisco, âz, tranc, slief*
'I think that Christ the saviour lived in this world *like* any other man, ate, drank, slept'

(24) Temporal (1195):
als *ich under wîlen zir gesitzé / sô si mich mit ir reden lât*
'*when* I sometimes sit by her, and she lets me speak to her'

(25) Causal (1483):
ich mag frou Barbel L. nit vil schriben, wenn ich sy wurd betrüb(en), als *ich wol waisß, von ganzem herzen ir daz gröst laid ist, das ir möcht zufallen*
'I do not want to write much to Mrs Barbel L, in case I might upset her, *because* I well know that this is the greatest sorrow that could happen to her'

In French, a similar development occurs with the particle *comme*, which again has a semantic range similar to 'as' and *als*. The origin here is Latin *quomodo*, meaning 'in which way', and from there the familiar range develops. 'De l'emploi comparatif procède, par une comparaison d'égalité appliquée à un rapport de simultanéité, l'emploi temporel et, de ce dernier, l'emploi causal' (Robert 1992, s.v. *comme*).

The examples above have demonstrated the path of change comparative > temporal > causal. The second stage of this development, the change from temporal to causal meaning, is extremely common, and is widely discussed in the literature (Heine et al. 1991*a*, 1991*b*, Hopper and Traugott 1993: 75–7). The development of the comparative meaning directly to a causal meaning has not been discussed so often, but there is no reason to assume that it is impossible. The following examples from Old Babylonian demonstrate some contexts in which both a comparative and causal interpretation for *kīma* are possible. Such contexts may have facilitated the development of the causal meaning of *kīma* in prehistoric times. (In the following examples, and in the rest of the chapter, *kīma* is glossed as *kīma* (rather than as 'when', 'because', COMP, etc.) whenever more than one interpretation is plausible.)

(26) *awâtim* *ša* *tašpur-am* *kīma abū-ka* *anāku*
matters.ACC REL you.wrote-to me *kīma* father-your I
lulammid-ka
let.me.inform-you
'let me inform you, as I am your father, about the matters which you wrote' (AbB 9: 250: 10)

(27) *kīma udammiqak-kunūši* *dummiqā-nim*
kīma I.did favours-to you(PL) do favours.IMP(PL)-to me
'as I have done you favours, do me favours' (AbB 9: 53: 5)

Both internal evidence and cross-linguistic parallels thus suggest that the original meaning of *kīma* was comparative, and that the temporal and causal meanings developed from there. As I explained above, the wide semantic range of *kīma* resulted from the fact that new meanings were acquired without the old ones being lost. It is interesting that a wide semantic range for adverbial subordinators was in general more common in older European languages than in their modern descendants. Kortmann conducted a survey of adverbial subordinators in the languages of Europe, and reports the following (1997: 3):

> What we find is a tendency away from polysemy[10] to monosemy and from more polysemous to less polysemous. This is a part of a historical phenomenon which has among other things been described as 'semantic streamlining' . . . Whereas, for example, more than half of the adverbial subordinators in Latin and Classical Greek were polysemous, the average proportion in the modern European languages has gone down to a third.

In Akkadian, the semantic range of *kīma* was expanded even further, when it developed into a complementizer in the Old Babylonian period. To demonstrate this wide semantic range in Old Babylonian, we can put the cart before the horse for a moment, and look at an example which shows how (after the development of *kīma* as a complementizer) various uses of *kīma* could coexist happily, even in adjacent sentences:

[10] I would prefer the term 'non-differentiation' to Kortmann's 'polysemy'. The term 'polysemy' implies that we are dealing with a list of distinct meanings, which is often not the case. I will use the neutral term 'wide semantic range'.

(28) *ana Šamaš-hāzir qibi-ma umma Lu-Ninurta-ma*
to Šamaš-hāzir say.IMP-P QUOT Lu-Ninurta-P
Šamaš liballiṭ-ka
Šamaš he.should.make live-you
'Tell Šamaš-hāzir, this is what Lu-Ninurta said: may Šamaš keep you in good health.'

aššum Ahum kīma lā ṣehru-ma rabû ul tīde
concerning Ahum *that* not child-P grown man not you.know
'Concerning Ahum, don't you know that he is not a child but a grown man?'

kīma awīlē ahhī-šu kīma PN_2 PN_3 u PN_4
like men.GEN brothers-his *like* PN_2 PN_3 and PN_4
eql-am apul-šu
field-ACC hand.IMP-him
'Like his gentlemen brothers, like PN_2 PN_3 and PN_4, hand over to him a field.'

kīma ēpiš ṣibût-im lā ša šuta"-îm šū-ma
that doer.of assignment-GEN not of neglect.INF-GEN he-P
ul tīde
not you.know
'Don't you know that he is on assignment and should not be treated neglectfully?'

lā tušta'aš-šum bēl-ī iqbi'-am-ma ašpurak-kum
not you.neglect-to him lord-my he.said-to me-P I.wrote-to you
'Don't treat him neglectfully! I am writing to you because my lord told me to.'

kīma tātapl-u-šu ša eql-am ātapal-šu
when you.handed-SUB-him REL field-ACC I.handed-him
meher ṭuppi-ja šūbil-am
reply.of tablet-my send.IMP-to me
'When you hand to him (a field), send me a reply to my letter of (the content): "I handed him a field".' (AbB 4: 53: 1)

4.2. Semantic bleaching of the causal adverbial conjunction *kīma*

We can now resume the real object of investigation of this chapter, and examine the mechanisms by which the complementizer *kīma* emerged from the adverbial uses of *kīma*. The main path through which the complementizer emerged was the weakening (or 'bleaching') of the causal meaning of *kīma* 'because' to a factive meaning 'that'. This bleaching occurred in particular 'bridging' contexts, in which both a causal and a factive interpretation of the *kīma* clause are possible. In §2.1, I mentioned examples of predicates such as 'be angry', which require arguments in a 'causal' or 'reason' semantic role. In sentences such as 'he was angry *because/that* the barley was not collected', the adverbial clause introduced by 'because', and the complement clause introduced by 'that' in fact describe the same situation.

In Babylonian, which is not particularly rich in abstract predicates of mental states, the bridging context for the process of semantic change was formed by speech-related verbs such as 'say', 'write', 'inform', or 'complain'. With these verbs, there can be a similar relation between a causal and a factive interpretation of the *kīma* clause:

(29) He complained to the governor
He informed the governor
He wrote to the governor
He said/spoke to the governor
} *kīma* (= *because/that*) the barley was not collected.

In the examples above, there is no fundamental difference between the causal and the factive interpretations of the *kīma* clause, since both describe essentially the same situation. If we take the situation with 'complain' as an example, the reason for the complaint in (29) is the same as the content of the complaint. To spell out the situation, we could say: '*because* the barley was not collected, he complained *that* the barley was not collected'. The only difference between the causal and factive interpretation is one of emphasis. The causal interpretation emphasizes the reason for making the speech act, whereas the factive interpretation emphasizes the content of the speech act.

It must have been through the use of *kīma* in such contexts that the process of semantic bleaching took place. The evidence from the Old Akkadian and early Old Babylonian periods is not abundant, so it is difficult to demonstrate such a process in detail. Nevertheless, the examples we do have suggest that speech-related verbs indeed formed the bridging context for the bleaching of the causal meaning of *kīma*. In Old Akkadian, *kīma* is not attested in the bleached factive meaning 'that'.[11] The first time we find *kīma* in this meaning is in the early Old

[11] There is one broken example in Old Akkadian of a *kīma* clause followed by the verb 'know'. This example is frustrating because it is broken in too many places to make it comprehensible. But it does not seem to be a finite complement. The suggested restoration by Kienast and Volk (1995) is:

ki-na-tu-ì-a in bu-bu-tim i-mu-tu kīma ŠE.BA *[i]m*[!?]*-ṭi-ù [i]ṣ-hi-ru*
workers-my in hunger-GEN they.die *kīma* rations decreased-SUB diminished-SUB
LUGAL *i-da ar-hi-iš [li]-šè-er*
king he.knows quickly [?]let-him-rectify[?] (SAB: Um 3)
'My people are dying from hunger, because the rations have become scarce—the king knows (about it)! He (someone else, not the king) should rectify[?] (the situation) quickly.'

But by their own admission, the suggested restoration does not agree very well at all with the traces of the broken signs. Another restoration, even less convincing, has *[ku]-ṭi-ù [m]a-hi-ru* instead of *[i]m*[!?]*-ṭi-ù [i]ṣ*[!]*-hi-ru*. This would read 'my people are dying from hunger, while (even) the Gutians are getting rations—the King knows (about it)!' Unfortunately, unless a compelling restoration is found, it is difficult to draw reliable conclusions from this example.

Babylonian period, in a group of letters from Ešnunna, dating from around 1900 BC (Whiting 1987. The two earlier groups of letters from Ešnunna, dating from earlier on in the twentieth century BC, contain no examples of 'bleached' *kīma*.) The first example we find is (30) below, with the verb *šūdûm* ('make known', 'inform'), and it is in precisely such a context where both a causal and a factive interpretation of *kīma* are possible.

(30) *PN šupur-ma kīma nār-um sekrat*
PN write.IMP-P kīma river-NOM blocked.STATIVE(FSG)
šūdi-šum
make known.IMP-to him
'write to PN and inform him because/that the river is blocked' (Whiting 1987: 40: 3')

In fact, throughout the Old Babylonian period, the great majority of examples of *kīma* clauses with speech-related verbs are indeed found in such 'ambiguous' contexts. A number of examples are given below:[12]

(31) *šumma alap awīl-im nakkapī kīma nakkapû bābta-šu*
if ox.of man-GEN gorer *kīma* gorer.SUB district-his
ušēdi-šum-ma
it.made known-to him-P
'if a man's ox is a gorer and his district (authorities) informed him because/that it is a gorer' (CH §251)[13]

(32) *kīma ana miks-i makās-i taprikā-ma adi inanna*
kīma to tax-GEN collect.INF-GEN you(PL).prevented-P until now
miks-u lā immaks-u mākis Bābili idbub
tax-NOM not collected-SUB tax collector.of Babylon he.complained
'the tax collector of Babylon complained because/that you prevented collecting the taxes so that taxes have not been collected yet' (AbB 11: 89: 7)

(33) *kīma ittī-ja ītawû alp-am šâtu alqû-šu*
kīma with-me he.spoke.SUB ox-ACC this.ACC I.took.SUB-(from) him
ašpurak-kum
I.wrote-to you
'I wrote to you because/that he spoke to me and I took this ox from him' (AbB 8: 26: 3')

[12] Some other examples are: AbB 2: 62: 6, 6: 179: 13, 9: 154: 14, 10: 210: 3, TCL 1: 26: 6, TCL 17: 58: 13.

[13] Example (31) is from the law code of Hammurabi. It is very interesting that the parallel passage from an older law code, that of Ešnunna, does not have a finite complement:

šumma alp-um nakkapī-ma bābt-um ana bēli-šu ušēdi-ma
if ox-NOM gorer-P district-NOM to owner-his it.made known-P
'if an ox is a gorer and the district informed its owner'
(Laws of Ešnunna §54, cf. also §56, §58)

(34) *kīma eql-um šū ihhaššah-u PN i[špur]-am*
kīma field-NOM this.NOM is needed.3SG-SUB PN he.wrote-to me
'PN wrote to me because/that this field is needed' (AbB 6: 6: 6)

(35) *aššum šigūš-im . . . kīma PN+ lā imhur-u ašpurak-ku*
about bitter barley-GEN *kīma* PN+ not he.received-SUB I.wrote-to you
'concerning the bitter barley, I wrote to you because/that PN+ didn't receive (it)' (AbB 9: 154: 12)

(36) *kīma 30 puhādī nēmetta-kunu ana Bābili lā tublānim*
kīma 30 lambs payment-your(PL) to Babylon not you(PL).sent
PN+ iqbi'-am
PN+ he.said-to me
'PN+ spoke/said to me because/that you did not send the 30 lambs, your payment, to Babylon' (AbB 2: 75: 5)

(37) *kīma šuddun-am lā nile''û ana bēli-ja aqbi*
kīma collect.INF-ACC not we.can to lord-my I.said
'I spoke/said to my lord because/that we were unable to collect (them)' (AbB 13: 33: 27)

(38) *kīma bīti napṭari-ja buzzû PN ahū-ka*
kīma warehouse-my pressed.STATIVE(3SG) PN brother-your
iqbi'-am
he.said-to me
'PN your brother spoke/told me because/that my warehouse was pressed (for payment)' (AbB 2: 97: 6)

(39) *kīma ana ugār-im rab-î[m] . . . eleppēt bā'irī*
kīma to water meadow-GEN great-GEN boats.of fishermen.GEN
ittanarra[dā-ma][14] *nūnī ibarr[ū] iqbû-[nim]*
they.keep going down-P fish.ACC they.catch they.said-to me
'they spoke/said to me because/that the fishermen's boats keep going down to the great water meadow and they are catching fish' (AbB 2: 62: 6)

(40) *kīma ṣābum Samharū ṣābum mādum-ma ana* ÁB.GUD.HI.A
kīma people Samharites people many-P to cattle
U_8.UDU.HI.A *u* ERIM *wāṣīt Sippar-Jahrurum šahāṭ-im*
sheep and people going out.of Sippar-Jahrurum attack.INF-GEN
ana libbu mātim ībirūnim turgumann-um . . . iqbi'-am
to hinterland they.came translator-NOM he.said-to me
'the translator [who has come from the camp of the Kassites] spoke/said to me because/that the Samharites are numerous and have come to the hinterland to attack cattle, sheep, and people leaving Sippar-Jahrurum' (AbB 7: 47: 6)

[14] This restoration is based on Huehnergard (1997: 418).

The examples above show the contexts in which the process of semantic bleaching of *kīma* could take place. As I mentioned, the large majority of the examples of *kīma* clauses with speech-related verbs is found in contexts where a causal interpretation is still plausible. Nevertheless, the repeated use of *kīma* in such contexts must have resulted in semantic bleaching. We do find some examples of speech verbs with *kīma* (although only a few), where the causal interpretation is no longer plausible:

(41) the woman took the barley and went away
kīma ittalkam ul iqbi'-am
kīma she.went not she.said-to me
'she did not tell me that she went' (AbB 2: 103: 7)

(42) concerning the sealed tablet that you had shown me
kīma āmur-u mahar šāpir Sippar ušanni-ma
kīma I.saw-SUB presence.of supervisor.of Sippar I.repeated-P
'I repeated in the presence of the supervisor of Sippar that I have seen (it)' (AbB 2: 173: 7)

(43) Just as I said myself
kīma $^{1}/_{3}$ MA.NA *kasp-am PN . . . ilqû mahar dajjānī*
kīma $^{1}/_{3}$ mina silver-ACC PN he.took.SUB presence.of judges.GEN
iqbi-ma
he.said-P
'he said in front of the judges that PN had taken $^{1}/_{3}$ mina of silver' (AbB 11: 158: 21')

(44) *kīma eql-am . . . ana rēdî iddin-u anna ītapal*
kīma field-ACC to soldiers.GEN he.gave-SUB yes he.answered
'he acknowledged that he gave a field to the soldiers' (AbB 2: 90: 15)

There is even one example where *kīma* seems to introduce a 'non-factive' complement, one which contains a false statement. In example (45) below (from a letter I quoted in the introduction), the sender reports having said something which is (and which he knows to be) untrue. A few lines later, he urges the recipient of the letter to do likewise. This is the only clear example in the corpus of a non-factive finite complement. (But perhaps *kīma* here is used in the meaning 'as if': 'I spoke as if you were not staying in town'?)

(45) *kīma āl-am lā wašbāta aqbi*
kīma town-ACC not you.live.STATIVE I.said
'I said that you were not staying in town' (AbB 7: 42: 13)

šūhiz-ma kīma āl-am lā wašbāta lidbubū
instruct.IMP-P *kīma* town-ACC not you.live.STATIVE let.them.speak
'instruct (the people) so that they say that you are not staying in town' (AbB 7: 42: 23)

It is possible that the bleaching of other adverbial uses of *kīma* also contributed to the emergence of the factive meaning. One potential additional route is the bleaching of the purpose meaning 'so that'. Across languages, purpose clauses are the most common source of infinitival complements (Haspelmath 1989). In theory, therefore, finite purpose clauses could also be the source of finite complements. In Babylonian, purpose clauses with *kīma* can be either infinitival, as in (46), or finite (47). When a finite purpose clause with *kīma* appears with manipulative verbs, the construction can be ambiguous in a similar way to the causal examples above. In (48) below, both a purpose interpretation and a factive interpretation are plausible from the context.

(46) *kīma lā nazāqi-ka eppuš*
kīma not irritate.INF-your I.(will)act
'I will act so as not to irritate you' (AbB 3: 2: 27)

(47) *kīma lā aturr-u-ma ina puhur ahhī-ja šumi*
kīma not I.(can)return-SUB-P in assembly.of brothers-my name.of
bīt a-bi lā azakkar-u tēteps-anni
house.of father.GEN not I.(can)mention-SUB you.did-to me
'you have treated me so that I cannot mention again the name of (my) family in the company of my peers' (TCL1: 18: 9)

(48) *kīma anāku eppeš-u qibi-šum*
kīma I I.(will)work-SUB say.IMP-to him
'speak to him so that I will work (it)' or: 'tell him that I will work (it)' (AbB 3: 2: 45)

Nevertheless, because there are so few examples like (48) above, it is difficult to assess whether they are significant. What seems clear, in any case, is that the main path of development of the complementizer was the bleaching of the *causal* meaning of *kīma*, and that the role of other adverbial meanings was at best ancillary.

I suggested in this section that speech-related verbs provided the bridging context for the weakening ('bleaching') of the causal meaning of *kīma*. In these bridging contexts, both a causal interpretation of *kīma* ('because'), and a factive interpretation ('that') are plausible from the context. In most examples of *kīma* clauses with speech verbs, a causal interpretation is still possible. But we do find a few examples where a causal interpretation is unlikely. These examples demonstrate that semantic bleaching did indeed take place with these speech-related verbs.

4.3. When do 'adverbial clauses' become 'complements'?

The process of semantic bleaching of *kīma*, which I described in the previous section, does not seem particularly problematic. But the structural element of the change requires more careful examination. In the 'ambiguous' examples above, where both a causal and a factive interpretation of *kīma* is possible, I glossed *kīma* as 'because/that'. But it may be argued that the difference between 'because' and 'that' should entail much more than just the strength of the causal undertone of *kīma*. The difference between 'because' and 'that' should be that 'because' introduces an adverbial clause, whereas 'that' introduces a complement clause, which is supposed to be a very different creature from an adverbial. An adverbial clause is a peripheral element. It is subordinate only on the sentence level, and is not a part of the verb phrase. A complement clause, on the other hand, is an argument of the verb, and at least according to general wisdom, functions as the object of the verb. Should we not expect, then, that when adverbial clauses turn into finite complements, some significant structural changes would co-occur with the semantic bleaching of *kīma*?

In fact, there is no evidence for any abrupt structural changes which accompanied the process of semantic bleaching of *kīma*. Moreover, this section will argue that no abrupt structural upheavals are required on theoretical grounds either. In order to demonstrate why, it may be helpful first to adopt a different gloss for the 'bleached' factive use of *kīma*. If the association between 'because' and 'that' seems confusing, the nature of the change may become clearer if instead of 'that', we gloss the 'factive' meaning of *kīma* as 'about the fact that'. The change from a causal to a factive interpretation would then be represented as follows: 'I complained *kīma* (= because of the fact that) the barley has not been collected' > 'I complained *kīma* (= about the fact that) the barley has not been collected'. (Of course, I do not want to imply that the way we gloss *kīma* makes the remotest difference to a process which occurred four thousand years ago. The different gloss may simply assist in illuminating for us the nature of the change.)

Section 2.1 explained why the equation between complement clauses and objects is problematic, and showed that finite complements do not always have to function as objects of the verb. With some verbs, finite complements may have the same distribution as nominal objects, but other finite complements are equally happy to be associated with intransitive verbs (such as 'complain'), or other predicates ('be angry', 'news'). The common denominator to all sentential complements is not their identification with the surface category 'object', but rather their intimate semantic link with the predicate, namely their status as arguments.

This interpretation of complementation is particularly important for the understanding of the emergence of finite complements in Akkadian. If finite complements always had to function as direct objects, we would need to postulate that a fairly spectacular reanalysis must have taken place hand in hand with the process of semantic bleaching of *kīma*. The adverbial clause, which was outside the verb phrase, and subordinate only on the sentence level, would need to be reanalysed overnight as the direct object of the verb. But there is no evidence that any such spectacular reanalysis took place at any given time. The reason for this is simple: finite complements with *kīma* emerged precisely in the context of verbs with which complements do not function as objects. The bridging context for the change in the meaning of *kīma* was formed by verbs such as 'inform', 'complain', and 'speak'. As we saw in §2.1, finite complements with these verbs do not function as objects, but rather correspond to nominal arguments in 'oblique' semantic roles ('inform *about* . . .', 'complain *about/because*', etc.).

Thus, the only change that needed to accompany the bleaching of *kīma* in the context of the speech-related verbs was a change in the status of the *kīma* clauses from peripheral elements to arguments. But as section 2.1 explained (following Langacker and Croft), the distinction between peripheral elements and arguments is itself a semantic distinction, and as such it is not binary, but rather one of degree. The emergence of finite complements from adverbial clauses can therefore be seen as a combination of gradual semantic processes, which do not need to involve any abrupt structural upheavals. The two processes are the bleaching of the causal meaning of *kīma* on the one hand, and the forging of an intimate link between the verb and the (erstwhile peripheral) adverbial clauses on the other hand. These two processes are intimately intertwined, and both stem directly from the semantic properties of the verbs that formed the bridging context.

We can thus sketch the following scenario for the emergence of the complements. The original use of causal *kīma* clauses is purely adverbial. The causal semantic role is explicitly expressed by the conjunction *kīma*, and the *kīma* clauses are peripheral elements. (They can modify any sentence, and they do not form any particular link with the verb.) But with some particular verbs (such as 'complain', or 'inform' in certain contexts), the reason for the action is not a peripheral element, but in fact an essential part of the interpretation of the action. This quality of the 'bridging' verbs can be imagined as a magnet which attracts the *kīma* clauses, and creates a more intimate link between the originally peripheral elements and the verb. Moreover, with these 'bridging' verbs, the reason for the action (the reason for making a speech act) is the same as the content of the speech act itself. The meaning of *kīma* in such contexts can then change from denoting the reason for making the speech act ('complain *because* of the fact that . . .') to denoting the subject or 'direction' of the speech act ('complain *about* the fact that . . .'). The combined outcome of these two processes was that the conjunction *kīma*, which had originally introduced peripheral elements and had an explicit causal meaning, turned into a factive conjunction which introduces sentential arguments. The adverbial clauses turned into finite complements.

4.3.1. *The emergence of finite complements as a distinct structural category*

The previous section argued that the emergence of complements consisted of a combination of semantic changes, which did not involve any abrupt structural upheavals. Nevertheless, are there no structural or surface consequences for these changes at all? This section will show that there are in fact structural consequences for the processes of semantic change, and that the 'complement' *kīma* clauses become distinct from other adverbial clauses in various respects. However, it should be remembered that these changes do not necessarily make finite complements 'function as' objects. The essential structural question that we have to answer is whether finite complements emerged as a separate syntactic category, distinct from adverbial clauses. The question of similarity with objects is only secondary, and will be discussed in the following section.

Various points make it clear that the *kīma* clauses in question do emerge as a separate category. First, the bleached *kīma* clauses quickly become distinct from other adverbial clauses in terms of the range of verbs that they are associated with. The semantic change occurred originally in the context of speech-related verbs. But quickly after (if not hand in hand with) the process of bleaching in such contexts, there is an extension in the use of the factive *kīma* clauses to knowledge and perception verbs, most notably to the verb 'know'.

On the one hand, such an extension is very natural. It is only a short step, for example, from the verb *šūdûm* (literally 'cause to know', 'inform') to *idûm* ('know'); from 'he caused the king to know *kīma* the river is blocked' to 'the king knows *kīma* the river is blocked'. But on the other hand, with the verb 'know', a causal interpretation of the *kīma* clause is no longer plausible from the context. The verb 'know' is outside the 'bridging context', because it no longer involves an action which requires a reason as a central part of its interpretation.

We already find *kīma* clauses with the verb 'know' (and with semantically related verbs like 'learn') in early Old Babylonian.[15] A few examples from early Old Babylonian are given in (49)–(53) below. Since causal *kīma* clauses do not normally appear with 'know', the distribution of the bleached *kīma* clauses sets them apart from the causal adverbial clauses.

(49) *kīma PN jā'um atta ula tīde*
kīma PN mine you not you.know
'don't you know that PN is mine?' (AbB 9: 209: 4)

(50) *kīma še'-um šū ša Sumu-lēl atta ula tīde*
kīma barley-NOM this.NOM of PN you not you.know
'don't you know that the barley belongs to Sumu-lēl?' (AbB 6: 177: 23)

(51) *kīma anhāku ula tīde*
kīma I.am.tired.STATIVE not you.know
'don't you know that I am tired?' (UET 5: 23: 14. Leemans 1960, p. 42)

(52) *kīma ana tāmart-im eql-um ibaššû ula tīdeā*
kīma to audience gift-GEN field-NOM there.is.SUB not you(PL).know
'don't you know that there is a field for audience gift?' (Al-A'dami 1967: pl. 17: 8)

(53) *kīma annikīam weri'-am lā dummuq-am lā*
kīma here copper-ACC not good-ACC not
amahhar-u-ka talammad
I.(will)receive-SUB-you you.(will)learn
'you will learn here that I will not accept from you copper that is not good quality' (UET 5: 81: 46. Leemans 1960, p. 40)

[15] And also in the Old Assyrian letters which are contemporary with early Old Babylonian.

Later on in the Old Babylonian period, other structural factors also combine to make the distinction between finite complements and adverbial clauses more marked. The most obvious factor is word order. Adverbial clauses are overwhelmingly preverbal in Akkadian, most often sentence-initial. The bleached *kīma* clauses inherited the preverbal position of the causal *kīma* clauses.[16] During the Old Babylonian period, however, we start finding that some complement clauses migrate to the right of the verb. Unfortunately, most of the examples cannot be dated accurately, but all seem to be from the middle or late Old Babylonian period. Some examples are given below:

(54) *ul tīde kīma kasap ekall-im u ṣibt-am*
not you.know *kīma* silver.of palace-GEN and interest-ACC
ikaṣṣarū
they.(will)collect
'don't you know that they will collect the silver of the palace and the interest?' (AbB 13: 65: 6)

(55) *amātū-ki ištenemmeā kīma lā bēles-sina anāku*
servants-your(FSG) they.(will)keep hearing *kīma* not lady-their I
'your servants will keep hearing that I am not their lady' (AbB 6: 188: 7')

(56) *ul tīde kīma ullânū-ka ah-am lā īšû*
not you.know *kīma* except-you brother-ACC not I.have.SUB
'don't you know that I don't have any brother except you?'

ul tīde kīma māt-um kalu-ša ša Marduk u Samsu-iluna
not you.know *kīma* land-NOM all of-it of Marduk and Samsu-iluna
šarr-im
king-GEN
'don't you know that the whole land belongs to Marduk and to the king Samsu-iluna?' (TCL 17: 55: 4)

Only complement *kīma* clauses migrate to post-verbal position. Normal adverbial clauses remain preverbal, and this clearly marks complements as a distinct group. In the Old Babylonian period, the post-verbal position of the comple-

[16] The *kīma* clauses are normally in sentence-initial position. More rarely, the subject of the main verb can appear in sentence-initial position, and the *kīma* clause then comes after the subject. The following two parallel examples from letters of King Abi-ešuh demonstrate the variation. The first example (repeated from (36)) has the order Complement–S–V, whereas the second example has the order S–Complement–V:

kīma 30 puhādī nēmetta-kunu ana Bābili lā tublānim PN+ iqbi'-am
[*kīma* 30 lambs payment-your(PL) to Babylon not you(PL).sent] PN+ he.said-to me
'PN+ told me because/that you did not send the 30 lambs, your payment, to Babylon' (AbB 2: 75: 5)

PN kīma puhādī nēmetta-ka ana ekall-im lā tublam iqbi'-am
PN [*kīma* lambs payment-your to palace-GEN not you.brought] he.said-to me
'PN told me because/that you did not bring the lambs, your payment, to the palace' (AbB 2: 64: 5)

ments is still optional, and fairly rare. But by the Middle Babylonian period, post-verbal position, as in (57) below, has become the norm with complements. (More examples are given in §7.2.) Thus, by the Middle Babylonian period, complements are always distinguished from adverbial clauses by word order, because they come after the verb, whereas adverbial clauses still come before the verb.

(57) *bēl-ī* *īde* *kī* *ultu* *ēlâ* *dilipt-u*
lord-my he.knows COMP since I.arrived trouble-NOM
mahratan-ni
confronts.STATIVE(FSG)-me
'my lord knows that since I arrived, trouble has befallen me'
(MB. BE 17: 43: 4)

It is interesting to note that the word-order properties of finite complements, which come to distinguish them from adverbial clauses, in fact also mark them apart from nominal objects. Like adverbial clauses, nominal objects remain preverbal throughout the history of Babylonian (except in the language of poetry, where word order is much freer). Word order, therefore, does not contribute to any similarity between finite complements and objects, since the position of finite complements is different from both adverbial clauses and nominal objects. (The reason for the migration of complements to post-verbal position must be related to their heaviness. Dryer (1980) reports that across languages, sentential complements often appear in post-verbal position, even in otherwise very strict verb-final languages.)

4.3.2. *Similarity with objects*

The previous section surveyed the surface indications for the emergence of finite complements as a separate syntactic category, distinct from other adverbial clauses. I claimed that the core defining feature for this distinct category is the status of its members as arguments, not their identification with objects. Nevertheless, it is still worthwhile to ask to what extent there emerges any similarity between finite complements and nominal objects. I claimed above that word-order properties in fact set finite complements apart from nominal objects. The similarity between finite complements and objects should be sought elsewhere. In this section, I argue that a perceived association between finite complements and objects must indeed have developed, due to the transitivity of the verbs with which *kīma* clauses began to mingle. The similarity is a consequence of the extension in the use of finite complements from speech-related verbs to more strongly transitive verbs like 'know', 'hear', and 'see'.

Across languages, speech verbs often display many intransitive properties, as Munro (1982) shows. (According to Hopper and Thompson 1980, speech verbs are only 'weakly transitive'.) In Akkadian, speech-related verbs often appear in intransitive constructions. Examples (58*a*, *b*, *c*) below demonstrate a few such constructions, where the unmarked speech verb *qabûm* is most easily translated as 'speak', rather than 'say'. In fact, in the early Old Babylonian period (which is the most relevant period for the emergence of finite complements) speech verbs are also syntactically intransitive when they are followed by direct speech with the quotative construction. As we shall see in chapter 5, the quotative construction with *umma* developed from a bi-clausal structure, in which the speech verb in the first clause is intransitive, and the direct speech is the complement of the quotative clause. This construction functions roughly on the lines of '[he spoke]$_{\text{SPEECH VERB}}$ [and this is what he said]$_{\text{QUOTATIVE CONSTRUCTION}}$ . . .'.

(58) (*a*) PN *ana šarr-im iqbi*
PN to king-GEN he.spoke
'he spoke to the king'

(*b*) *aššum māri-šu ana šarr-im iqbi*
about son-his to king-GEN he.spoke
'he spoke to the king about his son'

(*c*) *qibi-šum-ma lillik*
speak.IMP-to him-P he.should.go
'speak to him so that he should go' (~ tell him to go)
(cf. discussion of manipulation in §8.1)

We have seen already that finite complements do not 'function as' objects with the speech-related verbs which formed the bridging context for their emergence. The weak transitivity of these verbs does not induce any strong association between complements and nominal objects. The situation is different, however, when finite complements are extended to knowledge and perception verbs, which are more strongly transitive. Verbs like 'know', 'hear', and 'see' normally require an object.[17] When these verbs start appearing also with finite complements, a perceived association between these two categories is bound to emerge.

[17] Transitivity in the Akkadian verb is an issue which requires a detailed study on its own. The question of transitivity is complicated in Akkadian by the frequent use of zero anaphora. Especially inanimate and abstract objects are normally not taken up explicitly by anaphoric pronouns, as is demonstrated in the example below:

you wrote to me about something which you heard and which frightened you, saying:
ešme-ma attapalsah
I.heard-P I.threw myself to the ground
'I heard, and threw myself to the ground'
(~ I heard *it*, and threw myself to the ground) (AbB 1: 22: 10)

It could be claimed that such constructions are intransitive, since the verb does not have any overt object. Nevertheless, the use of such constructions with perception and knowledge verbs is different from the 'genuine' intransitive use with the speech verbs. With verbs like 'know', 'hear', and 'see', even if there is no overt anaphoric object, there is nevertheless a definite and immediately accessible 'latent' object in the context, as in the example above. (On 'latency' cf. Matthews 1981: 124 ff.) But in sentences such as 'I spoke to the king', there does not have to be an immediately accessible 'latent' object, and this use can thus be called truly intransitive.

If finite complements appear regularly with verbs which otherwise require a direct object (either overt or 'latent'), the relation between the finite complement and the verb is likely to be perceived as similar to the relation between the direct object and the verb.

The similarity must be especially salient when finite complements and direct objects appear close to one another. For example, in (59) below, the verb 'know' in the first line has a finite complement, whereas the verb 'know' in the second line has a nominal direct object ('my worries').

(59) *kīma še'-um šū ša Sumu-lēl atta ula tīde*
COMP barley-NOM this.NOM of Sumu-lēl you not you.know
'don't you know that this barley belongs to Sumu-lēl?

ištūma lumun libbi-ja lā tīdû
if indeed worries-my not you.know.SUB
u kasapka kalušu lū ersû
may also all your money be prepared
'If indeed you don't know (recognize) my worries, may also all your money be prepared' (AbB 6: 177: 23)

Some paratactic constructions also offer an explicit example for similarity between direct objects and finite complements. In some paratactic constructions with knowledge and perception verbs, an overt object in an anaphoric function is used to 'take up' the previous clause. These constructions are of the form: 'the barley was not collected, I know *this*$_{ACC}$ *matter*$_{ACC}$', as can be seen in examples (60)–(62) below.[18] In such examples, the object 'this matter' performs the same function as a complement clause in the sentence 'I know *kīma* the barley was not collected'. This parallel again must establish a perceived similarity between the relation of the finite complement to the verb, and the relation of the direct object to the verb.

(60) *inūma PN kaspam ana awīlim iddinu mahrīja kaspam ana awīlim iddin*
'when PN paid the gentleman, he paid the gentleman in my presence'
u anāku awâtim īde
and I matters.ACC I.know
'and I know the matters' (AbB 6: 4: 8)

(61) Long story
PN awâtim šināti īde
PN matters.ACC these.ACC he.knows
'Long story, PN knows these matters' (AbB 13: 181: 33)

[18] These are, however, not the usual paratactic constructions with knowledge and perception verbs. As I explained in note 17 (p. 52), in non-emphatic contexts, no anaphoric object is used. Thus, Akkadian has the equivalent of 'the barley was not collected, I know', not 'the barley was collected, I know *it*'. For further examples see §7.2.2.

(62) *ina Bad-tibira ṭāt-um ibbaši-ma awīlū ša ṭāt-am ilqû*
in Bad-tibira bribe-NOM occurred-P men.NOM REL bribe-ACC they.took
u šībū ša awâtim šināti īdû ibaššû
and witnesses.NOM REL matters.ACC these.ACC they.know there.are
'bribe(-taking) occurred in Bad-tibira, and there are people who took bribe (-money) and witnesses who know these matters' (AbB 2: 11: 7)

One structural consequence of the association between objects and finite complements with some verbs is the fact that we find examples (although extremely rarely) where finite complements also appear with 'passive' verbs, as in (63) below. In such constructions, the *kīma* clause can be said to function as the subject of the verb, and can be called a subject complement:

(63) *kīma* ERIM.DUSU *šū lā labirta-šunu ina*
COMP basket-carrying corvée work this.NOM not old function-their in
bīt nikkass-i innamer-ma
house.of accounting-GEN was seen.3SG-P
'that this basket-carrying corvée work was not their old function was found out in the accounting office' (AbB 10: 13: 15)

I have argued in this section that the association between finite complements and objects arises when finite complements spread out from their *Urheimat* with speech-related verbs, to more strongly transitive verbs. To the extent that a similarity develops between some finite complements and objects, this similarity is a consequence of the stronger transitivity of knowledge and perception verbs.

4.4. The development of finite complements with the 'proving verbs'

There is also an entirely different route through which finite complements developed with two particular verbs in Babylonian, *kunnum* and *burrum.* These two verbs, which I call the 'proving verbs', can be translated as 'prove', 'establish', or 'convict'. They are used mainly in legal contexts, and for our purpose they can be treated indiscriminately. Their structural behaviour is identical, and if there are any differences in meaning between them, these involve fine points of legal terminology which are not relevant to the linguistic issues at hand. (Detailed discussion of the precise legal use of these verbs can be found in Dombradi 1996.) The route of development of finite complements with the proving verbs was quite different from their path of emergence with the speech-related verbs which we followed in the previous section. The development of finite complements with the proving verbs proceeded from the comparative meaning of the conjunction *kīma* (rather than the causal meaning), and involved the merger of two different nominal arguments into one complement clause.

An imposing plethora of structures is used with the proving verbs, and these verbs are therefore often regarded as difficult by Assyriologists. The main reason for this structural variety is that we can observe various coexisting stages of a diachronic development, in which simpler (nominal) strategies were expanded and replaced by more elaborate (clausal) strategies. (A further complicating factor is contact between Akkadian and Sumerian. Contact is discussed briefly in §10.3.2.) The life-story of the proving verbs will be told in full in §11.3, where the variety of structures used with them is examined in the light of the motivation for the development of finite complementation. In this section, I examine only one aspect of this story, namely the emergence of finite complements through the merger of two arguments of the verb into one complement clause. To give a rough outline, this was the process in which constructions of the type 'I prove him as a thief' developed into complement clauses of the type 'I prove that he is a thief'. The stages in the development are sketched in (64) below:

(64) (i) Noun phrase: *kīma* a slave I prove-him
'I prove him as a slave'
(ii) Verbless clause: *kīma* he a slave I prove-him
'I prove him that he (is) a slave'
(iii) Verbal clause: *kīma* he ran away I prove-him
'I prove him that he ran away'
(iv) True complement: *kīma* he ran away I prove-Ø
'I prove that he ran away'

In the first stage (64 i), *kīma* is used in its comparative role, to equate between two distinct arguments of the verb.[19] For convenience, we can call these two arguments the 'criminal' argument ('he'), and the 'crime' argument ('a slave'). An example of such use in Babylonian is (65):

(65) *kīma waras-su ukān-šu-ma*
kīma slave-his he.proves-him-P
'he proves him as his slave' (CH §282)

The development of finite complements starts when the crime argument is extended from a noun phrase ('slave') to a clause. The extension could have started with verbless clauses, such as 'he a slave', as in (64 ii). Examples for such constructions are (66) and (67) below:

[19] The use of *kīma* to equate two elements is of course not restricted to the proving verbs. The examples below show similar use, but notice that in these examples (and as opposed to (65) above), *kīma* behaves as a preposition, and governs a noun phrase in the genitive:

ab-ī ì[R š]*uāti* *kīma qīšt-i* *ana jâši liddin-a*
father-my slave this.ACC *kīma* present-GEN to me he.should.give-to me
'my father should give me this slave as a present' (AbB 11: 60: 29)

bēl-ki *u* *bēlet-ki* *kīma kīs-i* *ša qāti-šunu* *liṣṣurū-ki*
lord-your(FSG) and lady-your *kīma* purse-GEN of hand-their let.them.keep-you(FSG)
'your lord and your lady should keep you like a purse in their hand' (AbB 6: 1: 11)

(66) *āl-ša* *kīma mārat* *awīl-im* *šī* *ubār-ši*
town-her *kīma* daughter.of gentleman-GEN she proves.3SG-her
'her town proves her, as/that she (is) a daughter of a gentleman' (AbB 6: 80: 5)

(67) *kīma mār* *Nippuri šū ubtirrū-šu*
kīma citizen.of Nippur he they.proved-him
'they proved him as/that he is a citizen of Nippur' (BE 6/2: 62, CAD s.v. *bâru* A3b)

From the equation between a noun phrase (criminal argument) and a verbless clause (crime argument), the next stage would be the extension of the crime argument to a verbal clauses, like 'he ran away' in (64 iii) above. Examples (68) and (69) demonstrate this construction:

(68) *kīma mimmû-šu* *lā* *halq-u* *bābta-šu . . .*
kīma property-his not lost.STATIVE-SUB quarter-his
ubār-šu-ma
it.(will)prove-him-P
'his quarter will prove him before the god that no property of his was lost' (CH §126)

(69) *kīma šum* *PN ušapšiṭ-u-ma* *šum-šu*
kīma name.of PN he.caused to erase-SUB-P name-his
ušašṭer-u . . . *PN+ ubtirrū*
he.caused to write-SUB PN+ they.proved
'they proved PN+ that he caused PN's name to be erased and his name written down' (AbB 4: 15: 14)

The motivation for the last stage in the process (64 iv) comes from the fact that in the third stage ('I prove *him* that *he* ran away'), the 'criminal' appears twice: once as the object ('him') of the main verb, but now also overtly as the subject of the *kīma* clause. The object of the main verb (the criminal) thus becomes redundant, and can be dispensed with. The last stage then becomes a 'true' finite complement clause, 'I prove Ø that he ran away':

(70) *kīma* *ištu* MU.3.KAM *ina bīt* *PN wašb-u*
COMP since 3 years in house.of PN he.lives.STATIVE-SUB
ubirrū-ma
they.proved-P
'they proved that he has been living in the house of PN for 3 years' (AbB 6: 181: 19')

(71) *PN ina pī ramāni-šu kīma dūr-šu*
PN in mouth.of own-his COMP permanent status-his
iššakk-um pagar-šu ubīr
privileged farmer-NOM self-his he.proved
'PN proved with his own mouth that his permanent status is (that of a) privileged farmer' (AbB 2: 43: 15)

It must be stressed that the succession of stages presented above is reconstructed. The examples quoted here do not necessarily form a chronological order. This is not only because most letters cannot be dated inside the Old Babylonian period, but more importantly because the different stages clearly coexisted during the Old Babylonian period. Nevertheless, direct evidence for a chronological shift may be deduced from the distribution of the examples. The last 'stage', true complement clauses with the proving verbs, does not appear in letters from the early Old Babylonian period. Nor is this stage represented in the conservative language of the law codes (Hammurabi and Ešnunna). The development of real finite complements with the proving verbs thus seems to have taken place only after the early Old Babylonian period.

The path of development presented in this section can be summarized briefly as follows. The process of change relies on the comparative meaning of *kīma*, which is used to equate two noun phrases ('I prove X *kīma* Y'). The function of *kīma* is then extended to equate a noun phrase and a clause ('I prove X *kīma* he is/did Y'). At this stage, the object (X) of the main verb becomes redundant and can be discarded. This finally results in a 'normal' finite complement ('I establish *kīma* X is/did Y').

4.4.1. *'Raising' and 'prolepsis'*

The 'intermediary' constructions discussed above ('I prove *him* that *he* is a slave') are similar to the phenomenon known as 'prolepsis' or 'raising'. 'Raising' is normally used in the context of infinitival clauses ('I prove him to be a slave'), whereas 'prolepsis' is the traditional philological term used with finite clauses ('I prove him, that he is a slave').[20] Raising is one of the most widely discussed issues in formalist linguistics (for references see Horn 1985). Prolepsis has been discussed mainly for the classical Indo-European and Semitic languages (Christol 1989, Givón 1991, Lehmann 1980, Milner 1980, Panhuis 1984, Touratier 1980, Zewi 1996). But prolepsis occurs in many other languages as well. The examples below demonstrate this construction in both ancient and modern languages:[21]

[20] The literal meaning of the term 'prolepsis' (anticipation) is not suitable for the Babylonian examples. The actual word order in Babylonian is not 'I prove him that he is a slave', but rather 'that he is a slave, I prove-him'. No anticipation is thus involved. Nevertheless, the structure itself is otherwise the same as the proleptic constructions in other Semitic and Indo-European languages, as in examples (72)–(79) below.

[21] There are also a number of Old Babylonian examples with the verb *idûm* 'know', which bear a superficial similarity to the structures with the 'proving verbs', but which are in fact of quite a

(72) *wa-yar' ĕlōhîm et hā-'ôr kî ṭôb*
and-saw.3MSG God ACC the-light COMP good
'and God saw the light, that it was good' (Biblical Hebrew. Genesis 1: 4)

(73) *viden me ut rapior?*
'don't you see me how I am being kidnapped?' (Latin. C. Lehmann 1988: 208)

(74) *Kuros ēidei auton hoti meson ekhoi tou Persikou strateumatos*
Cyrus knew.3SG him that centre.ACC hold.3SG of.the Persian army
'Cyrus knew him that he held the centre of the Persian army' (Ancient Greek. Milner 1980: 54)

(75) *eγó periméno ton jáni na fíji*
I expect.1SG the John.ACC SUBJUNCTIVE leave.3SG
'I expect John that he leave' (Modern Greek. Joseph 1992: 220)

different nature. The similarity of these structures to the 'raising' constructions is that the subject of the complement clause is found outside the clause. The crucial difference, however, is that the subject of the complement clause does not appear in the accusative case, as the object of the main verb, but rather in the nominative, in sentence-initial position. It is therefore topicalized with respect to the whole sentence. Some examples from Old Babylonian are given below (cf. also AbB 4: 56: 19, 4: 69: 29, 10: 18: 7):

aššum eqel PN+ ṣuhāri-ja a-wi-lum kīma jā'um ul tīde
concerning field.of PN+ servant-my man.NOM COMP mine not you.know
'concerning the field of PN+ my servant, the man, don't you know that (he is) mine?' (AbB 9: 198: 5)

aššum PN+ a-wi-lum kīma ana šuta''îm lā ireddû ul tīde
concerning PN+ man.NOM COMP to neglect.INF.GEN not is.suitable.SUB not you.know
'concerning PN+, a/the gentleman, don't you know that he should not be ignored?' (AbB 4: 55: 5)

A.ŠÀ *kīma mānaht-ī ul tīde-ma*
field COMP work-my not you.know-P
'the field, don't you know that (it is) my working field?' (AbB 3: 86: 4)

PN_1 kīma rihût PN_2 nīde
PN_1 COMP progeny.of PN_2 we.know
'PN_1 we know that (he is) progeny of PN_2' (Leichty 1989: iii. 29'–30')

This last example appears side by side with the 'normal' complement construction in the same document:

kīma PN_1 rihût PN_2 nīde
COMP PN_1 progeny.of PN_2 we.know
'we know that PN_1 is the progeny of PN_2' (Leichty 1989: ii. 2–3)

These examples should probably be understood by reference to topicalization, known in Semitic studies variously as 'extraposition', 'dislocation', or 'extraction'. Khan (1988: xxvi) defines extraposition as 'the syntactic construction in which a noun or nominal phrase stands isolated at the front of a clause without any immediate formal connection to the predication'. Noun phrases can be extracted out of most syntactic contexts, and as the examples above show, this includes finite complements.

(76) *sech-r-a-cualid*
although-P-him-you(PL).heard
as-n-é
COPULA(REL).PRESENT.3SG-NASALIZATION-him
'although you have heard him (that) it is He' (Old Irish. Genee 1998: 91)

(77) *sabi ton paire que vendrà*
I.know your father that he.will.come
'I know your father that he will come' (Occitan. Sauzet 1989: 242)

(78) *tu sais Jean qu'il aime le chocolat*
'you know Jean that he likes chocolate' (Colloquial French)

(79) *fyd zydta ruxs kaecaei cyd*
father knew light.ACC whence it.came
'the father knew the light whence it came'
(Ossete (Indo-Iranian). Christol 1989: 66)

(80) *wa-'ú-kta kho-má-kipha-pi*
I.AGENT-come-FUTURE STEM-I.PATIENT-fear-they.AGENT
'they fear me that I'm coming' (Lakota (Siouan). Pustet 1999)

Two points can be made about the nature of prolepsis in light of the Babylonian data. The first point concerns the status of the proleptic and 'raising' constructions with respect to 'normal' complement clauses. In generative literature, raising has been treated as a transformation, and is still regarded as a derived form, a variation on the more basic 'normal' complement structure. But a diachronic observation shows that, if anything, the proleptic constructions are a stage in the development of the 'normal' complement constructions, rather than vice versa. This point is not new, and has been raised by Heine and Reh (1988: 253) in their discussion of the phenomenon in African languages.

The second point concerns the way in which proleptic structures emerge. Here, the Babylonian data can shed new light on the discussion. In the literature, two routes have been suggested through which proleptic constructions emerge, but neither of them accounts for the Babylonian development. The first route is the reanalysis of a relative pattern. This can be demonstrated as follows:

(81) Relative structure: I know the man that $_{(=\text{REL})}$ is just
'Prolepsis': I know the man that $_{(=\text{COMP})}$ (he) is just

W. P. Lehmann (1980: 129) claims that the proleptic constructions in Indo-European derive from an earlier relative pattern:

> The late origin [of complements] is also clear from constructions which may be interpreted as transitional. Such is the pattern, found in Sanskrit as well as Greek, where the complement is a noun amplified by a descriptive clause . . . :

oîda tòn ándra hóti díkaiós esti
I.know the man that just he.is
I know that the man is just

The construction can be ascribed to an earlier relative pattern.

Givón (1991) suggests two routes for the emergence of proleptic structures. The first is the relative clause pattern which we have just mentioned. The second route is based on the combination of two arguments through the process of 'afterthought'. Givón (1991: 288) calls proleptic constructions 'accusative blends', and claims that they result from parataxis:

> The accusative blend is an intermediate construction that capitalizes on the systematic polysemy of many perception-cognition verbs, whereby such verbs can take either a *nominal direct object* or a *proposition* as their complement . . . The accusative blend involves cases where *both* complements are present together in the main sentence . . . [S]uch blends should be viewed as normal by-products of the polysemy of the verbs in question. That is, they represent normal spoken-language *parataxis*, whereby the speaker first chooses to consider the important *nominal topic* as the object of the verb, then—perhaps as an 'afterthought', and with intonational break—adds the proposition in which that nominal is the topical participant.

According to Givón, then, these structures develop in the following way:

(82) He saw the light.
Afterthought: He saw that it was good.
→ He saw the light, that it was good.

However, neither of these two routes, relative pattern or afterthought, can account for the development of proleptic structures in Babylonian. As we have seen, the proleptic structures in Babylonian do not emerge from augmenting one argument of the verb by a relative clause (*kīma* is never used as a relative). Nor can afterthought explain the Babylonian development. The 'proposition' (which I called the 'crime') precedes the verb in Babylonian, so there is no possibility that it is added as an afterthought. As we have seen, the proleptic structures in Babylonian emerged from the merger of two distinct arguments of the verb into one complement clause. Prolepsis is an intermediary stage in this development. At this stage, the 'crime' has been expanded to become a full clause, but the 'criminal' object is still present as a distinct argument of the main verb.

4.5. Structural parallels for the development of *kīma*

We have seen that the origin of the complementizer in Akkadian was the adverbial conjunction *kīma*. The development from adverbial to complementizer occurred initially through the bleaching of the causal meaning of *kīma* ('because'). In the introduction to this chapter, I mentioned that adverbial clauses are not a well-known cross-linguistic source of complementizers. Nevertheless, there are various parallels for the development of complementizers from adverbial conjunctions, and this section presents a few examples.

4.5.1. *English 'as'*

We have already seen parallels for the early development of *kīma* in §4.1 above. 'As' in English started as a comparative particle, and became a temporal and causal adverbial. In fact, the parallel between 'as' and *kīma* also extends further, to the development of *kīma* as a complementizer. 'As' can appear as a complementizer in English, at least in some dialectal use. One example from the OED is 'I don't know as you'll like the appearance of our place' (OED, s.v. 'as' B. 28).

4.5.2. *Twi*

A language which shows a close parallel to the Akkadian development is the African language Twi. Lord (1993) provides an extensive description of the meanings of the verb/conjunction *sɛ* in this language. There are no historical records to enable us to follow the development in Twi, but it is clear that the original meaning of *sɛ* is the comparative 'like'. The historical source of the conjunction *sɛ* is the verb *sɛ*, which is still used in Twi as a main verb meaning 'to be like', as in (83) below. In the well-documented process of reanalysis of serial constructions, the main verb develops into a preposition, and this results in constructions like (84). Once this step is completed, we are in a parallel situation to the 'initial stage' with *kīma*.

(83) *kofi sɛ ama*
Kofi be like Ama
'Kofi is like Ama' (all examples from Lord 1993: 153–70)

(84) *kofi yɛɛ adwuma no sɛ ama*
Kofi did work the like Ama
'Kofi did the work like Ama'

From the comparative meaning of *sɛ*, the whole familiar semantic range has developed, just as with Akkadian *kīma* or English 'as'. *Sɛ* can be used as a temporal adverbial ('when' or 'since', as in (85), (86)), as purpose adverbial 'so that' (87), and as causal adverbial 'because' (88):

(85) *sɛ kofi yɛ adwuma no â metua no ka*
if/when Kofi do work the CONDITIONAL I.will.pay him salary
'If Kofi does the work, I will pay him a salary'

(86) *efi sɛ wowoo me manyare peŋ*
since they.bore me I.NEGATIVE.sick
'Since I was born, I was never sick'

(87) *kofi yɛɛ adwuma no sɛ yaw bɛpɛ n'asɛm*
Kofi did work the so that Yaw will.like his.manner
'Kofi did the work so that Yaw would like him'

(88) *oguanee sɛ osuro*
he.ran away because he.was afraid

Finally, *sɛ* also became a complementizer, and is used to introduce complement clauses, as in (89) and (90) below. The development of *sɛ* thus offers a complete parallel to the development of *kīma.*

(89) *na ama nim sɛ kofi yɛɛ adwuma no*
PAST Ama know COMP Kofi did work the
'Ama knew that Kofi did the work'

(90) *ohwe sɛ kofi bɛba anaa*
he.look COMP Kofi will.come or.not
'he ascertained whether Kofi would come'

4.5.3. *Greek and other Indo-European languages*

The development of the two Greek complementizers, *hōs* and *hoti,* also shows resemblance to that of *kīma.* The parallel between *hōs* and *kīma* is especially striking. *Hōs* is an adverbial conjunction with a wide semantic range which largely overlaps with that of *kīma. Hōs* can introduce comparative, manner, temporal, result, and purpose clauses. Its original meaning seems to have been an adverbial of manner, 'by means of which, the way in which' (Cristofaro 1998*a*: 68).

The complementizer use of *hōs* developed from the adverbial conjunction. Cristofaro (1998*a*: 72) writes: 'The use of ὡς as a complementizer appears rather problematic, for complement clauses are subjects or objects of main predicates, and can therefore hardly be related to an oblique instrumental form.' In the light of the discussion in §2.1 and in this chapter, however, it seems to me that such a development is not problematic at all, but rather very natural. Complement clauses do not have to be subjects and objects. In fact, in Akkadian they emerged precisely in a context where they do not function as objects, and this may also have been the case in Greek.

The development of *kīma* has clear parallels also in Hittite and Latin. It is generally agreed that the origin of the conjunctions *kuit* and *quod* is a demonstrative/relative particle (for references see Holland 1984). But Hittite *kuit* and Latin *quod* have developed a range of adverbial uses (such as temporal and causal) which bears strong similarities to the adverbial meanings of *kīma.* It seems probable that these adverbial meanings of *quod* and *kuit* were the source of the later use of these particles as complementizers. Moreover, as Cuzzolin (1994*a*, 1994*b*) has shown, the process of the replacement of the Latin infinitive complements (AcI) by finite complements with *quod* started from verbs such as 'regret', 'resent', or 'be sorry', and from there extended to verbs such as 'know' and 'find out'. The parallels between this route and the development of *kīma* (from 'complain' and 'inform' to 'know' and 'learn') are not difficult to detect. In both cases, the process starts in contexts where a clear causal element is present, and from there extends to verbs such as 'know', where this causal undertone is no longer plausible.

4.5.4. *Semitic*

Cognates of the conjunction *kī*/*kīma* are used in most Semitic languages to introduce finite complements (Lipinski 1997: 535, Kogan and Korotayev 1997: 239). Only Arabic uses complementizers from a different source (*'an*/*'anna* and *mā*). The parallels between Akkadian on the one hand and the North-west Semitic languages on the other are especially close. The semantic range of the particle *kī* in North-west Semitic is essentially the same as in Akkadian (cf. k_1 and *ky* in Hoftijzer and Jongeling 1995). A few examples of the use of *kī* as a complementizer in North-west Semitic are given below:

(91) *w tnḫ b 'irty npš k (=kī) ḥy 'al'iyn b'l*
and will.rest in my breast my soul COMP alive mighty Baal
'and may my soul rest in my breast because/that mighty Baal is alive' (Ugaritic. KTU 1.6 III: 19' (Sivan 1997: 189))

(92) *w 'id' k (=kī) ḥy 'al'iyn b'l*
and I.know COMP alive mighty Baal
'so I know that mighty Baal is alive' (Ugaritic. KTU 1.6 III: 8)

(93) *wa-yēd'û kî 'êrummim hēm*
and-they.knew COMP naked.PL they
'they knew that they were naked' (Hebrew. Genesis 3: 8)

(94) *pr'h yd' k (=kī) 'bdk* [broken] . . .
Pharaoh he.knows COMP your servant . . .
'the Pharaoh knows that your servant . . .' (Aramaic. Letter of Adon. Hug 1993: 106)

Finite complements cannot be assumed to have existed in Proto-Semitic, since we have seen that in Akkadian, finite complements only developed in the historical period. The similarities between the Semitic languages therefore suggest that parallel developments of *kī*/*kīma* as a complementizer took place in the different languages. The main question in this regard is whether these parallel developments were independent or due to contact. The Semitic languages are very similar in syntactic structure, and this makes borrowing easier, but more difficult to detect. Nevertheless, we know that of all 'function words', conjunctions are particularly prone to borrowing (Thomason and Kaufman 1988: 74, Stolz and Stolz 1996, Matras 1998). We also know that there was prolonged contact between the languages, and it is difficult therefore to imagine the development of finite complements in these languages as entirely independent processes.

Moreover, there are parallel developments of complementizers in later periods, which are again difficult to regard as independent. In Neo-Babylonian (as we shall see in chapter 7), the older complementizer *kī* is replaced by the relative particle *ša*. This development is normally ascribed to Aramaic influence. In Aramaic, the complementizer *kī* is attested, as in (94) above, but the usual complementizer is the relative particle *dī/zī*, as in (95) below. The replacement of the complementizer *kī* by the relative particle also has a precise parallel in late biblical Hebrew, where the relative particles *ăšer/še* replaces the older complementizer *kī*, as in (96) below.

(95) *yāda‘ anâ dî 'iddānā' antûn zābnîn*
know I REL/COMP time you(PL) you(PL).gain
'I know that you are gaining time' (Daniel 2: 8)

(96) *yāda'tî še-gam zeh hû' ra‘yôn rûaḥ*
I.knew REL/COMP-also this COPULA notion.of wind
'I knew that this also is but a striving after wind' (Ecclesiastes 1: 18)

It is clear that there are close parallels between the developments of the complementizers in the Semitic languages, both in older periods (the original emergence of *kī* as a complementizer) and in younger periods (the replacement of *kī* by the relative particle). Nevertheless, in both cases, it seems very unlikely that the parallel developments in Semitic were entirely independent, and much more likely that they were at least encouraged by contact.

4.6. Conclusion

This chapter has described the emergence of finite complements in Babylonian. We have seen that finite complements developed from adverbial clauses, through a combination of two changes. The causal meaning of the conjunction *kīma* ('because') was bleached to a factive meaning ('that', or 'about the fact that'), and the *kīma* clauses forged an intimate link with the verb to become arguments. The bridging context for this process was provided by speech-related verbs such as 'complain', 'inform', and 'speak'. With these verbs, both a causal and a factive interpretation of the *kīma* clause is possible, and moreover, in some contexts the two interpretations describe the same situation. The repeated use of *kīma* in such contexts provoked the process of semantic bleaching. From speech-related verbs, the use of *kīma* was extended to knowledge and perception verbs, such as 'know', 'see', and 'hear'.

We also examined a different path through which finite complements emerged with the 'proving' verbs (later on in the Old Babylonian period). The development with the proving verbs involved the comparative meaning of *kīma* 'as'. The process consisted of the merger of two distinct arguments of the verb into one complement clause. This can be paraphrased as the change from constructions of the type 'I proved X as Y' to 'I proved that X is Y'.

Finite complements therefore developed through various routes and with different verbs, but the separate routes nevertheless were heading for the same destination. Finite complementation seems to be the end-point on which different paths all eventually converge. Lass (1997: 295) calls such points of convergence 'point attractors' or 'sinks'. Chapter 11 will try to explain why finite complementation is such a 'sink'. I shall suggest there that the reason lies in the relation between finite complementation and the alternative structures of the FDC. Finite complements are better equipped for dealing with more elaborate contexts than alternative strategies, because they combine flexibility and explicit marking of the dependence between clauses. The various strategies for expansion of simpler nominal clauses are thus likely to converge towards the stable 'sink' of finite complementation.

5

The Grammaticalization of the Quotative Construction

This chapter describes the development of the quotative construction in Babylonian (with *enma/umma*), which can serve as a 'model textbook example' of a process of grammaticalization. The construction started in the earliest period as a whole independent clause, which meant roughly '(this is what) X said'. In the following two thousand years, this construction followed a long path of reduction. Slowly but very surely, it underwent all the prototypical changes associated with grammaticalization: the independent clause was gradually reduced in phonetic form, in meaning, and in syntactic independence, to become a quotative marker, and finally to emerge as a general complementizer.

The first five sections of this chapter follow the process of grammaticalization of the *umma* construction from Old Akkadian to Neo-Babylonian. The final section of the chapter explores the cross-linguistic implications of the grammaticalization of *umma*. The historical development of the *umma* construction is illuminating because its long attested history offers a stark contrast to most reported instances of the grammaticalization of quotatives, in which the development has to be reconstructed on the basis of synchronic evidence.[22] The history of *umma* brings to light various intricacies of the grammaticalization process, which are lost when only synchronic evidence is available. The historical perspective also puts in context all the aspects in the behaviour of the construction which may appear irregular and unmotivated from a synchronic perspective.

Before we proceed to the detailed examination of the history of *umma*, Table 1 briefly sketches the main stages in the development (*X* stands for a pronoun or a person's name).

A word of caution is needed about the glossing and translation of *umma* in this chapter. The gradual nature of the change in the status of the *umma* construction makes glossing a difficult task. The quotative particle *umma* has always posed problems for Assyriologists, when trying to translate the Akkadian construction into idiomatic usage in languages which do not have a quotative particle. The desire to represent the quotative particle in languages such as English or German has resulted in the widespread but erroneous glossing of *umma*

[22] There is one notable exception, namely ancient Egyptian, cf. §5.8.2.

TABLE 1

Period	Form	Syntactic and semantic status	Rough 'translation'
Old Akkadian (2500–2200 BC)	*enma X (-ma)*	Whole independent clause. Introduces speech, but always on its own. Never appears after speech verbs.	'(this is what) X said/says'
Late Old Akkadian (2200–2000 BC)	*umma X (-ma)*		
Early Old Babylonian (2000–1800 BC)	*umma X-ma*	Still a whole independent clause which introduces speech on its own. But also starts appearing after speech verbs, in paratactic relation to them.	'(this is what) X said/says'
Later Old Babylonian (1800–1600 BC)	*umma X-ma*	Divergence: *umma X-ma* can still function as an independent clause which fully retains the meaning of speech, and introduces reported speech on its own. But this clause becomes almost obligatory after speech verbs. In such contexts, its contrastive function and independent speech meaning are weakened, and it becomes a reinforcing clause for reported speech.	'X said/says', or: Ø
Middle Babylonian (1500–1000 BC)	*ummā*	The loss of the active speaker *X* means that *ummā* is no longer syntactically independent. It can still appear after non-speech verbs, and in such contexts, it carries the speech meaning 'saying'. But it can no longer introduce speech on its own, and now has to depend on an antecedent. After speech verbs it can be regarded as a semantically empty quotative marker.	'saying' or: Ø
Neo-Babylonian (1000–500 BC)	*umma*	The use of *umma* as a grammatical marker is extended. It is no longer restricted to direct speech contexts, but appears also with verbs like 'fear' and 'hear', and in such contexts, can even introduce 'indirect' complements. *Umma* can now be considered a more general complementizer.	'saying', Ø, or: 'that'

as 'thus'.[23] The objective difficulty of translation is made even worse by attempts to find a uniform translation for a construction whose status has in fact changed very markedly during the history of the language. For this reason, it is important to realize that the glosses and translations for any specific example in this chapter should not be viewed as anything more than rough approximations, or convenient mnemonics. The real significance of the examples can only be understood in the light of the gradual historical development that we shall follow below.

5.1. Old Akkadian

In the earliest attested period (Old Akkadian), *enma* does not yet serve to introduce direct speech in unmarked contexts. Rather, Old Akkadian displays an older system, in which direct speech is introduced either without any formal marker (97), or with an enclitic particle *-mi* (98).[24] The enclitic *-mi*, if present, is suffixed to the first word of the reported speech, and is sometimes repeated after other important or stressed words.

(97) *iqabbi atta ward-am tašām-ma*
he.says you slave-ACC you.bought-P
'he says: "you bought the slave"' (SAB: Si 1: 8')

(98) *Gutium-ma-**mi** eql-am ula āruš a taqbi*
Gutians-P-**P** field-ACC not I.worked don't you.say
'don't say: "(because of the) Gutians, I could not work the field"' (SAB: Gir 19: 7)

[23] In most glossaries and text editions, *umma* is translated as 'thus' or 'folgendermaßen'. But 'thus' is one meaning that *umma* never had in any period. This chapter shows in detail how the phrase *enma/umma X* started with the full meaning of speech '(this is what) X said', and how it gradually developed into a bleached quotative marker, which should be left untranslated in many cases. But the transition from full speech meaning to bleached quotative particle did not in any stage involve the meaning 'thus' or 'like this'. In fact, in both older and younger periods, the meaning 'thus' or 'like this' was expressed by other particles. In Old Babylonian, we have common phrases such as *X kīam iqbi umma šū-ma*, which show that the adverbial 'thus' element was expressed by the word *kīam*, not *umma*. Similarly, in Neo-Babylonian we have phrases such as *akī agâ šuprašsu umma*, which show that the meaning 'like this' was expressed by *akī agâ*, not by *umma*. The general difficulties in rendering *umma* into English or German can be seen, for example, in the translation of the *umma X-ma* formula in the *Altbabylonische Briefe* series, which has changed several times from volume to volume.

[24] Von Soden (1995, §155*a*) assumes that *-mi* is a shortened form of *enma/umma*, but this seems highly unlikely. The particle *-mi* appears in a totally different position from *enma*, after the first word of the reported speech, and must therefore be the result of a reduction of quite a different sort of particle. I shall take the situation in Old Akkadian as the starting point for describing the development of the new particle *enma*. See Kraus (1975) for a detailed discussion of the uses of *-mi*.

In Old Akkadian, we find the phrase *enma X* mainly in the introduction formula in the beginning of letters, as in (99) or more elaborately (100):

(99) *enma X ana Y*
enma X to Y
'this is what X says to Y'

(100) *enma X ana Y qibi-ma*
enma X to Y say.IMP-P
'this is what X says, say to Y . . .'

However, the phrase *enma X* is not restricted to the letter opening formula. We also find it in the text itself, used to introduce a new sender or addressee, or to indicate the beginning of an important delivery. We can see this in examples from Old Akkadian letters (101), royal inscriptions (102), and legal documents (103):

(101) [*enma* PN_1] *ana* PN_2 *ašma-ma ahtadu* *enma anāku-ma*
enma PN_1 to PN_2 I.heard-P I.was happy *enma* I-P
'This is what PN_1 says to PN_2: I heard (his letter) and was happy (about it). (And now) this is what I say (i.e. answer): ". . ."' (SAB: Gir 37: 1)

(102) *enma Narām-Sin dann-um šar kibrāt-im arba'-im*
enma Narām-Sin strong-NOM king.of corners-GEN four-GEN
'this is what Narām-Sin the strong, king of the four corners (of the earth) said ". . ."' (Gelb and Kienast 1990: Nar C5: 82)

(103) *5 šībūtum šūt enma* PN_1 *ana* PN_2
5 witnesses REL *enma* PN_1 to PN_2
'witnesses (to the fact) that PN_1 said to PN_2: ". . ."' (Gelb 1984: 266: i)

Whatever the stylistic status of the phrase *enma X*, its syntactic status as an independent clause is unquestionable. The phrase *enma X* never follows a speech verb in Old Akkadian. It is not syntactically dependent on a speech verb, and in fact, it is never dependent on any other verb either. *Enma* is the head of the independent clause *enma X*.

The etymology of the word *enma*, and the internal structure of the phrase *enma X* are obscure. As Kraus (1975) has already explained, the structure *enma X* (*ana Y*) does not obviously correspond to any synchronic structure in Old Akkadian. It cannot be a genitival structure (like 'word of X'), because the X is always in the nominative, rather than the genitive. *Enma X* also does not look like a verbal structure (like 'X said'), because the word order would require the verb after the subject, not before it. When the construction *enma X* appears on the stage of history, it is already a fossilized form, whose internal structure was in all likelihood opaque for the Old Akkadian speakers themselves.[25]

[25] Two etymologies have been suggested for *enma*. In his dictionary, von Soden (1965–81) says that *enma* is related to Hebrew *hinnēh*, Ugaritic *hn*, which are 'presentative' focus particles. According to this etymology, *enma* would consist of *en* (cognate with *hinnēh*, *hn*) and the emphatic particle *-ma*.

Nevertheless (regardless of etymology and internal structure), the use of *enma X* makes clear that its meaning must have been roughly equivalent to '(this is what) X said'. *Enma X* must have encapsulated the meaning of speech because it always introduces speech, and always does so on its own, never after verbs like 'say' or 'write'. Moreover, the Akkadian phrase *enma X* is equivalent, both in its use as a letter opening formula, and in bilingual lexical lists, to the Sumerian formula *X na.(b)e.a* ('X PREFIX.say.SUBORDINATION'), which means transparently: '(this is) what X said'. For this reason, the most important point to remember for the following discussion is that the *enma X* clause, *as a whole unit*, encapsulated the meaning of speech. (That is, its meaning was roughly equivalent to '(this is what) X said', or 'these were the words of X'.)

From the late Old Akkadian period (Ur III), *enma* appears as *umma*. The form of the construction in the few Akkadian letters from this period is either *umma X*, or *umma X-ma* with the emphatic particle *-ma*. But the syntactic status of *umma* has not changed. Example (104), from a sale document, shows that the *umma* construction still functions as an entirely independent clause. The

The connection between 'presentative' focus particles and quotative particles is attested elsewhere in Semitic. In Hebrew, a form of the particle *hinnēh* can appear after the verbs 'see' and 'dream' (cf. §10.4). It is also probable that the Hebrew particle is cognate with Arabic *'inna*, which is also used as a quotative particle and as a complementizer. There are also possible parallels in Old Aramaic and Ethiopic (Testen 1998: 46 ff.). A different etymology has been suggested by Baumgartner (1974), who relates *enma* to Hebrew *n'um* ('speech').

With our present state of knowledge, the etymology of *enma* is more a matter of artistic creativity than real science. We are not even sure of the phonetic value of the sign EN in *en-ma*, although *en* seems the most plausible possibility. Moreover, as this chapter demonstrates, the etymology of *enma* is in fact of little importance to its subsequent route of grammaticalization. Nevertheless, to me it seems tempting to try to relate *enma* to a *verb* meaning 'say'. The temptation arises because the usual source for quotative particles is verbs of speech, and also because if *enma X* did derive from an expression meaning '(this is what) X said', then it can be shown to be directly parallel to the equivalent Sumerian letter-opening formula. The problems with this suggestion are first that the VS word order seems wrong for Akkadian, and second that *enma* does not look like a verb. With some imagination, such problems could be overcome, but the result is of course entirely speculative. If we think of the phrase *enma X* not in terms of the synchronic rules of Old Akkadian, but as a fossilized form from an older period, it may become easier to reconcile the structure to a verbal one. Akkadian SOV order is a borrowing from Sumerian. The original Semitic order is VSO, and this order survives in early Akkadian personal names which are mostly of the VS type (cf. the list of early pre-Sargonic personal names in Westenholz (1988: 110), which contains only VS sequences). If we assumed the phrase *enma X* originated at a time when VS order was still the rule, the word order would be explained. But can *enma* derive from a verb? The verb *n'm* ('to deliver a speech') occurs once in biblical Hebrew (Jeremiah 23: 31) and is apparently related to Arabic *na'ama* ('whisper', 'groan', 'sigh') and possibly to Hebrew *nūm* ('speak') (Baumgartner 1974, Klein 1987, s.v. *n'um*). If this verb ever existed in pre-Akkadian, the third person form could have been something like *in'um* or *inūm*. If we think of the verb in the subordinative form, not the subordinative in *-u* but the form in *-a* (which is found sporadically in Old Akkadian, and which is claimed by Gelb (1969) to be the original form), then we get *in'uma or inūma*. There is the disappearance of a long syllable to account for, but this seems to bring *enma* a little closer to a verb related to *n'um*. As I said, the appeal of this hypothesis would be the Sumerian equivalence. If *enma* is a subordinative form of 'he spoke', then *enma X* would be a direct translation of the Sumerian formula: *X na.e.a.* (*na*-prefix; *e-* 'say'; *-a* the subordinating particle, meaning '(this is) what X said').

reported speech here does not even follow *umma* directly. The *umma* clause appears in conjunction with a speech verb ('swear'), but *umma* actually precedes the verb, and seems to serve as a general introduction to the situation:

(104) *umma PN nīš šarr-im itma*
umma PN life.of king-GEN she.swore
šumma GÉME *arugimānī ir-tá-ši-ì anāku lū*
if slave woman claims.ACC she.(will)acquire I EMPH
GÉME
slave woman
'This was what PN said, she swore by the life of the king "if the slave girl acquires legal claims I will become a slave woman (myself)"' (Steinkeller 1989, p. 326)

We shall see that in later periods, *umma* does become dependent on speech verbs, and this is also reflected in its position (after the verb, rather than before it). For comparison, example (105) below shows the Old Babylonian equivalent to (104) above. In Old Babylonian, the *umma* construction appears after the speech verb, and directly before the reported speech:

(105) *nīš Samsu-iluna šarr-im kīam itma umma šī-ma*
life.of Samsu-iluna king-GEN thus she.swore *umma* she-P
'by the life of Samsu-iluna the king, thus she swore, *umma* she-P: ". . ."' (RA 69: 120)

5.2. Early Old Babylonian

By the time of the early Old Babylonian letters, proliferation in the use of *umma* is already evident. The *umma* clause has now lost any solemn connotations which it may have had, and is now used to introduce direct speech in conversation, in normal 'I said, he said' contexts:[26]

(106) PN gave the barley of PN_2 . . . to the diviner
umma anāku-ma miššu anni'-um
umma I-P what this-NOM
umma šū-ma awīl-um ittalak-ma [b]a-ri-u₄
umma he-P man-NOM he.went away-P they are starving
'I said: "what is this (supposed to mean)?" He said: "the man went away and they are starving".' (AbB 5: 141: 11)

[26] Nevertheless, in the early Old Babylonian period, direct speech without any marker is still very common. This is also the case in the law code of Hammurabi, which is written in the middle Old Babylonian period, but in conservative (if not archaizing) language. All instances of reported speech in the code follow the earlier patterns, and there are no examples of *umma* introducing direct speech.

At this period, *umma X-ma* was still an entirely independent clause. In most cases in early Old Babylonian, *umma X-ma* introduced reported speech on its own, and did not stand after any speech-related verb, just as in the example above. The meaning of *umma X-ma* by itself sufficed to introduce speech, so it must still have contained the speech meaning '(this is what) X said'. Nevertheless, from the earliest Old Babylonian texts, we find cases where *umma X-ma* appears after speech-related verbs, as well as after other verbs, in paratactic relation to them. We can see this use in the first and second lines of (107) below, an example from the earliest group of Old Babylonian letters, from Ešnunna, which date from around 1990 BC.[27]

(107) *šipir bēli-ja ellikam-ma umma šūt-ma* . . . [4 lines]
messenger.of lord-my he.came-P *umma* he-P
'The messenger of my lord arrived, and this is what he said ". . ."'

⌜*a-ap-pá-al-šu*⌝ [*um-m*]*a anāku-ma* . . . [5 lines]
I.answered-him *umma* I-P
'I answered, (and) this is what I said ". . ."'

umma šūt-ma bēl-ī išpuran-ni 1 alp-am idn-am-ma
umma he-P lord-my he.sent-me OX-ACC give.IMP-to me-P
ana Samium lurde
to Samium let.me.lead
'He said: "my lord sent me, give me an ox so that I take (it) to Samium".'

umma anāku-ma 1 alp-um ša taqabbi'-u [*ú-la i*]*z-za-az*
umma I-P OX-NOM REL you.say-SUB is not available
'I said: "the ox you are talking about is not available".' (Whiting 1987: 30: 17)

Although the *umma* clause was still entirely independent in this period, the appearance of *umma* in parataxis after speech verbs sets the scene for the future stages of grammaticalization. Once the *umma* clause starts appearing regularly after speech-related verbs, the conditions for the incipient process of grammaticalization are fulfilled. At the core of this process lie two axes of reduction, the semantic and the syntactic. When the *umma* clause is used frequently after speech verbs, its semantic content can be eroded, since the meaning of speech

[27] Another example of the *umma* clause after a speech-related verb is the following:

[. . .] *ašpurak-kum umma anāku-ma litma'ā*
I.wrote-to.you *umma* I-P let.them.swear
umma atta-ma '. . .'
umma you-P
umma anāku-ma '. . .'
umma I-P
'I wrote to you, (and) this is what I said: ". . .", this is what you said ". . .", this is what I said ". . ."' (Whiting 1987: 21: 1)

is supplied by the speech verb. On the syntactic axis, when the *umma* clause appears regularly after speech verbs, and when its semantic content has been eroded, the erstwhile paratactic sequence of two independent clauses ('I answered' + *umma* I-P) can be reinterpreted as a sequence containing a main verb and a dependent quotative phrase.

5.2.1. *Semantic bleaching, the appearance of* umma *with the verb 'say'*

The first clear signs that something has changed point to 'bleaching' of the speech meaning of the *umma* clause. These signs come from the behaviour of *umma* with the unmarked speech verb *qabûm* ('say', 'speak', 'tell'). As I explained above, the *enma*/*umma* clause initially encapsulated the meaning of speech. It is therefore important to notice that in the earliest Old Babylonian texts (the first group of letters from Ešnunna), *umma* appears after speech verbs such as 'write' (*šapārum*) or 'answer' (*apālum*),[28] but it does not appear after the unmarked speech verb *qabûm*.

The reason why *umma* does not initially appear after 'say' must be that whereas paratactic sequences such as *ašpurakkum umma anāku-ma* (I.wrote.to you *umma* I-P) would have meant 'I wrote to you, this is what I said . . .', the sequence *aqbikum umma anāku-ma* (I.said.to you *umma* I-P) must have seemed redundant, because it would have meant 'I said to you, this is what I said'. Therefore, the point at which *umma* starts following the unmarked speech verb 'say' is a very important landmark on the road to semantic bleaching.

With other speech-related verbs, the juxtaposition of the *umma* clause after the verb was fairly easy, and followed from naturally occurring parataxis. But the association of *umma* with the unmarked 'say' does not seem to have been entirely painless, because a simple juxtaposition would have meant 'I said and this is what I said'. It seems that the first appearances of *umma* with the verb 'say' were of an emphatic nature, and formed a sort of hybrid pattern of two earlier constructions. In this pattern, the reported speech is bracketed between the *umma* construction and the verb 'say', as schematized in (108):

(108) *umma X-ma* + 'reported speech' + X said.

The first step for linking *umma* to the verb 'say' was thus a sort of amalgamation (for emphatic purpose) of the two earlier constructions (*umma* clause (on its own) + 'reported speech', and 'reported speech' + 'say'). We find this hybrid pattern the first time we encounter *umma* with the verb 'say', in the second group of letters from Ešnunna (roughly fifty years later than the first group). Two (out of three)[29] of the examples are of this form:

[28] Cf. (107) above, and note 27 (p. 72). But in both cases the context is not secure.

[29] The third is in broken context but seems to show the later order where *umma X-ma* follows the verb *qabûm*:

⌜*iq*⌝*-bi-ú-*⌜*ni-im-ma*⌝[?] *umma šunu-ma*
they.said-to me-P[?] *umma* they-P (Whiting 1987: 34: 10)

(109) *umma anāku-ma atta lū bēl-ī-ma anāku lū warad-ka*
umma I-P you EMPH lord-my-P I EMPH servant-your
aqbi-šum
I.said-to him
'I said: "you really are my lord and I really am your servant" I said to him' (Whiting 1987: 34: 20)[30]

(110) *umma anāku-ma adi balṭāti atta-ma lū bēl-ni aqbi-šum*
umma I-P until you.live you-P EMPH lord-our I.said-to him
ula išme'an-ni
not he.heard-me
'I said: "as long as you live you are our lord" I said to him, (but) he didn't listen to me' (Whiting 1987: 34: 28)

For an idiomatic translation of these examples, we can compare them with spoken registers in English, where reported speech is often introduced by formulae such as 'I said to him I said ". . ."'. In German (and indeed sometimes in colloquial English), there is a closer approximation, because the reported speech can be bracketed by speech verbs: 'Da hab' ich zu ihm gesagt: ". . ." hab' ich gesagt'. In Babylonian, we find this type of bracketing not only in the texts from Ešnunna, but also in early Old Babylonian letters from other sources:

(111) *umma šū-ma 4 lahrātim āhuz iqbi*
umma he-P 4 ewes.ACC I.took he.said
'he said: "I took four ewes" he said' (AbB 9: 259: 9)

(112) *umma atta-ma wēdiššika-ma tūr awāt-am ṣuhār-um*
umma you-P on your own-P return.IMP matter-ACC boy-NOM
lā irašše taqbi-šum
not he.(will)get you.said-to him
'you said "return alone so that the boy doesn't get a cause for complaint" you said to him' (RA 75: 103)

We can see the original emphatic nature of this pattern in another early Old Babylonian example, which is a variation on a common idiomatic phrase. Many Old Babylonian letters end with a warning which literally means 'don't say "you didn't write to me"', but can be translated idiomatically as 'don't say I didn't warn you!'.[31] In this common formula, the direct speech 'you didn't write to me'

[30] Whiting interpreted this text differently, taking the verb *aqbišum* to start a new sentence. But since this pattern is a recurring one, I think the interpretation given here is the correct one.

[31] The sentiment is not confined to Old Babylonian. Similar expressions are used in letters from Old Akkadian (cf. example (98) in the main text) to Neo-Babylonian (as in the following example):

PN lā iqabbi umma ul tašpur
PN not he.(should)say *umma* not you.wrote
'PN mustn't say "you didn't write"' (Cole 1996: 37: 29)

precedes the speech verb 'don't say' without any marker, as in (113) below. But the early Old Babylonian example in (114) adds *umma X-ma* before the direct speech, thus giving the bracketing pattern we have seen above:

(113) *ul tašpur-am lā taqabbi*
not you.wrote-to me not you.(should)say
'don't say "you didn't write to me"'
(~ don't say I didn't warn you!)

(114) *umma atta-ma ul tašpur-am lā taqabbi*
umma you-P not you.wrote-to me not you.(should)say (AbB 6: 177: 34)

As I said, it is not difficult to understand why it was initially easier for *umma* to follow speech-related verbs such as 'write' and 'answer' than to appear after the unmarked verb 'say'. The combination of *umma* with 'write', for example, is straightforward, through naturally occurring parataxis: 'I wrote, and this is what I said . . .'. But *umma* was not originally used with the unmarked speech verb 'say', because the simple juxtaposition of 'say' and the *umma* clause must have seemed redundant. The route for the combination of the *umma* clause with 'say' was through a bracketing pattern, a hybrid of two earlier constructions, which probably started as an emphatic form.

This hybrid bracketing pattern becomes rare in letters later in the Old Babylonian period. (But as we shall see in §5.7 below, the phenomenon of bracketing of reported speech does not disappear entirely.) Once the connection between the verb 'say' and *umma* was established, it may have been by analogy with the other speech verbs that the *umma* construction 'realigned' itself after the verb 'say'. This realignment then resulted in the standard pattern in later Old Babylonian: 'say' + *umma X-ma* +'reported speech'. Already in the nineteenth century BC, *umma X-ma* appears regularly with *qabûm* in the normal formula, as in (115) and (116) below. The frequent appearance of *umma* with *qabûm* must mean that semantic bleaching of the speech meaning had already taken place.

(115) *ana PN aqbi-ma umma anāku-ma ittī-ka lullik*
to PN I.said-P *umma* I-P with-you let.me.go
'I said to PN: "let me go with you"' (Al-A'dami 1967: pl. 9: 5)

(116) *ana PN kīam qibi umma atta-ma*
to PN thus say.IMP(2MSG) *umma* you-P
'speak to PN in this way, say: ". . ."' (Al-A'dami 1967: pl. 5: 29)

5.3. Later Old Babylonian

By the middle Old Babylonian period, *umma X-ma* has established itself as the common and unmarked way of introducing direct speech. Direct speech without any marker, or with the enclitic marker *mi*, becomes rare in the colloquial language of the letters, compared to the ubiquitous *umma*.

5.3.1. *Divergence*

What happens to the *umma* clause in this period is the phenomenon which has been called 'divergence' (Hopper 1991: 24, Hopper and Traugott 1993: 116). The construction which undergoes grammaticalization can lose syntactic and semantic independence in some contexts, but can retain its original independence in other contexts. An obvious example of such divergence is the English construction 'be going to', which has been grammaticalized as a future marker in some contexts (117*a*), but in other contexts retains its original meaning (117*b*). The reason for divergence is of course that it is not one element in isolation that undergoes grammaticalization, but the whole construction in context. In some contexts (for example before other verbs), the repeated use of 'be going to' may cause the bleaching of its original physical meaning ('walk'). But in other contexts (for example before noun phrases denoting a location), the construction can happily retain its original meaning.

(117) (*a*) I *am going to* read a book this evening.
(*b*) I *am going to* the dining room.

The development of *umma* in Old Babylonian is similar. On the one hand, the *umma* clause can still be entirely independent. It very often introduces direct speech without any verb, and in such cases it functions as a whole independent clause, which contains the meaning of speech:

(118) *umma Ipiq-Damu-ma kasp-um jā'um ul ša ummiān-im*
umma Ipiq-Damu-P silver-NOM mine not of money lender-GEN
umma Dulluqum-ma kasp-um ša ummiān-im
umma Dulluqum-P silver-NOM of money lender-GEN
'Ipiq-Damu said: "the silver is mine, not the money-lender's" (but) Dulluqum said "the silver is the money-lender's"' (AbB 11: 159: 11)

(119) *ana as-îm umma atta-ma*
to physician-GEN *umma* you-P
'say to the physician ". . ."' (AbB 11: 53: 8)

(120) *pīqat umma PN-ma*
perhaps *umma* PN-P
'perhaps PN might say ". . ."' (AbB 4: 49: 11)

(121) *aššum ša umma bēl-ī-ma*
concerning REL *umma* lord-my-P
'concerning what my lord said ". . ."' (AbB 12: 31: 8)

In the examples above, the *umma* clause maintains both its syntactic and semantic independence. But in a different environment, when the *umma* clause follows speech verbs, its independence is clearly eroded. Thus, when speech verbs are present, the phrase *umma X-ma* becomes almost obligatory after them:

(122) *lā taqabbî umma atti-ma*
not you.say *umma* you(FSG)-P
'don't say ". . ."' (AbB 1: 134: 22)

(123) *aššum ša tašpur-am umma atta-ma*
concerning REL you.wrote-to me *umma* you-P
'concerning what you wrote to me ". . ."' (AbB 12: 7: 4)

Direct speech without any marker is much rarer in the letters. Since even the most common speech verbs are almost always followed by *umma*, it is clear that *umma* in such an environment is losing its contrastive role (or in other words, its semantic content). The syntactic repercussions of the loss of its contrastive role are not yet evident in Old Babylonian, but they will become apparent in Middle Babylonian.

5.3.2. *'Deletion'*

We have seen that the *umma* clause has now diverged and has a dual role. On the one hand, it can retain its independence, and introduce speech on its own (124). On the other hand, it is almost obligatory after speech verbs (125):

(124) *pīqat umma PN-ma*
perhaps *umma* PN-P
'perhaps PN might say ". . ."' (AbB 4: 49: 11)

(125) *pīqat nappāhū iqabbû-kum umma šunu-ma '. . .'*
perhaps smiths they.say-to you *umma* they-P
'perhaps the smiths might say to you ". . ."' (AbB 4: 50: 8)

From a purely synchronic perspective, this variation may seem strange. This variation has also encouraged erroneous interpretations. For example, Buccellati (1996: 487) calls examples like (124) above, in which the *umma* clause still stands on its own, cases of 'verb deletion'. According to his analysis, the construction *umma X-ma* + 'reported speech' derives from an underlying construction *umma X-ma* + 'he.said' + 'reported speech', where the speech verb has been deleted. But from the historical development which we have followed so far it should be clear that no deletion of any kind is involved. Rather, what occurs is optional 'verb addition'. The optionality of the speech verb during the Old Babylonian period is the result of an intermediary stage in the grammaticalization process of a new direct speech marker. Old Babylonian is the stage between Old Akkadian, when a speech verb was never used with *enma*, and Middle Babylonian when *umma* loses the ability to stand on its own.[32]

[32] The 'optionality of speech verbs' is not a phenomenon limited to Akkadian. Frajzyngier (1996: 125 ff.) discusses it at length in Chadic languages, and claims that it also occurs in Bantu. He refers to it as 'verb omission'. By using comparative data from a large number of Chadic languages, he postulates the diachronic scenario which we can actually observe.

5.3.3. *The range of verbs which* umma *can follow*

In some contexts, as we have seen, *umma* is still the only carrier of the speech meaning. This is not only the case when it does not follow any verb, but also when it follows non-speech verbs such as 'come' or 'seize':[33]

(126) *PN+ iṣbatan-ni umma šū-ma*
PN+ he.seized-me *umma* he-P
'PN+ seized me, and said ". . ."' (TCL 1: 2: 10)

The main category of verbs which *umma* follows is of course speech verbs, as we have seen above. In Old Babylonian *umma* only makes very modest headway in discarding its active speech meaning entirely. *Umma* in Old Babylonian is restricted to contexts where active speech is present, at least metaphorically. Thus, we may find *umma* introducing 'talking to oneself' (which, nowadays, we tend to call 'thinking'), as in (127) below. But we do not find *umma* further afield, with verbs such as 'hear' and 'fear', which are more distant from prototypical speech situations.

(127) *umma anāku-ma ana nuppuš libb-i ša šāpiri-ja*
umma I-P to set at ease.INF.of heart-GEN of superior-my
ṭupp-ī lušābil
tablet-my let.me.send
'I "thought": let me send a tablet of mine to set my superior's mind at ease' (AbB 13: 34: 9')

[33] In fact, the appearance of direct quotation after motion and action verbs is quite common across languages, since these verbs seem to be a natural extension of speech situations. (Reasons are discussed in Romaine and Lange 1991: 265.) This is the case both in languages which use a quotative marker for direct speech, and in languages which do not. Below are some examples from languages without a quotative particle. These examples are from colloquial registers, all meaning: 'so he says: "what do you want?"':

go	American English:	he goes	'what do you want?'
come	Swedish:	*och så kom han då*	'*Vad vill ni?*' (from Romaine and Lange 1991)
		and so he came	'what do you want?'
do	Modern Hebrew:	*az hu ose li*	'*ma ata roce?*'
		so he does to me	'what do you want?'

In fact, Tannen (1986: 315) counted in her discourse samples of American English that 13 per cent of quotations were introduced by the verb 'go'. She also found the phenomenon (but less frequently) in spoken Modern Greek. A similar phenomenon occurs in languages which use quotative particles. Georgian offers very clear evidence that even a clitic particle *-tko* (suffixed to the end of the reported speech) can appear with verbs of action.

exlave ak moiq'vane, puls gačukeb-tko
right now here fetch him the money I shall present it to you-QUOTATIVE
'fetch him here right now (telling him that) I shall present him with the money'
(Hewitt and Crisp 1986: 122)

It is even possible that in Sanskrit, the verb *go* itself developed into a direct quotation marker. Dorothy Disterheft (personal communication) suggests that the quotative particle *iti* is a reduced form of the verb form *eiti* (go.3SG.PRESENT).

Notice, however, example (128) from Old Babylonian, which suggests a way for the later extension of the range of *umma* to the verb 'hear':[34]

(128) *ina pī PN kīam eštenemme umma šū-ma . . .*
in mouth.of PN thus I.keep hearing *umma* he-P
'from the mouth of PN thus I keep hearing, *umma* he: ". . ."' (AbB 3: 71: 17)

It was probably the presence of the speaker *X* in the *umma* construction which prevented the further extension in the range of verbs that *umma* could follow. Throughout the Old Babylonian period, the element *X-ma* in the *umma* construction is obligatory,[35] and it must have been the high salience of this element which ensured that the phrase *umma X-ma* was still restricted to contexts which involve active speech.

5.4. Middle Babylonian

In the Middle Babylonian period, we find the *umma* construction further along the grammaticalization 'cline'. First, the construction has undergone reduction in form: the obligatory person marker *X-ma* in the *umma* construction disappears. As a consequence, *umma* also loses its syntactic independence and its role as a head of a clause.

5.4.1. *The disappearance of the person marking* X-ma

By the Middle Babylonian period, the obligatory *X-ma* after *umma* has entirely disappeared. Instead of *umma X-ma*, with a variable *X*, we now find the invariable form *ummā* (written *um-ma-a*).[36] There is a gap between the Old Babylonian texts and the Middle Babylonian texts, a 'dark period' of at least two hundred years. We cannot, therefore, trace the disappearance of *X-ma* historically. But the seeds of the development are already sown in the Old Babylonian period, and it is not difficult to reconstruct how and why the change occurred. The basic cause for the disappearance of the person marker after *umma* is simple: when *umma* starts appearing after speech verbs, the speaker is marked on the verb (or in the verbal clause), and thus the marking of the person after *umma* becomes redundant.

[34] In Mari, where the invariable element *ummami* is often used instead of *umma X-ma*, *ummami* does appear after the verb *šemûm* already in OB (e.g. Charpin et al. 1998: 523 (p. 498): 25).

[35] There is only a handful of exceptions, such as: *šarrum kīam iqbišunūšim umma ana qištīkunu lā tegiā* (AbB 4: 111: 9), *ṭuppi bēlija kīam illikam umma* '. . .' (AbB 13: 33: 6). (See AbB 13: 33 fn. b for other examples.) The use of *X-ma* is not obligatory in other OB dialects, e.g. in Mari *ummami* is regularly used instead.

[36] In the contemporary stage of the other dialect of Akkadian, Middle Assyrian, this construction was reduced further to *mā*. In Middle Babylonian, there are still some examples of the use of the older construction, but these are restricted to the (old) letter introduction formula *ana X qibima umma Y-ma* (e.g. in BE 17: 80: 1).

The process can be illustrated schematically as follows: when *umma X-ma* introduces speech on its own, *umma* carries the speech meaning, and *X* is the sole identifier of the speaker. But when *umma* starts appearing after speech verbs, the weight of the identification of the speaker shifts to the verbal clause. The two patterns can be contrasted in the parallel examples (124) and (125) above, repeated here as (129*a*, *b*). In (*a*), *umma* appears without a speech verb, and *PN-ma* is the only identifier of the speaker. In (*b*), the speakers ('the smiths') are identified as the subject of the verb 'say', and the person marker after *umma* is only a pronoun ('they') which refers back to the verbal clause.

(129) (*a*) *pīqat umma PN-ma*
perhaps *umma* PN-P
'perhaps PN might say ". . ."' (OB)

(*b*) *pīqat nappāhū iqabbû-kum umma šunu-ma*
perhaps smiths they.say-to you *umma* they-P
'perhaps the smiths might say to you ". . ."'

Thus, when *umma* follows speech verbs, the element *X-ma* is most often a pronoun which only refers back to the speaker in the verbal clause. In such cases, *umma* does not carry any new information. Only rarely does the element *X-ma* serve in a contrastive role after speech verbs, as in examples (130) and (131) below. (Notice, however, that in these cases, *umma* does not normally follow the speech verb directly, but is separated from the verb by the coordination particle *-ma.*)[37]

(130) *ašpurak-kum-**ma** umma **atta**-ma*
I.wrote-to you-P *umma* **you**-P
'I wrote to you and this is what you said: ". . ."' (OB. AbB 1: 23: 6)

(131) *PN+ ašāl-**ma** umma **šū**-ma*
PN+ I.asked-P *umma* **he**-P
'I asked PN+, and this is what he answered: ". . ."' (OB. AbB 4: 68: 33)

However, since in the vast majority of cases, the element *X* only refers back to a speaker which was already identified in the verbal clause, the contrastive function of the *X* is very limited. It is not surprising, therefore, that the X became a redundant agreement marker, and from there the road to its disappearance was open.

[37] In fact, when *umma* appears with the verb *šâlum* 'ask/question/inquire' in OB, as in (131), *umma* normally introduces the answer, rather than the question. A further example of such use is given below (cf. also AbB 11: 165: 9, 13: 79: 1):

tašālan-ni-ma umma anāku-ma
you.asked-me-P umma **I**-P
'you asked me and this is what I answered: ". . ."' (Kienast 1978: 166: 5)

5.4.2. *Further syntactic and semantic reduction*

The syntactic consequences of the disappearance of *X-ma* are evident in Middle Babylonian. The clause *umma X-ma* is now reduced to a single invariable word *ummā*. As such, *ummā* can no longer identify the speaker. The result of this reduction is that *ummā* no longer appears on its own, and now has to depend on an antecedent to supply the identity of the speaker. *Ummā* can still appear after non-speech verbs, as in (132) below, and in such contexts *ummā* is the only carrier of the speech meaning. But with a few exceptions,[38] *ummā* in Middle Babylonian can no longer introduce a whole independent clause, and is now syntactically dependent on its antecedent verb. Accordingly, I gloss *ummā* in (132) as 'saying'.

(132) *eql-a ša PN+ . . . ana PN$_2$ ittadin ummā bēl-ka iqbâ*
field-ACC of PN+ to PN$_2$ he.gave *ummā* lord-your said.to me
'he gave the field of PN+ to PN$_2$, saying "your lord ordered me (to do it)"' (BE 17: 48: 9)

The loss of *X-ma* also encourages further semantic reduction. Even if *ummā* can still introduce the speech meaning on its own, *ummā* is found most often after speech verbs. In the context of speech verbs, *ummā* can now be regarded as a grammatical marker, since it is both obligatory, and does not carry any new information:

(133) *PN+ ana mārti-šu išappara ummā šumma mimma*
PN+ to daughter-his he.writes *ummā* if anything
iqtabûnik-ki qibī ummā amāt-a ana šarr-i
they.say-to you(FSG) say.IMP(FSG) *ummā* matter-ACC to king-GEN
našāku
I.bring.STATIVE
'PN+ used to write to his daughter: "if they say anything to you, say (to them) 'I will bring the matter to the king'"' (PBS 1/2: 21: 6)

(134) *mannu iqabbi ummā ul mārat šarr-i šī*
who he.(would)say *ummā* not daughter.of king-GEN she
'who would say: "she is not a king's daughter"?' (EA 4: 13)

Moreover, the loss of *X-ma* eliminates the last obstacle for the extension of *ummā* from a quotative marker to a more general complementizer. The disappearance of the active speaker from the *umma* construction facilitates the further erosion in the speech meaning of *ummā*. We now find an example of *ummā* following the verb 'hear' (135). As opposed to the Old Babylonian example (128)

[38] There is one context in which *ummā* still introduces a clause, but this is only in a frozen formulaic expression in the introduction of letters. Many MB letters contain the phrase *ummā ana Y-ma* (*ummā* to Y-P). Here, it is clear that *ummā* introduces the speech of the writer of the letter, and the frozen expression can be translated as 'this is what I say to Y'.

above ('from the mouth of someone I heard, this is what he said ". . ."'), in (135) there is no mention of the active speaker at all. Here *ummā* has reached the stage where it is no longer restricted to situations of active speech. We shall see below that this tendency becomes much stronger in Neo-Babylonian.

(135) *aššum šarrāni ša limīt-i šem-ê ummā hurāṣu* [. . .]
so that kings of region-GEN hear.INF-GEN *ummā* gold
'so that the kings of region will hear: "[there is much]? gold"' (EA 11: r20)

5.5. Neo-Babylonian

By the Neo-Babylonian period, the process of grammaticalization has progressed to such an extent that *umma* can be considered a general complementizer. The following examples are not meant to provide a thorough description of the use of *umma* in Neo-Babylonian. They only seek to demonstrate the degree of reduction which *umma* has reached.

The reduction in the status of *umma* can be seen both in form and in meaning. The phonetic form is further reduced in Neo-Babylonian from *ummā* (written *um-ma-a*) to *umma* (written *um-ma*).[39] The syntactic status is now that of an entirely dependent particle. *Umma* cannot stand on its own, and has to depend on an antecedent. *Umma* normally depends on verbs, but we also find a few cases where it depends on nouns, as in (136) below. (In §5.7 below, we shall see another structural indication for the reduced syntactic status of *umma* in Neo-Babylonian: the repetition of *umma* within reported speech.)

(136) *amāt ša itti libbi-kunu kuṣṣupākunu anāku īde*
matter REL with heart-your(PL) you(PL).think.STATIVE I know
umma
umma
'I know what you think in your hearts, namely: ". . ."' (ABL 301: r3)

Umma can still appear after non-speech verbs such as 'go', and carry the speech meaning, as in (137). But most often, *umma* appears after speech verbs, as in (138), where (as already in the Middle Babylonian period) *umma* does not have any independent semantic role.

(137) *PN kī illika umma kigallānu ašaṭṭar*
PN when he.came *umma* pedestals I.(will)inscribe
'when PN came saying "I will inscribe the pedestals"' (Cole and Machinist 1998: 178: 4)

[39] The longer form *ummā* is retained only in the formulaic introductory phrase *ummā ana Y* (*ummā* to Y) which survives from the Middle Babylonian period, and often comes after the salutation in the beginning of a letter. There are only negligibly few examples where the longer form is used in other contexts, e.g. ABL 1420: 6, Cole 1996: 21: 20.

(138) *mamma ša iqabbâkka umma*
whoever REL he.says.to you *umma*
šēpīt šar Bābili lā taṣabbat bēl dabābi-ka šū
feet.of king.of Babylon not you.grasp enemy-your he
'whoever tells you "don't grasp the feet of the king of Babylon", he is your enemy' (ABL 1236: 8)

But the most striking change in Neo-Babylonian is the expansion in the range of verbs which *umma* can follow. First, as opposed to the Old Babylonian period, *umma* now regularly appears after the verb 'ask':

(139) *ašāl-šu umma mannu išpuru-kunūšu iqabbâ umma PN+*
I.asked-him *umma* who he.sent-you(PL) he.says.to me *umma* PN+
iltapran-nāšu
he.sent-us
'I asked him "who sent you?", he told me "PN+ sent us"' (ABL 1028: 8')

More importantly, *umma* starts appearing after verbs which, although speech-related, are increasingly further away from prototypical speech situations. These verbs may describe (at least metaphorically) an act of speech, but they have increasing emphasis on the mental activity associated with the situation, rather than the speech act itself. The following are examples with the verbs 'agree' (140), 'become hostile' (141), 'worry' (142), and 'fear' (143), (144):

(140) *anīni ul nimangur umma PN bēl-āni baliṭ*
we not we.agreed *umma* PN lord-our he.lives.STATIVE
'we did not agree, saying: "PN our lord is alive"' (ABL 576: 14)

(141) *ālāni ma'dūte lapāni-šu ittikirū umma*
towns many in front-his they.became hostile *umma*
ina qātē-ka ul nillak
in hands(DUAL)-your not we.(will)go
'many towns have become hostile to him, saying "we will not follow you"' (ABL 839: 10)

(142) *PN akanna inamziq umma [ū]mussu anāku [a]l-ta-ad-da-ad . . .*
PN here he.worries *umma* daily I I.bear misfortune[?]
'PN here is getting worried, saying: "daily I bear misfortune[?]"' (BIN 1: 86: 17)

(143) *gabbi iptalhū umma ana qātē kalbāni muššurāni*
all they.feared *umma* to hands(DUAL).of dogs we.are.delivered
'they all feared: "we are delivered to the dogs"' (ABL 1431: r3)

(144) *kī aplahu umma ana hiṭṭi-ja lā i-ta-ri*
when I.feared *umma* to fault-my not it.(will)turn
'when I feared "let it not turn into my fault"' (Parpola 1993: 120: 9)

In Neo-Babylonian, *umma* also appears regularly with the verb 'hear'. In some cases, *umma* is still used in a strictly quotative function even after the verb 'hear'. For example, in (145) below, *umma* introduces the exact words of the original speakers, and is very similar to the Old Babylonian example in (128) above:

(145) *ina pī ša* LÚ.GAL.MEŠ *alteme umma madaktu ina Dilbat*
from mouth of overseers I.heard *umma* camp in Dilbat
nišakkan
we.(shall)place
'I heard from the mouth of the overseers: "we shall pitch camp in Dilbat"' (ABL 804: r8)

Nevertheless, the verb 'hear' also provides the clearest indications that *umma* has moved away from its role as a quotative marker. Most often, we find *umma* without any explicit indication of the original speakers, as in the example below:

(146) *altemû umma šar Aššur ana kutalli kī issûni . . . madākti*
I.heard *umma* king.of Assyria to rear when he.withdrew camp
ittadû
he.lay down
'I heard that when the king of Assyria withdrew to the rear, he pitched camp . . .' (ABL 901: 5)

Moreover, *umma* in Neo-Babylonian loses the most important property which previously distinguished it as a 'direct speech' marker. The reported speech after *umma* need no longer retain the deictic system of the original 'speaker'. In (147) below, the deictic system of the reported 'speech' has shifted from the (implicit) speaker to the hearer: the speaker would have said: 'your' or 'his' instead of 'my'. The same is the case in (148), where the possessive 'my' refers to the hearer, not to any speaker. In such examples, Neo-Babylonian *umma* can be regarded as a general complementizer, and be translated as 'that'.

(147) *altemû umma ṣābē-ja ša halqū [ah]ū-a*
I.heard *umma* men-my REL lost.STATIVE(PL) brother-my
iptaṭar-šunūtu
he.ransomed-them
'I heard that *my* brother ransomed *my* men who were lost' (Cole 1996: 24: 11)

(148) *kī ašmû umma bēl-ī ina nakuttu ašibu*
as I.heard *umma* lord-my in peril he.lives.STATIVE
'as I heard, *my* lord is living in peril' (Cole 1996: 29: 5, cf. no. 83: 4, 8)

5.6. Recapitulation: from Old Akkadian to Neo-Babylonian

We have followed the development of the *umma* construction in some detail. The changes from Old Akkadian to Neo-Babylonian involve a marked reduction in the semantic, syntactic, and phonetic content of the *umma* construction. What started as a whole clause with the meaning '(this is what) X said' eventually became a bleached and entirely dependent grammatical marker.

In Old Akkadian and Old Babylonian, *umma* was the head of the independent clause which introduced direct speech, and meant roughly '(this is what) X said'. Throughout the Old Babylonian period, *umma X-ma* was used as an independent clause, but this clause also started appearing after speech verbs, initially in simple parataxis ('he wrote to me, and said . . .'). The regular appearance of the *umma* clause after speech verbs meant that it gradually lost its contrastive function, and induced bleaching in its semantic content. The syntactic consequences of the semantic bleaching were manifested in the Middle Babylonian period, when the active speaker *X-ma* disappeared, and the *umma* construction was reduced to an invariable *ummā*. With the disappearance of *X-ma*, *ummā* was no longer the head of an independent clause, and now needed an antecedent on which to depend. By the Neo-Babylonian period, *ummā* was further reduced to *umma*. The use of *umma* was extended from direct quotations to other contexts, so that *umma* appeared regularly with the verbs 'fear' and 'hear', with which it did not even need to retain the deictic system of the original 'speaker'. Neo-Babylonian *umma* can therefore be regarded as a general complementizer.

The syntactic reduction of *umma* and the extension in its use have important implications for the Functional Domain of Complementation as a whole. These will be discussed in detail in chapter 7. In Neo-Babylonian, *umma* can be regarded as an alternative complementizer, and the *umma* construction is in direct competition with other structures in the FDC. In particular, the verb 'hear' only appears with *umma*, and does not appear with the older complementizer *kī*(*ma*). The distribution between the *umma* construction and finite complements in Neo-Babylonian is no longer based simply on the opposition between 'direct speech' and 'indirect' finite complements. Rather, the opposition now is between the domain of speech, and the non-speech domain. We find the complementizer *kī* (and the relative particle *ša*) in the non-speech domain ('know', 'see' etc.), whereas *umma* reigns in the speech domain (which includes the verb 'hear' in the meaning 'hear it said').

5.7. Bracketing of reported speech in the different periods

Section 5.2.1 above mentioned that in early Old Babylonian, the first way to combine the *umma* clause with the unmarked speech verb 'say' (*qabûm*) was through a type of bracketing construction, probably used for emphatic purpose. I said that this particular bracketing construction disappeared fairly quickly in the language of the letters. Nevertheless, the phenomenon of bracketing direct speech does not disappear in Old Babylonian. First, the construction from §5.2.1 is still found, although rarely, in legal documents also from later Old Babylonian, as in the examples below:

(149) *umma šunu-ma PN_1 kīma rihût PN_2 nīde iqbû*
umma they-P PN_1 COMP progeny.of PN_2 we.know they.said
'they said: "we know that PN_1 is the progeny of PN_2," they said'
(Leichty 1989, p. 352: iii. 25')

(150) *umma šū-ma hablāku iqtabi*
umma he-P I.am wronged.STATIVE he.said(PERFECT)
'he said: I have been wronged' (Edzard 1970, n. 54: 15)

But in the later Old Babylonian period, more elaborate formulae are preferred, especially in letters of more official nature. The circumstances which are dealt with in the letters from the Old Babylonian chancery become increasingly complex, and the reports often involve multiple speakers in nested constructions, such as 'you wrote to me that X said that Y said that . . ., but Y claimed that X said that . . .'. In such bureaucratic language, the reported speech is often not only preceded by *umma X-ma*, but is also bracketed by the expression *kīam iqbi* (thus he.said). The particle *kīam*, to be translated 'thus', or 'like this' is another variation on the comparative meaning of the element *kī*. The following example is repeated from a letter I quoted in the introduction, printed here in abridged form:

(151) *ana Sin-iddinam qibi-ma umma Hammurabi-ma*
to Sin-iddinam say.IMP-P *umma* Hammurabi-P
aššum . . . ša ašpurak-kum-ma
concerning [the sending the overseers . . .] REL I.wrote-to you-P
umma atta-ma
umma you-P
umma waklū tamkārī-ma
umma overseers of the merchants-P
ina kīma inanna ebūrum warki ebūrim i nillik
as it is right now harvest time, let us go after the harvest
kīam iqbû-kum-ma
thus they.said-to you-P
tašpur-am . . .
you.wrote-to me
'Tell Sin-iddinam, this is what Hammurabi said: concerning the sending to Babylon of the overseers of the merchants . . . that I wrote to you about, you said as follows "the overseers of the merchants said as follows 'as it is right now harvest time, let us go after the harvest'", thus they told you and you wrote to me.' (AbB 2: 33: 1)

The bracketing of reported speech seems to occur in a variety of languages. Munro (1982: 311) reports that such patterns are found in Lahu (Tibeto-Burman), Gahuku (New Guinea), and the Yuman family (American Indian). (I have already mentioned colloquial German in §5.2.1 above.) Example (152) is from Chickasaw (Muskogean, American Indian):

(152) *Jan-at* *aachi-kat* *'Ish-ī'sh-a'chi'* *aash-tok*
Jan-SUBJECT say-SAME you-take-FUTURE say-PAST
'Jan said "you take it" he said' (Munro 1982: 311)

In the history of Babylonian, the bracketing strategy does not survive beyond the Old Babylonian period. In Neo-Babylonian, a different device develops. Instead of bracketing, *umma* can now be repeated before every clause of the reported speech, in order to mark that the following clause still belongs to the reported speech. This can be seen in the following example:

(153) *ana ekalli altapra*
to palace I.wrote
umma LÚ.ŠAMÁN.MÁL.LÁ.MEŠ *ša šarru ina pānīja ipqidu Enūma Anu Enlil iltandū*
umma the apprentices whom the king appointed in my charge have learnt the *E-A-E*
umma mīnu hiṭūa šarru itti ummânīšu rēša ul iššī
umma what's my fault that the king hasn't summoned me with his scholars?
šarru iqtabi
king he.said
umma lā tapallah
umma don't be afraid
umma rēška anašši
umma I will summon you
'I wrote to the palace: "The apprentices whom the king appointed in my charge have learnt the *Enūma Anu Enlil.* What is my fault that the king has not summoned me with his scholars?" The king (then) said: "Don't be afraid, I will summon you".' (Parpola 1993: 171: 17)

This use of *umma* in Neo-Babylonian is another indication of its increasing reduction and dependence. In Old Babylonian, when *umma* introduces reported speech, even long stretches of speech are reported verbatim, without any internal modification. In Neo-Babylonian, the use of repeated *umma* before every clause can most easily be understood if we think of it as '(and) that': 'he said *that* . . . (and) *that* . . . (and) *that* . . .'.

5.8. The development of *umma* in cross-linguistic perspective

Quotative particles are not common in modern European languages, but are found in many other languages of the world. The most well-known sources from which quotative particles emerge are verbs of saying. The grammaticalization of verbs of saying into quotative particles has been studied for various languages, most notably in Africa (Lord 1993, Frajzyngier 1996), but also in East Asia

(Matisoff 1991: 398). Many languages of the Near East (ancient and modern) also have quotative particles which originated from verbs of saying (Turkish *diye*, Ancient Egyptian *r-ḏd*, Hittite *wa(r)*,[40] and biblical Hebrew *lēʾmōr*).

On the surface, the development in Babylonian is different from all these languages on two accounts. First, *umma* does not obviously derive from a speech verb (cf. note 25, p. 69). Secondly, the *umma* construction starts as a whole clause *enma/umma X-ma*, not just a single word. Nevertheless, on closer inspection the differences appear very superficial, and the route of grammaticalization of the *umma* construction and of speech verbs turns out to be very similar. The reason for the similarity is that what is crucial in determining the route of grammaticalization is not the lexical properties of an element, but rather the context in which the element is used. Since the *umma* clause (as a whole unit) is used precisely in the same contexts that would accommodate a speech verb, its path of grammaticalization is the same as that of speech verbs.

5.8.1. *A Hebrew parallel*

To demonstrate the similarity between the development of *umma* and the grammaticalization of speech verbs, we can look at a parallel to the development of *umma* in biblical Hebrew. Here, the historical development has to be reconstructed from coexisting synchronic constructions, but the comparison is nonetheless compelling. The Hebrew verb *ʾmr* ('say') can be used in different grades of grammaticalization, from a full verb to a quotative marker. This section does not presume to describe the intricacies of use of reported speech in biblical Hebrew. (For detailed studies on reported speech in Hebrew cf. Goldenberg 1991, Miller 1995.) It only outlines the various grades (or 'stages') of grammaticalization of the verb 'say', for the purpose of comparison with the Babylonian *umma* construction.

Within the biblical Hebrew corpus, we can observe four different grades in the grammaticalization of the verb *ʾmr* ('say'). Examples of these are given in (154) below. First, *ʾmr* can appear as a full verb, which carries the meaning of speech on its own, as in (i). Then, *ʾmr* regularly appears after other speech verbs, as in (ii). In such constructions, although *ʾmr* is still syntactically independent (it is a finite verb which appears in parataxis after other speech verbs), its semantic content is already reduced.

Example (iii) demonstrates a more reduced form of the verb *ʾmr*, the particle *lē-ʾmōr* (to-say.INF). This form is no longer syntactically independent. Finally, in (iv), the use of *lēʾmōr* has been extended further, and it can appear not only in the context of speech, but also after verbs such as 'hear'.

[40] The particle *wa(r)* is regarded by most scholars as a fossilized form of the root **uer* 'say' (Forston 1998: 21).

(154) Grades of grammaticalization of *'mr*:

(i) *wa-yō'mer ēl-āw Abnēr lēk . . .*
and-said.3MSG to-him Abner go.IMP(MSG)
'and Abner said to him: "Go!"' (2 Samuel 3: 15)

(ii) *wa-taggēd l-Dāwid wa-tō'mer . . .*
and-told.3FSG to-David and-said.3FSG
'and she told David and said: ". . ."' (2 Samuel 11: 5)

(iii) *wa-ydabbēr ĕlōhîm el Nōah lē-'mōr . . .*
and-spoke.3MSG God to Noah to-say.INF
'and God spoke to Noah saying: ". . ."' (Genesis 8: 15)

(iv) *w-kol Yisrā'ēl šām'û lē-'mōr hikkâ Šā'ûl*
and-all Israel heard.3MPL to-say.INF smote.3MSG Saul
et nṣîb Plištîm
ACC garrison.of Philistines
'and all Israel heard that Saul had smitten a garrison of the Philistines' (1 Samuel 13: 4)

Purely in terms of their function in the sentence, these four grades in the use of *'mr* can be compared to the different stages in the grammaticalization of *umma* in (155):

(155) Stages of grammaticalization of *umma*:

(i) *umma PN-ma*
'PN said . . .'

(ii) *PN iqbi umma šū-ma*
PN he.spoke *umma* he-P
'PN spoke and said'

(iii) *PN iqbi umma*
PN he.spoke *umma*
'PN spoke, saying'

(iv) *PN išme umma*
PN he.heard *umma*
'PN heard:'

Stage (155 i), where *umma X-ma* stands on its own and alone carries the speech meaning, corresponds to grade (i) of *'mr*, where the verb introduces the speech meaning on its own. In stage (ii), the *umma* clause is now semantically reduced, but it still functions as a 'finite' independent clause, because the speaker is identified in the clause (by the element *X-ma*). In stage (iii), *umma* no longer carries the identity of speaker, and in this respect it functions as a 'non-finite' clause, corresponding to the infinitival form *lē'mōr*. Finally, stage (iv), where *umma* has been extended beyond the contexts of speech, corresponds to the identical development of *lēʾmōr.*[41]

Of course, we cannot talk directly about *umma* being 'finite' or 'non-finite', because it is not a verb. But the whole phrase *umma X-ma* does carry the person category, whereas *umma* on its own does not. In this respect, the relation between them is similar to the relation between the finite forms of *ʾmr* and the non-finite form *lēʾmōr.*

The close parallel between the development of *umma* and grammaticalization of speech verbs into quotatives shows that the etymology and internal structure of the *umma* construction are not the important factors in its process of grammaticalization. In order for the process of grammaticalization to take place, the only crucial ingredients are a clause which means roughly '(X) says/said', and the regular appearance of this clause in paratactic sequences after verbs of speech. From there, the road to reduction is open. Whether this clause originally consists only of the single verb 'say' (as in most of the reported examples) or whether it starts out as a more elaborate clause (but with approximately the same meaning), as in Akkadian, the subsequent route is similar.

5.8.2. *Extension beyond 'fear' and 'hear'*

In Neo-Babylonian (and in Hebrew), the extension in the use of the erstwhile quotative particle did not continue beyond verbs such as 'hear' and 'fear'. *Umma* is never used with the verb 'know', for example. But in many languages, the original quotative marker can be extended much further, to be used with all complement-taking verbs. In ancient Egyptian, for example, an infinitival form of the verb 'say' (*r-ḏd*) underwent precisely the same process of grammaticalization as we have seen in Babylonian. From its use to enforce speech after non-speech verbs, *r-ḏd* developed into a quotative particle after verbs of speech, and then to a more general complementizer. But as opposed to the situation in Babylonian, the development went further in Egyptian. By the eighteenth dynasty, *r-ḏd* appeared (although rarely) after the verb 'know' (*rh*) (Gardiner 1957, §224), and in later Egyptian, *r-ḏd* became the normal complementizer for all complement-taking verbs (Sweeney 1986).

Another example comes from Ewe (spoken in Ghana, Togo, and Benin). Here, the development has to be reconstructed from synchronic evidence, but it seems that precisely the same process occurred with the verb *bé* (Lord 1993). *Bé* in Ewe

[41] The range of uses of *lēʾmōr* in Hebrew and *umma* in Neo-Babylonian is actually very similar. They appear after the same verbs and in the same contexts. Moreover, just as we have seen for *umma* in Neo-Babylonian, Hebrew *lēʾmōr* can also depend not only on verbs, but on nouns. Thus compare example (136) from Neo-Babylonian, where *umma* depends on the noun 'word/matter', with (2 Chronicles 11: 2): 'and the word of yhwh was to Shemaiah the man of God *lēʾmōr.* ". . ."'. The repeated use of *umma* in reported speech as in (153) also has parallels with Hebrew *lēʾmōr*, as in 2 Samuel 3: 12: 'Abner sent messengers to David *lēʾmōr* "to whom does the land belong?" *lēʾmōr* "make your covenant with me . . ."'.

was originally a full lexical verb meaning 'say', and can still function as such, as in example (156). But the verb *bé* also underwent grammaticalization, to become a quotative particle, as in (157). The use of this particle has also been extended much further, and *bé* can function as a complementizer after a wide range of verbs, including 'know' (158) and 'want' (159). (All examples are from Lord (1993: 184 ff.).)

(156) *mebé mewoe*
I.say I.do.it
'I said "I did it"'

(157) *meyó vinyéa bé adzó*
I.call child.my say adzo
'I called my child Adzo'

(158) *atá nyá bé kofí wo doá*
Ata know say Kofi do work
'Ata knew that Kofi did the work'

(159) *medí bé máfle awua dewó*
I.want say I.buy dress some
'I want to buy some dresses'

We can never know whether the development of *umma* in Neo-Babylonian was arrested only by the death of the language, or by other factors. But had Babylonian continued to be spoken for a few more centuries, a similar extension in the use of *umma* may well have taken place.

Part III

Functional History: The Changes in the Functional Domain of Complementation from 2500 BC to 500 BC

6

The Functional Domain of Complementation in Babylonian

This study makes a strict division between structural change (in Part II), and functional change (in this Part). Part II followed the emergence of new structures: finite complements and the quotative construction. This Part examines functional replacement: the changes in the functional roles of different structures. The following three chapters trace the changes in the relative roles of the various structures in the FDC throughout the historical period. Chapter 7 will examine the structures used with knowledge, perception, and speech verbs; chapter 8 will describe verbs of manipulation and modality; and chapter 9 will describe the structures used in the '*wh*-functional domain'. This chapter offers a brief introduction to the Functional Domain of Complementation in Babylonian. It surveys first the range of verbs in the FDC (§6.1), and the range of structures used with them (§6.2). Section 6.3 then explains the difference between subordinate and independent clauses in Babylonian. Finally, section 6.4 examines briefly the relation between syntax and semantics in the choice of structures in the FDC.

6.1. The verbs in the FDC

The main semantic categories in the Babylonian Functional Domain of Complementation are listed below, together with the most common verbs in each of the groups:[42]

(i) Speech: *qabûm* ('say', 'speak'), *dabābum* ('speak', 'complain'), *šapārum* ('write'), *apālum* ('answer'), *šâlum* ('ask')
(ii) Manipulation: *qabûm* ('tell', 'order'), *šapārum* ('order in writing'), *magārum* ('let', 'agree')
(iii) Perception: *amārum* ('see'), *šemûm* ('hear')
(iv) Knowledge and acquisition of knowledge: *idûm* ('know'), *lamādum* ('learn')

[42] The list is based on Noonan's classification (1985), but with modifications: I omit groups which are not found in Babylonian, and introduce groups such as 'proving' which are of special importance. Another group which does exist in Babylonian, but which I do not treat here, is phasal and achievement verbs, such as *qerēbum* ('start'), *kašādum* ('finish'), *ṣabātum* ('begin'), *gamārum* ('finish'), *egûm* ('be negligent').

(v) Fearing: *palāhum* ('fear')
(vi) Proving: *kunnum* and *burrum* ('establish', 'prove', 'convict')
(vii) Modality: *le'ûm* ('be able to')

A few points should be made about this list and about the range of verbs in the FDC. The first point is that Babylonian is very poor in 'complement-taking verbs', when one compares it to modern European languages. Babylonian is especially poor in verbs which denote abstract mental states and attitudes. One will look in vain for verbs such as 'suppose', 'assume', 'imagine', 'pretend', 'guess', 'doubt', 'regret', or 'hope'. Concepts such as 'think' are normally expressed using the terminology of speech. 'I thought', for example, will typically appear as 'I said', or 'I said in my heart'.

There are also various verbs in Babylonian which are similar in meaning to complement-taking verbs in modern European languages, but which nevertheless are not used in the same contexts as the corresponding European verbs. For example, Babylonian has a verb *mašûm* ('forget'), but whereas we find the Babylonians forgetting a matter, or forgetting a person, we do not find them forgetting 'to do something' or forgetting 'that something happened'. In translation, we can sometimes paraphrase the original with a complement structure, as in (160) and (161) below. But in Babylonian, the verb is only used with nominal objects, in constructions such as 'have you forgotten me?' or 'have you forgotten the matter about which I told you?'.

(160) *ṣibût-um ina qāti-ja amši-ma ul aqbi-kum*
wish-NOM in hand-my I.forgot-P not I.said-to you
'a wish was in my hand, I forgot (it) and did not tell you'
(~ I had a wish, but I forgot to tell you) (AbB 6: 57: 20)

(161) *aššum enkētim u erbī ša una''id-u-ka*
about fish.GEN and locusts.GEN REL I.informed-SUB-you
lā tamašši leqe'-am
not you.forget take.IMP-for me
'don't forget about the fish and locusts that I informed you, get (them) for me'
(~ don't forget to get for me the fish and locusts that I informed you about') (AbB 2: 141: 7)

The reader may also have noticed that the list of modality verbs is rather short. Babylonian does not use periphrastic verbs such as 'should', 'must', or 'want to'. The modal nuances are either implicit in the 'present' verbal form (cf. §3.5.3), or expressed explicitly with the precative form of the verb, or with the particle *lū* (cf. §3.5.5). Moreover, 'causative' verbs are entirely absent. Causative constructions in Babylonian (like in other Semitic languages) are based on internal verbal inflection. For example, the causative form of the verb *wabālum* 'bring' is *šūbulum* 'send'; the causative form of *dabābu* 'talk' is *šudbubum* 'make someone talk'.

The final point that should be noticed is that manipulative verbs are not lexically distinct from normal speech verbs. We have already seen in chapter 4 that the general speech verb *qabûm* can be used either intransitively ('speak', 'talk') or followed by reported speech ('say'). But the same verb can also be used for the manipulative senses 'tell' or 'order' (as well as for 'promise' and 'ask'). What distinguishes the manipulative senses ('tell', 'order') from non-manipulative senses ('say', 'speak') is only the construction in which the verb is used. In chapter 8 we shall examine in more detail the difference between manipulative and non-manipulative constructions with speech verbs.

6.2. The structures in the FDC

Chapters 7 and 8 will present a detailed diachronic survey of the structures used in the Babylonian FDC. As a means of introduction, Table 2 on the following page demonstrates (with constructed Old Babylonian examples) the main structures used in the FDC, and the typical verbs with which they are used. Since all these structures will be discussed in more detail in the following chapters, only a few merit a special introduction at this stage.

The 'as you know' construction is not normally considered in surveys of complementation, so its inclusion here may appear surprising. Nevertheless, we shall see that at least in the Old Babylonian period, the 'as you know' construction and finite complements in fact perform very similar functions, and are almost interchangeable in some contexts. The 'as you know' construction should thus be considered as a part of the FDC.

Infinitive complements also require a few words of introduction, mainly to explain the limited scope of their treatment in this study. Infinitive clauses appear in a variety of forms and flavours in Akkadian. The introduction (§3.5.4) has already explained that the infinitive can be used both in nominal constructions (with arguments in the genitive) and in verbal constructions (with arguments in the nominative or accusative). A further axis of variation is the function of the infinitive clause in the main clause. The infinitive verb may function as the direct object of the main verb (and take the accusative case), or it may be governed by various prepositions, such as *ana* ('to'), *ina* ('in'), *aššum* ('about'). The treatment of the object of the verb in the infinitive clause produces further varieties. When an infinitive clause is governed by a preposition, the object of the infinitive verb may appear in the accusative, but it may also undergo 'case attraction', and be governed directly by the preposition. (For examples of these two different constructions, see (283) and (284) in chapter 8.) In this study, however, I make no attempt to describe systematically the range of structural variation in infinitival complementation. (A very detailed study of the different infinitive structures in Akkadian was conducted by Aro 1961.) Here, I shall only distinguish between the infinitival varieties when the differences between them are directly relevant to their function within the FDC.

TABLE 2

Finite complements	*kīma alp-am ilqû atta tīde* COMP OX-ACC he.took.SUB you you.know 'you know that he took an ox'
	kīma alp-am ilqû atta tešme COMP OX-ACC he.took.SUB you you.heard 'you heard that he took an ox'
	kīma alp-am ilqû ubirrū(-šu) COMP OX-ACC he.took.SUB they.proved-(him) 'they proved that he took an ox'
Asyndetic parataxis	*alp-am ilqe lū tīde* OX-ACC he.took EMPH you.know 'he took an ox, may you know!'
'As you know' construction	*kīma tīdû alp-am ilqe* as you.know.SUB OX-ACC he.took 'as you know, he took an ox'
	kīma tešmû alp-am ilqe as you.heard.SUB OX-ACC he.took 'as you heard, he took an ox'
Infinitive complements	*alp-am leq-âm ul ele"i* OX-ACC take.INF-ACC not I.can 'I cannot take an ox'
	alp-am leq-âm taqbi-šum OX-ACC take.INF-ACC you.said-to him 'you told him to take an ox'
	alāk-šu ešme go.INF-his I.heard 'I heard (of) his going'
	ina alp-im leq-êm ubirrū-šu in OX-GEN take.INF-GEN they.convicted-him 'they convicted him of taking the ox'
	ana alp-im leq-êm palhāku to OX-GEN take.INF-GEN I.fear(STATIVE) 'I am afraid to take the ox'
Coordination	*qibi-šum-ma alp-am lilqe* say-to him-P OX-ACC he.should.take 'tell him and he should take an ox' (~ tell him to take an ox)
	ešme-ma alp-am ilqe I.heard-P OX-ACC he.took 'I heard and he took an ox' (~ I heard that he took an ox)

For example, we shall see in chapter 8 that the difference between the nominal and the verbal construction is relevant to the distinction between manipulative and non-manipulative speech verbs.

Table 2 also makes clear that this study separates two types of paratactic constructions: asyndetic parataxis (without a coordination morpheme), and coordination (with the particle *-ma*). The reason for the distinction between the two types of parataxis is that the two constructions have quite different roles. As we shall see, asyndetic parataxis is used mainly with the verb 'know', whereas coordination with *-ma* is used most prominently for manipulation, but also for verbs of perception and modality. The following section explains why both paratactic constructions are easily distinguishable from subordinate clauses.

6.3. The difference between independent and subordinate clauses

In a cross-linguistic perspective, it is not always possible to make a simple binary distinction between independent and subordinate clauses. In Babylonian, however, such a distinction can easily be drawn, not only on the basis of the presence or absence of a subordinating morpheme, but also on the basis of other morphological and lexical features. Babylonian has a special verbal form, the 'subordinative' (§3.5.8) which is used in finite subordinate clauses (relatives, adverbials, and complements). There are also other elements which distinguish subordinate clauses from independent ones: the negation word *ul* appears only in independent clauses, whereas the word *lā* appears in subordinate clauses (but also in some types of independent clauses).

The two parallel (constructed) examples below demonstrate the difference between a finite subordinate complement (162), and asyndetic parataxis (163). The two constructions are not distinguishable only by the presence or absence of the complementizer *kīma*, but also by the different form of the verb 'receive' (independent form *imhur*, as opposed to subordinative form *imhuru*), as well as by the different negation words.

(162) *kīma še'-am* ***lā*** *imhur-**u*** *bēl-ī* *īde*
COMP barley-ACC not he.received-**SUB** lord-my he.knows
'you know that he didn't receive the barley'

(163) *še'-am* ***ul*** *imhur-Ø* *bēl-ī* *īde*
barley-ACC *not* he.received lord-my he.knows
'he didn't receive the barley, my lord knows (this)'

We can see the same difference in a real example from an Old Babylonian letter, (164) below. Here, the same clause is repeated first as an independent clause and then as a subordinate clause:

(164) *šum* *PN ušapšiṭ-Ø-ma* *šum-šu . . .*
name.of PN he.caused to erase-P name-his
ušašṭer-Ø
he.caused to write
u *kīma* *šum* *PN ušapšiṭ-u-ma* *šum-šu*
and COMP name.of PN he.caused to erase-SUB-P name-his
ušašṭer-u *. . . ubtirrū*
he.caused to write-SUB they.proved
'he caused PN's name to be erased and his name to be written down, and they proved that he caused PN's name to be erased and his name to be written down' (AbB 4: 15: 11)

The distinction between the subordinate and independent form of the verb is not marked morphologically in all cases (for example, plural forms are mostly unchanged). Nevertheless, since the verbal distinction is maintained very consistently, there must have been a clear distinction between subordinate and independent clauses in the mind of the speakers. Precisely for this reason, paratactic structures cannot be, and could not have been, regarded as subordinate structures without a complementizer (like the English construction 'I know he is ill'). In the following chapters, therefore, I refer repeatedly to 'paratactic structures' (both asyndetic parataxis and coordination) and to 'subordinate clauses' as two distinct and easily distinguishable constructions.

6.4. Syntax–semantics correlations

Finally, a few words should be said about the choice of structures used with the different semantic groups. There are various approaches which try to link the syntax and semantics of complementation. In this study, I do not concentrate on the motivation for the *synchronic* distribution of structures within the FDC at any given period, because my main aim is to trace the diachronic changes in the FDC. Nevertheless, it is useful to sketch the general distribution of the structures in the FDC according to the main semantic groups.

One general principle for the cross-linguistic relation between form and function in complementation has been suggested by Givón (1980; 1990, ch. 13). Givón argued that a strong principle of iconicity underlies the relation between the degree of semantic and syntactic integration of the clauses. The stronger the semantic bond between two events, the tighter the syntactic integration of the two clauses will be. Complement-taking verbs can thus be arranged in a 'binding hierarchy', according to the strength of semantic integration between the main event (represented by the main clause) and the dependent event. The degree of semantic integration between the events can be determined by factors such as the control of the participant in the main event on the realization of the dependent event, the identity of participants between two events, or the determination of the time reference of the dependent event with respect to the main event

(Cristofaro 1998*b*: 18). On the basis of such criteria, the main groups of verbs in the FDC can be arranged on a scale from highest to lowest degree of semantic integration, as in (165) below.

(165) modality > manipulation > perception > knowledge > speech

The degree of syntactic integration between the complement clause and the main clause reflects the extent to which the dependent clause is treated as an embedded argument of the main clause. For example, in more tightly integrated complement clauses, there will be morphological treatment and reduction of the verb in the complement clause, and the subject of the complement clause will acquire case marking from the main clause. The main structures in the Babylonian FDC can be arranged on such a scale of syntactic integration, as demonstrated in (166) below:

(166) infinitival complements > finite complements > ('as you know' construction) > coordination with *-ma* > asyndetic parataxis, direct speech

Givón's general claim, then, is that structures on the left of the scale in (166) (more tightly integrated syntactic structures) will appear with the verbs on the left hand of the scale in (165), and vice versa. In broad outline, this principle is supported by the Babylonian data. The loosest syntactic structures (asyndetic parataxis and direct speech) appear mostly on the right hand of the scale above, with verbs of speech and knowledge. The tightest syntactic structure, the infinitive clause, is most prominent on the left hand of the scale, with modality and manipulation. Moreover, successful manipulation, or 'causation' is so tightly integrated that it is not expressed with a bi-clausal structure, but rather with a verb-internal causative form. The middle of the scale (verbs of perception) can appear with most syntactic structures.

Nevertheless, the relation between the degree of semantic and syntactic integration is not always a perfect match. As we shall see in chapter 8, manipulative verbs consistently appear with two structures on the opposing sides of the syntactic integration scale: infinitive complements (tightly integrated), and coordination with *-ma* (loosely integrated). The distribution between these two structures is determined purely on the basis of tense, and does not reflect any difference in the semantic integration between the two events.

7

Verbs of Knowledge, Perception, and Others

This chapter examines all the main semantic categories of verbs in the Functional Domain of Complementation, except modality and manipulation. The chapter presents a diachronic survey of the different structures used with these verbs, from Old Akkadian to Neo-Babylonian. Section 7.1 starts with an overview of the main developments in the FDC over the period 2500 to 500 BC. The following sections discuss the changes in each of the semantic categories: knowledge (§7.2), perception (§7.3), speech (§7.4), proving (§7.5), fearing (§7.6), and the 'what have I done that . . .' construction (§7.7).

7.1. Overview: the main changes from Old Akkadian to Neo-Babylonian

The FDC in Old Akkadian cannot be described in great detail, but the picture which emerges is the complete domination of parataxis in the FDC. There are no examples of finite complements in the Old Akkadian documents, and even infinitive complementation is not as highly developed as in the Old Babylonian period. Because there are only a few texts from that period, one could argue that finite complements may have existed, but are simply not attested in extant documents. But a few facts make this unlikely. First, finite complements are not attested in the earliest Old Babylonian texts either. They achieve currency only in the middle Old Babylonian period, and become more common later. Their absence in Old Akkadian thus shows a general trend, not just an isolated coincidence. More importantly, the argument against their existence is not purely *ex silentio*. In Old Akkadian, we find paratactic constructions in places where we would expect to find finite complements, as we shall see in the following sections.

The most important development from Old Akkadian to Old Babylonian is the emergence of finite complements. In Old Babylonian, finite complements take over functions which were earlier expressed by parataxis, and we now find finite complements with verbs of knowledge, perception, speech, and, later, 'proving'. The second important development is the flowering of infinitive complementation. The infinitive reaches its structural and functional zenith in Old Babylonian. Infinitive clauses are most elaborate and most flexible at this period, and they are also more widely used throughout the FDC than in any other period.

The available corpus of Middle Babylonian texts is small compared to Old Babylonian and Neo-Babylonian, and so the shape of the FDC in Middle

Babylonian cannot be described in as much detail. The major discernible change between Old Babylonian and Middle Babylonian is the beginning in the decline of infinitive complementation.

In the Neo-Babylonian period, there are two important developments which change the shape of the FDC. The first development is the almost complete disappearance of infinitive complementation, which is noticeable with verbs of perception, proving, and mental states (but most strongly with manipulative verbs, which are discussed in the next chapter). The place of infinitive complements is taken mainly by finite complements and by the *umma* construction.

The second major change in Neo-Babylonian is caused by the emergence of *umma* as a complementizer. This development (which we followed in chapter 5) brings about a realignment in the FDC, along the lines of the distinction between the domain of speech and the domain of non-speech.[43] In the Old Babylonian period, *umma* constructions were used only with direct speech, whereas in other contexts (indirect speech, perception, knowledge) other strategies were used. But in Neo-Babylonian, the line between *umma* and the traditional finite complements has been redrawn. The *umma* construction is now used not only for 'direct speech', but also in all contexts which are related to speech (including 'hear it said'). The traditional finite complements are no longer used with speech verbs or with 'hear (it said)', but now only appear with verbs in the non-speech domain.

Overall, the main changes in the FDC throughout its history can be seen as

TABLE 3

	Old Akkadian	Old Babylonian	Neo-Babylonian
Finite complements with *kīma* (later *kī* and *ša*)		knowledge, perception, (speech), proving	knowledge, perception, proving, fearing
Asyndetic parataxis	knowledge, proving	knowledge	knowledge
'as you know'		knowledge, perception, speech	perception, speech
Coordination	manipulation, perception, modality	manipulation, perception	manipulation, perception
Infinitive	manipulation	manipulation, modality, perception, speech, proving, fearing	
umma construction	(direct) speech	(direct) speech	speech, perception, mental states, fearing, manipulation

[43] Frajzyngier (1991) uses the terms *de dicto* and *de re* to refer to the distinctions between these two domains.

a combination of three major developments: the rise of finite complements, the flowering and then decline of the infinitive, and the emergence of the erstwhile quotative construction as an alternative complement structure. Table 3 presents a brief overview of the main changes in the FDC in the history of Babylonian. The table lists the major structures used with the different semantic categories in the FDC (in Old Akkadian, Old Babylonian, and Neo-Babylonian). Included here are also the categories of manipulation and modality, which will be discussed in more detail in the next chapter.

7.2. Knowledge verbs

7.2.1. *Old Akkadian*

In Old Akkadian, the verb *idûm* 'know' is only attested with asyndetic parataxis, as in the example below:

(167) *ana Iribum Ubarum eqel Gakuli šūlu'-am iqbi . . .*
to Iribum Ubarum field.of Gakuli dispossess.INF-ACC he.said
'Ubarum told Iribum to dispossess the field of Gakuli . . . (but instead)'
eqel Bazi . . . uštēli Ubarum ula īde
field.of Bazi he.dispossessed Ubarum not he.knew
'Iribum dispossessed the field of Bazi, Ubarum didn't know (this)'
mahar laputtî ukīn-šu
in.front.of inspectors.GEN he.proved-him
'Ubarum proved him (Iribum) in front of the inspectors'
(~ Ubarum proved in front of the inspectors that he told Iribum to dispossess the field of Gakuli, but that instead, without his knowledge, Iribum dispossessed the field of Bazi) (Foster 1990: 2: 1)

7.2.2. *Old Babylonian*

The most important development in the Old Babylonian period is the appearance of finite complements, which are now most commonly found with the verb 'know'. A few examples of finite complements with 'know' are given below:

(168) *kīma napišti māt-i eql-um-ma ul tīde*
COMP soul.of land-GEN field-NOM-P not you.know
'don't you know that the soul of the land is the field?' (AbB 9: 48: 14)

(169) *kīma bēl-ī atta awīl-um Sippar u Bābili kalu-šu*
COMP lord-my you gentleman-NOM Sippar and Babylon all of-it
īde
knows.3SG
'all Sippar and Babylon knows that you, my lord, are a gentleman' (AbB 2: 83: 29)

(170) *kīma ālānû ana šipirt-im ša bīti-šu uznā-šu*
COMP émigré.NOM to message-GEN of home-his ears(DUAL)-his
ibaššiā atta ul tīde
they.are attentive you not you.know
'don't you know that an émigré "pricks up his ears" for a message from his home?' (TCL 17: 19: 10)

(171) *Gimillum īde kīma elepp-um iṭb-û*
Gimillum he.knows COMP boat-NOM sank.3SG-SUB
'Gimillum knows that the boat sank' (TCL 17: 8: 7)

Finite complements are also found with semantically related verbs, such as 'learn' and 'believe':

(172) *kīma ina qātī-ja lā ibaššiā-ma lā ahmid-u*
COMP in hands(DUAL)-my not they.are-P not I.hid-SUB
talammadī
you(FSG).(will)learn
'you will learn that they (the stones) are not in my hands and that I did not hide (them)' (AbB 9: 61: 22)

(173) *kīma ina sūni-ki nīl-u-ma aqtīp*
COMP in lap-your(FSG) he.lies.STATIVE-SUB-P I.believe(PERFECT)
'I believe that he lay in your lap' (i.e. 'slept with you') (TCL 1: 10: 23)

Two other constructions provide the functional competition for finite complements with the verb 'know': asyndetic parataxis, and the 'as you know' construction. Asyndetic parataxis is generally restricted to the verb 'know'. In the asyndetic constructions, the two clauses are juxtaposed without any coordination marker between them. The order of the two juxtaposed clauses is interchangeable, as can be seen from the examples below:

(174) *ul tīde ana kâšim-ma taklāku*
not you.know in you.GEN-P I.trust.STATIVE
'don't you know? I put my trust in you' (AbB 13: 74: 13)

(175) *atta tīde inūma šakkanakk-um . . . ina Agaga eqel šukūsi*
you you.know when governor-NOM in Agaga allotment

erēš-am ušaddi'an-niēti alpī-ja ana Diniktim ana
cultivate.INF-ACC prevented-us oxen-my to Diniktum to

erēš-im assuh-ma
cultivate.INF-GEN I.took away-P
'you know, when the governor prevented us from sowing the allotment in Agaga, I transferred my oxen to work in Diniktum' (AbB 8: 7: 6)

(176) *PN ṭupšarr-um aššum eql-im anna īpul bēl-ī īde*
PN scribe-NOM about field-GEN yes he.answered lord-my he.knows
'PN, the scribe, answered yes concerning the field, my lord knows'
(AbB 2: 90: 5)

(177) *še'-am ištu ašariš ul alqe'am-ma ana Isin ul allikam*
barley-ACC from there not I.took-P to Isin not I.went
atta tīde
you you.know
'I have not taken barley from there and gone to Isin, you know!'
(TCL 18: 150: 14)

(178) *ina āl sunq-im wašbāku tīde atta*
in town.of famine-GEN I.live.STATIVE you.know you
'I am living in a town of famine, you know!' (AbB 9: 240: 9)

In most contexts, asyndetic parataxis with the verb 'know' can be functionally interchangeable with finite complements. The following example shows the two constructions used in the same breath:

(179) *kīma PN jā'um atta ula tīde*
COMP PN mine you not you.know
u 10 MA.NA KÙ.BABBAR *ittī-šu atta ula tīde*
and 10 mina silver with-him you not you.know
'don't you know that PN is mine? and there are 10 mina of silver with him, don't you know?' (AbB 9: 209: 4)

Nevertheless, there is one important difference between the two constructions. With finite complements, the syntactic embedding of the complement clause into the main clause imposes a strong degree of cohesion between the two clauses (cf. Givón 1990: 515 ff.). On the other hand, asyndetic parataxis allows for a great variety on the scale of cohesion between the two clauses, from more tightly integrated ones (such as example (179) above) to a much looser relation. In emphatic contexts, for example, where the verb 'know' is preceded by the emphatic particle *lū* (cf. §3.5.5), only asyndetic parataxis occurs in Old Babylonian:

(180) *kīam awās-su lū tīde*
thus word-his EMPH you.know
'such was his statement; you should indeed know' (Whiting 1987: 44: 10)

(181) *šumma ṣuhār-ī ša ēzib-u-kum sarr-um šūri'-aš-šu*
if servant-my REL I.left-SUB-to you liar-NOM send.IMP-to me-him
ik-ta-la-ni lū īde
he.deceived[?].me EMPH I.know
'If my servant that I left you is a liar, send him to me. He deceived[?] me, I indeed know.' (Kienast 1978: 175: 5)

Another example with looser integration between the two clauses can be seen in (182) below. Here, the two clauses are separated by the coordination morpheme *u* (on the difference between *-ma* and *u* cf. §3.5.6). The function of *u* here is mainly emphatic, precisely like the word 'and' in the English translation:

(182) *ana bīti abī-ka udammiq u atta tīde*
to house.of father-your I.did favours and you you.know
'I did favours for your family and you know (it)!' (AbB 11: 5: 8)

An example of an even looser relation is (183) below, where the verb 'know' comes after a whole sequence of clauses which describe a complex event. In this case, the verb 'know' has an overt nominal object 'these matters', which performs an anaphoric function:

(183) When I was staying in Kār-Nabium, he presented the emblems of the palace to me. I sent my servants . . . to Nukar, but Pirhum, a servant of Marduk-nāṣir . . . robbed them of it. One man from Nukar was killed in the clash.
Ṭāb-ṣillum awâtim šināti īde
Ṭāb-ṣillum matters.ACC these.ACC he.knows
'Ṭāb-ṣillum knows (about) these matters' (AbB 13: 181: 33)

The second very common alternative to finite complements with the verb 'know' is the 'as you know' construction. This construction is similar to the English equivalent: 'as you know, he has gone', instead of 'you know that he has gone'. As I explained in the previous chapter, the 'as you know' construction has not been discussed in surveys of complementation, although it performs a very similar function to that of finite complements. In Babylonian, there is an additional similarity between the 'as you know' construction and finite complements: the conjunction *kīma* is used in both. The 'as you know' clause mostly precedes the main clause ((184)–(186)), but sometimes can also follow it (187):

(184) *kīma tīdû ša ana Bābili illak-u rīqūssu*
as you.know.SUB REL to Babylon he.goes-SUB empty-handed
alāk-am ul ile"i
go.INF-ACC not he.can
'as you know, he who goes to Babylon cannot go empty-handed' (AbB 11: 16: 12)

(185) *kīma tīdû ina āl-im mahrī-ka imērū-ja izzazzū*
as you.know.SUB in city-GEN presence-your asses-my they.stay
'as you know, my asses are staying with you in the city' (AbB 12: 72: 11)

(186) *aššum eql-im ša PN kīma tīdû ištu* MU.40.KAM *eql-am*
about field-GEN of PN as you.know.SUB since 40 years field-ACC
ikkal
he.eats
'about the field of PN, as you know, he has been living from the field for 40 years' (AbB 4: 73: 5)

(187) *awīl-um šū ah-ī kīma tīdû*
man-NOM this.nom brother-my as you.know.SUB
'this man is my brother, as you know' (AbB 1: 119: 7')

In Old Babylonian, the 'as you know' construction is very common, in fact more frequent than finite complements. As in English, this construction is generally used when what would have been the complement clause represents presupposed information. In Babylonian, however, it seems that the 'as you know' construction is sometimes used not only in order to stress the presupposed nature of the information, but also for structural reasons. The 'as you know' construction retains the heavier and more complex clause as a main clause, and can thus be used to avoid what would otherwise be too heavy and complex a (pre-verbal) finite complement. The following example can perhaps demonstrate this point:

(188) *kīma tīdû ša harrān-im ša pānī-ja u amât u*
as you.know.SUB of journey-GEN REL face-my or I.die or
balṭāku ul īde
I.live.STATIVE not I.know
'as you know, in the journey ahead of me, either I die or I live, I don't know'
(~ you know that I don't know whether I'll die or live in the journey ahead of me) (AbB 12: 124: 6) (cf. AbB 12: 67: 12)

Because the 'as you know' construction retains what would have been the complement clause as the main clause, it can also link the 'as you know' clause to a longer story, just like asyndetic parataxis in example (183) above.

(189) *kīma bēl-ī īdû*
as lord-my he.knows.SUB
ištu Hammurabi li-bi-it-tim ša [uru]*ba-ṣu in-na-du-ú i-na pí-ha-at ša Bāṣu wašbānu* GIŠ.MÁ *mēhertam u muqqelpītam tamkāram ša ṭuppi šarrim našû nuba''ama nušetteq tamkāram ša ṭuppi šarrim lā našû ana Bābili nutarraššu*
'As my lord knows, since the bricks of the town Bāṣu were laid in the time of Hammurabi,[44] we reside in the province of Bāṣu; and (as for) the

[44] The scribe seems to have got into a muddle over the grammatical structure of this sentence, but the general meaning seems clear nevertheless.

boats which go up and down stream, the merchant who has a tablet (i.e. 'permit') from the king, we inspect him and let him pass, and the merchant who does not have a tablet from the king, we return him to Babylon.' (AbB 2: 84: 4) (cf. AbB 13: 60: 1)

7.2.3. *Middle Babylonian*

Finite complements appear with the verb 'know' in Middle Babylonian, but there are changes in their structure. In §4.3.1, we saw that even by the time of the later Old Babylonian period, finite complements start appearing after the verb. In Middle Babylonian, post-verbal position becomes the norm. Another change is in the complementizer itself, which now has the shorter form *kī*.[45] A few examples are given below:

(190) *bēl-ī īde kī* 3 SÌLA ŠE.NUMUN *PN īriš-u*
lord-my he.knows COMP 3 litre sown land PN he.cultivated-SUB
'my lord knows that PN cultivated sown land (requiring) 3 litres (of seed)' (BE 17: 42: 16)

(191) *bēl-ī īde kī ultu ēlâ dilipt-u*
lord-my he.knows COMP since I.arrived trouble-NOM
mahratan-ni
confronts.STATIVE.FSG-me
'my lord knows that since I arrived, trouble has befallen me.' (BE 17: 43: 4)

(192) *bēl-ī īde kī ištēn šamm-u ibbattaq-u-ma lā*
lord-my he.knows COMP one herb-NOM is.left out-SUB-P not
išallimū
they.(will)get well
'my lord knows that one (medicinal) herb is left out, and they will not get well' (PBS 1/2: 72: 13)

Parataxis is now the only main competition to finite complements with the verb 'know'. One example is (193) below, here with the emphatic use of the coordination particle *u*, like in (182) above from Old Babylonian.

(193) *hīṭū-a ana bēli-ja ja'nu u bēl-ī īde*
wrongdoing-my to lord-my there isn't and lord-my he.knows
'there is no wrongdoing of mine against my lord, and my lord knows (it)' (PBS 1/2: 73: 37)

[45] We cannot tell with certainty whether the change from *kīma* to *kī* was due to phonetic reduction, or a result of the functional replacement of *kīma* by the already existing conjunction *kī*. The change occurred entirely during the dark age after the Old Babylonian period. Nevertheless, what is clear is that all the main functions of *kīma* in Old Babylonian are taken over by the shorter form *kī* in Middle Babylonian.

The 'as you know' construction, which was so common in Old Babylonian, entirely disappears in Middle Babylonian with the verb 'know'. It is not clear why this happened, but the disappearance shows that the common use of the 'as you know' construction in Old Babylonian was more than just stylistic preference.

7.2.4. *Neo-Babylonian*

The main structure with the verb 'know' in Neo-Babylonian is again finite complementation. During the Neo-Babylonian period, the older complementizer *kī* is gradually replaced by the relative particle *ša*. (This development is often ascribed to Aramaic influence, cf. §4.5.4.) In the early Neo-Babylonian letters from Nippur (*c.*755–725 BC), *ša* is not yet attested as a complementizer, and only the older complementizer *kī* is used, as in (194) below. Then, in the letters from Nineveh (*c.*725–625 BC), *ša* appears as a complementizer (196), but is still less frequent than *kī* (195).

(194) *anāku īde kī kurummatu ibaššû*
I know COMP allowances there.are
'I know that there are allowances' (Cole 1996: 97: 25)

(195) *šarru bēl-ī ul īde kī uqnû īlûni*
king lord-my not he.knows COMP lapis lazuli arrived
'does the king my lord not know that the lapis lazuli has arrived?' (ABL 1240: 18')

(196) *šarru īde ša lū ma'da marṣāk*
king knows COMP EMPH much I.am ill.STATIVE
'the king knows that I am very ill' (ABL 327: 5)

In the late Neo-Babylonian letters (from the second half of the sixth century) *ša* has mostly replaced *kī*, as in (197) and (198). The older complementizer *kī* is now mostly restricted to the context of oaths, as in (199) below.[46] It is interesting to note further that as opposed to the situation in Old Babylonian, finite complements in Neo-Babylonian can also appear after the particle *lū*, as in example (199).

(197) *bēlu īde ša šarru ana muhhi išmû-ma*
lord he.knows COMP king about he.heard-P
'the lord knows that the king heard about (it)' (CT 22: 3: 15)

[46] Instances of *kī* outside oaths in the late NB letters are rare. One example is given below:
atta tīde kī agurrī šatta agâ lā nilbin
you know COMP bricks year this not we.spread
'you know that we have not made baked bricks this year' (YOS 3: 125: 32)

(198) *atta bēlu īde ša šatta uṭṭatu ina Eanna ja'nu*
you lord know.3SG COMP this year barley in Eanna there.isn't
'you, lord, know that this year there is no barley in Eanna' (YOS 3: 8: 6)

(199) *Bēl u Nabû lū īdû kī ūmu agâ šipirtu*
Bēl and Nabû EMPH they.know COMP day this message
altapar-akkunūtu
I.sent-to you(PL)
'(may the gods) Bēl and Nabû indeed know that today I sent you a message' (CT 22: 21: 5)

The only competition to finite complements with the verb 'know' is now asyndetic parataxis:

(200) *ul tīde nišē mušāhize šunu*
not you.know people instructor they
'don't you know? they are people (in need) of an instructor?' (YOS 3: 9: 51)

(201) *uṭṭatu ša PN₁ lū tīde ana muhhi PN₂ . . . šu-ṭur-ru*
barley of PN₁ EMPH you.know to PN₂ write.IMP
'the barley of PN₁—you should know—write on the account of PN₂'
(CT 22: 76: 21)

The 'as you know' construction, which was so common in Old Babylonian, has already disappeared with the verb 'know' in the Middle Babylonian period, and is not found in Neo-Babylonian either.

7.3. Perception

7.3.1. *Old Akkadian*

As with the verb 'know', the only structure attested with perception verbs in Old Akkadian is parataxis. Here, it is not asyndetic parataxis, but coordination with the particle *-ma*, as in the example below:

(202) *mīnam tāmur-ma 'à-i-śa* LU[NGA] BAPPIR G[IG]? *u-śu-ṣi-[ma]*
how you.saw-P PN peasant bad bread? he.gave out-P
taštapu
you.were.silent
'how did you see, and PN, the peasant, gave out bad bread, and you remained silent?'
(~ why did you remain silent when you saw that PN, the peasant, gave out bad bread?) (SAB: Ga 6: 5)

7.3.2. *Old Babylonian*

The common structures used with perception verbs in Old Babylonian are finite and infinitive complements, but coordination with *-ma* is still used as well.

Finite complements appear with perception verbs when 'non-immediate' perception is implied, for example when 'hear' means 'hear it said', and 'see' means 'realize':

(203) *kīma ṣuhār-u šū mār-ī tātamar*
COMP lad-NOM this.NOM son-my you.saw
'you saw that this lad is my son' (AbB 1: 74: 20)

(204) *kīma enš-um ana dann-im . . . lā iššarrak-u Sippar kalu-šu līmur*
COMP weak-NOM to strong-GEN not is.given-SUB Sippar all of-it let.it.see
'let all of Sippar see that the weak is not put in the power of the strong' (AbB 7: 153: 50)

(205) *kīma pāni dīn-i lā ubbal-u āmur*
COMP face.of judgement-GEN not he.(will)bring-SUB I.saw
'I saw that he will not be lenient with the judgement'
(literally: 'not bring the face of the judgement') (AbB 3: 21: 27)

(206) *kīma immerī tīšû ešme-ma*
COMP sheep.ACC you.have.SUB I.heard-P
'I have heard that you have sheep' (AbB 2: 160: 6)

In the same context (non-immediate perception), the 'as you know' construction can be used as well:

(207) *kīma bēl-ī atta tešmû alpī nakr-um itbal*
as lord-my you you.heard.SUB oxen.ACC enemy-NOM he.took
'as you my lord have heard, the enemy has taken away the cattle' (AbB 2: 86: 4)

With immediate perception, neither finite complements nor the 'as you know' construction are used, and the main construction employed is infinitive complementation:

(208) *warkānuma kīma atluk-ī išmû urdam-ma*
afterwards when go away.INF-my she.heard.SUB she.came down-P
'afterwards, when she heard me going away, she came down' (AbB 1: 27: 13)

(209) *āl-am ša ina qātī-šunu še'-am zabāl-am īmur-u aṭrud-ma*
town-ACC REL in hands(DUAL)-their barley-ACC carry.INF-ACC it.saw-SUB I.sent-P
'I sent the town that saw (them) carrying barley in their hands' (AbB 3: 70: 13)

At least with the verb 'hear', infinitives can be used also to express non-immediate perception (when 'hear' means 'hear it said'), as in (210) and (211) below.[47] In such contexts, infinitive complements compete with finite complements (such as (206) above) and there are no obvious differences in meaning between them.

(210) *PN u PN_2 . . . ana ṣēri-ka alāk-šunu ešme*
PN and PN_2 to presence-your go.INF-their I.heard
'I heard that PN and PN_2 visited you.' (Whiting 1987: 45: 6)

(211) *epēš-ka dummuq-am lušme*
work.INF-your good-ACC let.me.hear
'I want to hear that you worked well.' (AbB 6: 220: 36)

The coordination construction with the particle *-ma* (which we saw in Old Akkadian in (202) above) is still used in Old Babylonian, although it is now rarer.[48] This construction emphasizes an element of volition or intention in the act of perception. It is used not simply for 'see' but rather for 'inspect' or 'observe', as in (212) and (213) below. In examples (214) and (215) below, we should probably understand the verb 'hear' accordingly, as 'find out by hearing', 'make enquiries'.

(212) *šumma tanaṭṭalā-ma ina mīl-im ša illâm kārū*
if you(PL).watch-P in high water-GEN REL it.rises banks.NOM
mê šunūti lā . . .
water.ACC those.ACC not
'if you watch and in the rising high water, the dam banks cannot [hold in] that water' (AbB 4: 109: 6)

(213) *šumma tattaplasī-ma tulû-ša lā damiq*
if you(FSG).inspect-P breast-her not good
'if you inspect and her breast is not good' (AbB 1: 31: 17)

[47] Other nominalized (or lexicalized) verbal forms are also used with the verb 'hear':

mu-ṣa-ša iš-te-me
go out(NOMINALIZED FORM)-her I.heard
'I heard that she left' (AbB 6: 57: 34)

ištu sili'ta-ka ešmû
since illness-your I.heard.SUB
'since I heard (about) your illness' (AbB 7: 62: 7)

[48] In Old Assyrian *-ma* is more common with perception verbs, especially with the verb *šemû* (Stola 1972: 80). In OB, there is also one possible example of coordination with the verb 'know' (AbB 6: 55: 5), but the example is very uncertain, and should probably be interpreted otherwise. Frankena reads: *i-de-e-ma awātkima rabi'atti i-qá-bu-ki-i[m] ma-gi-ir* ('I know and your word is (of) great (influence), one tells you "agreed"'). Von Soden, however, reads differently: *i-de e-ma awātkima rabi'atti i-qá-bu-ki ma-gi-ir* ('I know: wherever your word is great, one tells you "agreed"').

(214) *ina ahīt-im* *ešme-ma* ÉNSI.MEŠ *ina* ERIM.MEŠ . . .
in neighbourhood-GEN I.heard-P managers in workers
šutemṭû
be short of.STATIVE.PL
'I heard in my neighbourhood and the managers were underprovided with workers'
(~ I heard in my neighbourhood that . . .) (AbB 13: 78: 1)

(215) *nišemme-ma PN+ ana šê . . .* *leqê* *ana mahrī-ka*
we.hear-P PN+ to barley.GEN take.INF.GEN to presence-your
illikam
he.went
'we hear and PN+ went to you to take barley'
(~ we hear that PN+ went to you to take barley) (AbB 7: 167: 3)

7.3.3. *Neo-Babylonian*

There are not sufficient examples to draw a detailed picture of the use of perception verbs in Middle Babylonian. In Neo-Babylonian, it is easier to discuss the verbs 'hear' and 'see' separately, because their behaviour is very different. In the Neo-Babylonian period, the structures used with the verb 'hear' are considerably different from those used in Old Babylonian. The main strategies in Old Babylonian were finite complements with *kīma* and infinitive complements. Neither of these structures is used in Neo-Babylonian. Infinitive complements have mostly disappeared from the FDC, except for some frozen lexicalized constructions, which have lost all vestige of verbal behaviour. Finite complements with *kī* or *ša* are not used with the verb 'hear' either. Instead, 'hear' appears with the erstwhile quotative marker *umma*, as in examples (216) and (217) below. As we saw in chapter 5, *umma* in Neo-Babylonian should not be considered only as a quotative marker, since it is no longer restricted to introducing direct speech. *Umma* is now the complementizer for the domain of speech. It is used with speech verbs, and also with verbs (such as 'hear it said') that are related to the domain of speech.

(216) *altemû umma šar* *Aššur* *ana kutalli kī* *issûni . . .* *madākti*
I.heard *umma* king.of Assyria to rear when he.withdrew camp
ittadû
he.lay down
'I heard that when the king of Assyria withdrew to the rear, he pitched camp . . .' (ABL 901: 5)

(217) *altemû umma ṣābē-ja* *ša* *halqū* [*ah*]*ū-a*
I.heard *umma* men-my REL lost.STATIVE(PL) brother-my
iptaṭar-šunūtu
he.ransomed-them
'I heard that my brother ransomed my men who were lost'
(Cole 1996: 24: 11)

The 'as you know' construction, however, is still used with the verb 'hear':

(218) *kī ašmû šar Elamti mišid*
as I.heard king.of Elam is.stricken.STATIVE
'as I heard, the king of Elam has had a stroke' (ABL 839: 8)

(219) *kī ašmû musukkannu šū . . . ina pāni abī-ja ibašši*
as I.heard Magan tree this with father-my there.is
'as I heard, my father (still) has that Magan tree' (UET 4: 185: 4)

The differences in the use of the verb 'see' between Old Babylonian and Neo-Babylonian are less radical. The verb 'see' appears with finite complements, as in (220), (221) below. (It seems that the new complementizer *ša* replaced the older *kī* more quickly with the verb 'see' than with 'know'.)

(220) *āmur ša šarru bēli-ja rīmānû š[ū. . .]*
I.saw COMP king lord-my bull-like he
'I saw that the king my lord is bull-like' (ABL 587: r12)

(221) *atta bēlu īmuru ša lū ma'du sa-ma-ak-ka*
you lord saw.3SG COMP I am very hard pressed
'you, lord, saw that I am very hard pressed' (YOS 3: 8: 11)

In Old Babylonian, the two alternatives to finite complements with the verb 'see' were infinitive complements and coordination with *-ma*. In Neo-Babylonian, infinitive complements are no longer used. The only alternative to finite complements is coordination, as in the examples below:

(222) *kī ša īmurū-ma ṣābē šaplānu-šunu ma'du*
when REL they.saw-P soldiers beneath-them many
'when they saw that there were many soldiers beneath them' (ABL 520: 25)

(223) *aššu īmurū-ma ṭēmu ša māt Aššur lapāni-šunu irīqu . . .*
because they.saw-P report of land.of Aššur before-them was.distant
'because they saw that a report from the land of Assyria remained distant' (ABL 1241: 9)

7.4. Speech

The most common structure with speech verbs throughout the history of Babylonian is direct speech. Since direct speech was discussed in detail in chapter 5, it will not be taken up in this section. This section only describes the alternatives to the quotative construction with *umma*. We shall start the survey with Old Babylonian, since in Old Akkadian only direct speech is attested.

7.4.1. *Old Babylonian*

Was there indirect speech in Old Babylonian? According to the standard grammar of Akkadian, the answer is negative: 'Da es im Akkadischen keine

Ausdrucksmittel für die indirekte Rede gibt, können Aussagen jeder Art nur in Form der direkten Rede zitiert werden' (von Soden 1995, §155*a*). The reality, however, is more complex. We saw in chapter 4 that speech-related verbs were instrumental in the development of finite complements in Old Babylonian. Speech-related verbs formed the bridging context in the process of semantic bleaching of the conjunction *kīma* from a causal adverbial to a factive complementizer. We also saw that *kīma* clauses appear with speech verbs in Old Babylonian mostly only when some shade of causal meaning is still present, as in examples (224) and (225) below (cf. (31)–(40) in chapter 4). It seems, therefore, that even if speech verbs were instrumental in the process of change from causal adverbial clauses to finite complements, the *kīma* clauses with speech verbs may not have become fully emancipated from their original causal meaning.

(224) *kīma bariāku ul aqbi-kum*
COMP I.starve.STATIVE not I.said-to you
'didn't I say/speak to you that/because I am starving?' (TCL 1: 26: 6)

(225) *kīma eql-um šū ihhaššah-u PN i[špur]-am*
COMP field-NOM this.nom is needed-SUB PN he.wrote-to me
'PN wrote to me that/because this field is needed' (AbB 6: 6: 6)

Nevertheless, we do find some examples, although only a few, such as (226)–(228) below, where any causal interpretation of the *kīma* clause is implausible. Here the *kīma* clauses are purely factive finite complements. But finite complements with speech verbs normally go about their business under a more mundane name, 'indirect speech', and it is indeed difficult to interpret the examples below as anything other than indirect speech:

(226) The woman took the barley and went away.
kīma ittalkam ul iqbi'-am
COMP she.went not she.said-to me
'she did not tell me that she went' (AbB 2: 103: 7)

(227) *kīma āmur-u mahar šāpir Sippar ušanni-ma*
COMP I.saw-SUB presence.of governor.of Sippar I.repeated-P
'I repeated in the presence of the governor of Sippar that I saw (it)' (AbB 2: 173: 7)

(228) *kīma eql-am . . . ana rēdî iddin-u anna ītapal*
COMP field-ACC to soldiers.GEN he.gave-SUB yes he.answered
'he acknowledged that he gave a field to the soldiers' (AbB 2: 90: 15)

We have to conclude, therefore, that the syntactic mechanism for indirect speech clearly existed in Old Babylonian, but that this mechanism was used only rarely compared to the ubiquitous direct speech construction. *Kīma* clauses with speech verbs seem to have been avoided when no shades of causal meaning were present.

Apart from direct speech and *kīma* complements, we find infinitive complements with speech verbs in Old Babylonian, as in (229) below. We also find other nominalized forms, the most common of which is the abstract nominalization suffix *-ūt*, as in (230), (231). The abstract nominalization with *-ūt* can serve in identical contexts to infinitives, as can be seen from (229) and (230).

(229) *wašāb-šu ina āl-im mahrī-ka iqbû-nim*
stay.INF-his in town-GEN presence-your they.said-to me
'they told me (of) his staying in the city in your presence' (AbB 9: 62: 18)

(230) *ina Ik-barî ina bīt PN . . . wašb-ūs-su*
in Ik-barî in house.of PN stay-NOMINALIZATION-his
iqbû-nim
they.said-to me
'they told me (of) his staying in Ik-barî in the house of PN' (AbB 13: 21: 10)

(231) *še'-am ša ahī-šu halq-ūt-su iqbû-nim*
barley-ACC of brother-his lost-NOMINALIZATION-its they.said-to me
'they told me that the barley of his brother was lost' (AbB 2: 128: 5')

Finally, the 'as you know' construction can also be used with speech verbs:

(232) *annikīam kīma iqbû-ni mādiš šuzzuq*
here as they.said-to me very he.is upset.STATIVE
'as they told me here, he is very upset' (AbB 10: 169: 9)

7.4.2. *Middle Babylonian*

As in earlier periods, the most common strategy in Middle Babylonian is direct speech, but finite complements are used as well, as in (233), (234).

(233) *inanna ana bēli-ja altapra kī qan-û nadû*
now to lord-my I.wrote COMP reed-NOM laid down.STATIVE.SUB
'now I have written to my lord that the reed is laid down' (BE 17: 3: 23)

(234) *inanna kī mār šiprija ašāluma*
when I asked my messenger
iqb-â kī girr-u rūqat-u
he.said-to me COMP journey-NOM is far.STATIVE(3FSG)-SUB
'when I asked my messenger, he told me that the journey is far' (EA 7: 30)

Although the 'as you know' construction has disappeared with the verb 'know' in Middle Babylonian, it is still used with speech verbs:

(235) *kī iqbû-ni ina māt-i ša ahī-ja gabbu ibašši*
as they.said-to me in land-GEN of brother-my everything there.is
'as they told me, there is everything in the land of my brother' (EA 7: 33)

(236) *kī iqbû-nim-ma*
as they.said-to me-P
girru dann[at] mû batqū u ūmū emmū šulmāna ma'da banâ ul ušēbilakku
'the journey is hard, the water cut off and the weather hot, so I'm not sending you many beautiful gifts' (EA 7: 53)

7.4.3. *Neo-Babylonian*

Finite complements with the complementizer *kī* (and the original relative particle *ša*) are no longer used with speech verbs in Neo-Babylonian. We now only find speech verbs with the *umma* construction. As I explained in the beginning of this chapter, the emergence of *umma* as an alternative complementizer causes a realignment in the FDC in Neo-Babylonian along the lines of speech and the domain outside speech. *Umma* is now the only complementizer for the domain of speech, and this naturally includes speech verbs.

7.5. Proving

The life-story of the proving verbs will be told in detail in chapter 11, and so this section presents just a brief outline. In Old Akkadian, only parataxis is attested with the proving verbs (cf. (167) above). In the Old Babylonian period, a profusion of structures is used with the proving verbs, as we shall see in §11.3. The reason for such abundance is that we can observe a range of coexisting stages of various parallel attempts to expand simpler (nominal) strategies to more flexible (clausal) strategies. We have already met a few of the structures concerned. Section 4.4 examined the path along which finite complements developed with the proving verbs, and presented some intermediary structures on the way towards 'real' finite complements. Here, only one example is repeated, a 'real' finite complement (237). We shall see in §11.3 that in addition to finite complements, the proving verbs also appear with parataxis, infinitive complements (238), and various nominal strategies (only one example given here, (239) below):

(237) *kīma ištu* MU.3.KAM *ina bīt PN wašb-u*
COMP since 3 years in house.of PN he.lives.STATIVE-SUB
ubirrū-ma
they.proved-P
'they proved that he has been living in the house of PN for 3 years' (AbB 6: 181: 19')

(238) *ina še'-im zabāl-im āl-um ukīn-šunūti*
in barley-GEN carry.INF-GEN town-NOM convicted.3SG-them
'the town convicted them of carrying (= stealing) barley' (AbB 3: 70: 9)

(239) *še'-am ša . . . ina eql-im šuāti PN ilteq-û . . .*
barley-ACC REL from field-GEN this.GEN PN he.took-SUB
birrā-ma
establish.IMP(PL)-P
'establish the barley that PN has been taking from this field'
(~ establish how much barley . . .) (AbB 4: 79: 27)

In Neo-Babylonian, the infinitive complements have disappeared. The main structure used with the proving verb *kunnum* (*burrum* is no longer used) is now finite complementation, as in examples (240) and (241):

(240) *ina ūmu mukinnu ana PN+ uktinnu ša*
in day witness to PN+ he.proved COMP
uṭṭatu ša Bēlti ša Uruk ana kaspu iddinu
barley of Lady of Uruk for silver he.gave
'on the day that a witness proves against PN+ that he sold barley belonging to the Lady of Uruk' (YOS 7: 24: 1)

(241) *ina ūmu mukinnu lū bātiqu ittalkam-ma*
in day witness or denouncer he.came-P
ana PN+ uktinnu ša uṭṭatu ina qāt ikkaru . . . imhuru
to PN+ he.proved COMP barley from hand.of farmer he.received
'on the day when a witness or a denouncer comes and proves against PN+ that he received barley from the peasant' (TCL 12: 106: 1)

In Neo-Babylonian, the verb *kunnum* is also used in the meaning 'testify', and in this case it seems that the *umma* construction is the preferred option:

(242) *iššālu-ma iqbi eli ramni-šu ukīn umma . . .*
he.was asked-P he.said on self-his he.testified *umma*
'he was questioned, and then he spoke and testified against himself: . . .' (TCL 13: 138: 18)

(243) *PN ina pānī-šunu uktīn umma . . .*
PN before-them he.testified *umma*
'he testified before them: . . .' (CT 22: 38: 23)

7.6. Fearing, mental states

In Old Akkadian, the verb *palāhum* ('fear', 'be afraid') in attested only with nominal objects. In Old Babylonian, this verb still appears most frequently with simple nominal objects: 'be afraid of someone/something'. But we now find it also with infinitival complements. In 'control' contexts ('be afraid to do something'), the infinitive complements are introduced by the preposition *ana*, as in (244) and (245) below. In other contexts, the infinitive complement is introduced by the preposition *aššum* (246).

(244) *ana epēš-im annîm kī lā taplah*
to do.INF-GEN this.GEN how not you.feared
'how were you not afraid to do this?'
(idiomatic for: how did you dare act like this?) (AbB 2: 53: 17)

(245) *ana ṣāb-im sahār-im kīma lā palhāku*
to men-GEN search.INF-GEN COMP not I.fear.STATIVE
tammarī
you(FSG).(will)see
'you will see that I am not afraid to search? for people' (AbB 6: 63: 9')

(246) *aššum awāt-im lā naṣār-im [ana m]īnim taplahī*
about word-GEN not keep.INF-GEN why you(FSG).feared
'why were you afraid that the word would not be kept?' (AbB 11: 38: 5)

In Middle Babylonian, the verb 'fear' still appears only with infinitive complements:

(247) *šūr-a . . . [an]a naš-ê palhāku*
reed-ACC to take.INF-GEN I.fear.STATIVE
'I am afraid to take the reed' (PBS 1/2: 28: 2)

But in Neo-Babylonian, the infinitive complements disappear with the verb 'fear', and are replaced by two other structures: finite complements and the *umma* construction. The verb 'fear' thus occupies the border area between the domains of speech and non-speech. The data are insufficient to determine the precise distribution between the two constructions with the verb 'fear', but it seems likely that finite complements would have been used when no element of speech is emphasized, as in (248) below, whereas *umma* would have been used when the element of speech is more marked, as in (249).

(248) *lā taplah kī šangû Sippar qīpi ṭupšarrūti*
not you.feared COMP temple administrator of Sippar resident scribes
īmur[ū] . . .
they.saw
'were you not afraid that the temple administrator of Sippar, the resident, and the scribes saw . . .?' (CT 22: 39: 18)

(249) *kī aplahu umma ana hiṭṭi-ja lā i-ta-ri*
when I.feared *umma* to fault-my not it.(will)turn
'when I feared "let it not turn into my fault"' (Parpola 1993: 120: 9)

Some other verbs of mental states also appear with finite complements for the first time in the Neo-Babylonian period:

(250) *libbū-a il-ṣi kī tāri'*
heart-my rejoices COMP you.became pregnant
'my heart rejoices that you are pregnant' (CT 22: 40: 6)

(251) *naqutta lā ta-ri-ša-' ša ṭēm-a lā tašammā'*
worries not you.(should)get COMP report-my not you.hear
'you should not become worried that you don't hear from me' (CT 22: 6: 7)

(252) *pān ša bēli-ja lā ibi''išu ša ṣēnu ikūšā'*
face of lord-my not it.(should)be bad COMP sheep were.delayed
'my lord should not be annoyed that the sheep were delayed' (BIN 1: 83: 12)

7.7. 'What have I done that you (should) treat me like this?'

Section 2.1 examined a rarely discussed structure, which I called the 'what have I done . . .' construction. The interpretation of finite complements as semantic arguments, rather than as surface objects, suggested that the clause 'that you (should) treat me like this' in this construction could be seen as a finite complement. I suggested that just as there can be complement-taking verbs (such as 'know'), adjectives ('happy'), and nouns ('news'), there can also be a whole clause ('what have I done') that should be seen as a complement-taking predicate.

In Old Babylonian, finite complements are not used to express the 'what have I done' sentiments. Instead, coordination with *-ma* is used for this purpose: 'what have I done, and (=so that) you treat me like this?'. These constructions can be seen in examples (253)–(256). (Notice especially (253), where the construction appears twice.)

(253) *anāku ṭēm-ī imtaqut-ma mahar awīlē sābî ṭapulta-ka*
I mind-my it.fell-P in front.of brewers slander-your
aqabbi
I.(should)say
mīnam tēpuš-anni-ma ṭaplāti-ka adabbub
what you.did-to me-P slanders-your I.(should)speak
'Did I go out of my mind and I should slander you in front of the brewers? What have you done to me and I should slander you?'
(~ did I go out of my mind that I should . . .) (AbB 5: 138: 8')

(254) *mīnam tāmuran-ni-ma ina rēqēnum-ma têrt-ī ana šanîm*
what you.saw-me-P in absence-P office-my to someone else
taddin
you.gave
'what did you see me and you gave my office to someone else in my absence?'
(~ what did you think I was that you gave . . .) (AbB 9: 1: 21)

(255) *mīnum amātum-ma ištu* 6 KASKAL.GÍD.DA *rīqūs-su*
what matter-P after six 'double-hours' empty handed-his
taṭarradaš-šu
you.send-him
'what is the matter and you send him empty handed after a journey of six "double-hours" (*c*.65 kms)?' (AbB 13: 77: 11)

(256) *atti bīt-ki ana kaspim tanaddinī-ma kīam tašpur-īm*
you(FSG) house-your for silver you.(will)give-P thus you.wrote-to me
'do you want to sell your house for silver and you wrote to me like this?' (AbB 2: 135: 13)

In the Neo-Babylonian period, however, we find finite complements (with both complementizers *kī* and *ša*) used to express precisely the same sentiments:

(257) *mannu anāku ša dibbi agâ šarru bēli-ja išappar-a*
who I COMP words these king lord-my he.(should)write-to me
u mamma ibaššû ša iqabbû umma . . .
and what there.is COMP he.says *umma*
'who am I that the king my lord should write these words to me, and what is the matter that he should say ". . ."?' (CT 54: 4: r8)

(258) *manna anāku ša arah ūmī* 2 GÚ.UN *kaspu ana tēlīt*
who I COMP whole month 2 talents of silver for harvest tax
ušellu
I.produce
'who am I that I (should be able to) produce two talents of silver as harvest tax per whole month?' (YOS 3: 17: 29)

(259) [*anāku u*]*l šukkallu kī lā palhāta*
[I no]t minister COMP not you.fear.STATIVE
'am I not a minister that you are not afraid?' (UET 4: 183: 14)

7.8. Conclusion

Three major developments interweave to shape the changes in the Functional Domain of Complementation over the history of Babylonian. These are the emergence of finite complements and the extension in their use, the decline of infinitive complementation, and the development of *umma* as an alternative complementizer for the speech-domain.

The FDC in Old Akkadian was dominated by parataxis. Finite complements emerged in the Old Babylonian period, and started taking over functions which were earlier expressed by parataxis. In Old Babylonian, finite complements 'conquered' verbs of knowledge, perception, speech, as well as the proving verbs. In the Neo-Babylonian period, finite complements were extended further to verbs of fearing and other mental states, and also to the 'what have I done . . .' construction.

The second major development is the flowering and then decline of infinitive complementation. The infinitive reaches its structural and functional peak in Old Babylonian. Infinitive complements are most elaborate and most flexible at this period, and they are also most widespread. Infinitive complements are used with almost any category in the FDC: perception, speech, proving, and fearing (and of course manipulation, which will be discussed in the following chapter). But from the Middle Babylonian period, the infinitive complements begin to decline, and by the Neo-Babylonian period they have almost entirely disappeared from the FDC. Their place is mainly taken by finite complements and the *umma* construction.

The third important development is the realignment of the FDC in the Neo-Babylonian period, following the emergence of *umma* as an alternative complementizer. In Neo-Babylonian, *umma* has come to be the complementizer for the whole of the speech domain, not just for direct speech.

8

Manipulation and Modality

This chapter describes the structures used with verbs of manipulation and modality. The expression of manipulation remained quite stable in the history of Babylonian, at least until the Neo-Babylonian period. From Old Akkadian to Middle Babylonian, manipulation was expressed with two different structures, which appeared in complementary distribution on the basis of tense. Infinitive complements were used for past manipulation, and coordination was used for non-past manipulation. The only major disruption to this system occurred in the Neo-Babylonian period, when infinitive complements almost entirely disappeared from the FDC, and were replaced by the *umma* construction. Table 4 summarizes the main structures used with manipulation in the history of Babylonian.

TABLE 4

	From Old Akkadian to Middle Babylonian	Neo-Babylonian
Past: 'you told PN to go'	*ana PN alāk-a(m) taqbi* to PN go.INF-ACC you.said 'you said to PN to go'	*ana PN taqbi umma alik* to PN you.said *umma* go.IMP 'you said to PN: "go!"'
Non-Past: 'tell PN to go'	*ana PN qibi-ma lillik* to PN say.IMP-P he.should.go 'speak to PN, and he should go'	*ana PN qibi-ma lillik* to PN say.IMP-P he.should.go 'speak to PN, and he should go'

8.1. Manipulation: non-past

Throughout the history of Babylonian, from the earliest to the latest period, manipulation in the present or future is expressed by the coordination constructions with *-ma*. The structure of the construction is transparent. The first clause contains the verb of manipulation followed by the coordinating particle *-ma*. The second clause codes the action of manipulation, and the verb is normally in the precative mood (cf. §3.5.5). The following examples demonstrate this stable use from Old Akkadian to Neo-Babylonian:

(260) 1 DÚSU.NÍTA *ana PN liqbi-ma lišēri'-am*
1 stallion to PN he.should.say-P he.should.send-to me
'he should tell PN (about) 1 stallion, and he should send (it) to me.'
(~ he should tell PN to send me one stallion) (OAkk. SAB: Su 2: 28)

(261) *qibi-šum-ma nār-ī literr-am*
say.IMP-to him-P canal-my he.should.return-to me
'speak to him and he should return my canal to me'
(~ tell him to return my canal to me) (OB. AbB 9: 252: 20)

(262) *ana PN qibi-ma* SIG$_4$ *li-še-ri-im-ma ina bīt-i*
to PN say.IMP-P bricks he.should bring-P in house-GEN
liṣṣur
he.should.keep
'~ tell PN to bring bricks and keep (them) in the house'
(MB. PBS 1/2: 29: 16)

(263) *bēl-ī lišpuram-ma mê ana X liddinū*
lord-my he.should.write-P water.ACC to X let.them.put
ṣuppātī-šunu limalû
pools.ACC-their let.them.fill
'~ my lord should write (to them) to put water into the X and to fill their pools' (MB. PBS 1/2: 56: 19)

(264) *šarru bēl-a liqbi-ma bītu ina Nīnua lukallimū-šunu*
king lord-my he.should.say-P house in Nineveh let.them.assign-them
'~ the king my lord should tell them to assign them a house in Nineveh'
(NB. ABL 960: r6)

(265) *PN ṣulli-ma qātē-a liṣbat*
PN beseech.IMP-P hands(DUAL)-my he.should.seize
'~ beseech PN to seize my hands (= help me)' (NB. UET 4: 184: 7)

When the whole action takes place in the future, the second clause can also appear in the 'present' verbal form, rather than in the precative:

(266) *šumma lā taddin ašapparam-ma ipir šatti-ša ina bīti-ka*
if not you.gave I.(will)write-P yearly ration-her from house-your
tanaddin
you.(will)give
if you did not give, I will write, and you will give her yearly rations from your house' (OB. AbB 2: 129: 14)

There are also a few examples of this construction without the particle *-ma*. This use is almost exclusive to the verb *šapārum* ('order in writing'), as in example (267) below:[49]

[49] Some other examples are in AbB 2: 18, 2: 19, 13: 27, 13: 43.

(267) *šupur PN litrûnik-kum*
write.IMP PN let.them.bring-to you
'write, (and) let them bring PN to you'
(~ write to them to bring PN to you) (OB. AbB 2: 12: 14)

The most important point to note about the use of coordination with manipulative verbs is that coordination is by no means a structure specific to the FDC. The coordination construction used with manipulative verbs is identical in all respects to the general patterns of result clauses in Akkadian. As explained in §3.5.6, coordination with *-ma* codes various logical relations, including very frequently the relation of purpose or result, 'so that'. Akkadian does not have a specific structure for 'tell him to go'. Such commands are instead expressed as purpose clauses: 'speak to him, and (= so that) he should go.'

To demonstrate this, the following examples show sequences of clauses coordinated by *-ma*. Some of these clauses involve manipulative speech verbs ('say/tell', 'write/order in writing'), and some involve other verbs. In (268) for example, there are three clauses in coordination with *-ma*. In translation, we can treat the coordinating structure after 'write' differently from the coordinating structure after 'give'. We can translate the first with a complement, and the second as a purpose clause. But the original does not make any distinction between the two structures. The same principle can also be seen in (269) and (270).

(268) *bēl-ī lišpur-ma miksat eqli-ja liddinū-nim-ma*
lord-my he.should.write-P shares.of field-my they.should.give-to me-P
lā eberri
not I.(will)starve
'my lord should write so that they give me the shares of my field so that I don't starve'
(~ my lord should write to them to give me the shares of my field so that I don't starve) (OB. AbB 13: 4: 19')

(269) *šupur-šunūšim-ma ana PN liqbûnim-ma še'-am*
write.IMP-to them-P to PN they.should.speak-P barley-ACC
lišābil-am-ma nipûs-su luṭrus-su
he.should.send-to me-P distrainee-his let.me.send-him
'write to them so that they speak to PN so that he sends me barley so that I send him his distrainee' (OB. AbB 11: 106: 26')

(270) *li-ib tamkār-im šâtu liṭībū-ma*
heart.of merchant-GEN this.GEN let.them.make good-P
ana māri-šu lišpuram-ma mār-u lipṭuran-nêti
to son-his let.him.write-P son-NOM let.him.set free-us
'let them soften the heart of this merchant, so that he writes to his son, so that his son buys us free' (OB. AbB 2: 46: 15)

8.2. Manipulation: past

8.2.1. *Old Akkadian to Middle Babylonian*

Reported manipulation in the past is coded with infinitive complements until the Middle Babylonian period. A few examples are given below:

(271) *ana Tabal alāk-am aqbi-šim*
to Tabal go.INF-ACC I.said-to her
'I told her to go to Tabal' (OAkk. SAB: Eš 3: r12)

(272) *ana Iribum Ubarum eqel Gakuli šūlu'-am iqbi*
to Iribum Ubarum field.of Gakuli dispossess.INF-ACC he.said
'Ubarum told Iribum to dispossess the field of Gakuli' (OAkk. Foster 1990: 2: 1)

(273) BÙR IKU A.ŠÀ *šarr-um nadān-am iqbi'-am*
one bur field king-NOM give.INF-ACC he.said-to me
'the king told me to give one bur field' (OB. AbB 4: 114: 10)

(274) *her-â kī aqb-âkku ul tehri*
dig.INF-ACC when I.said-to you not you.dug
'when I told you to dig, you didn't dig' (MB. PBS 1/2: 50: 38)

(275) *bēl-ī ana Nippur alāk-a išpur-a*
lord-my to Nippur go.INF-ACC he.wrote-to me
'my lord wrote to me to go to Nippur' (MB. PBS 1/2: 58: 5)

In the Neo-Babylonian period, as we shall see below, the use of infinitive complements declined drastically, and they were no longer employed to express past manipulation. In fact, the decline in the use and flexibility of the infinitive structures can be seen already in Middle Babylonian. In the Old Babylonian period, the infinitive reached both its functional and its structural zenith. Infinitive structures were not only very common, but the infinitive clauses themselves could be more elaborate. In particular, the infinitive clause very often contained the object of the verb, as in the following examples:

(276) *mimma nudunn-âm ša PN ana mārtiša iddinuma*
whatever dowry-ACC REL PN gave to her daughter and
ana bīt PN_2 *ušēribu ana PN turr-am niqbi*
brought into the house of PN_2 to PN return.INF-ACC we.said
'we ordered (them) to return to PN all the dowry that PN had given to her daughter and had brought into the house of PN_2' (AbB 9: 25: 10)

(277) *bēl-ī ana PN še'-am makās-am iqbi*
lord-my to PN barley-ACC collect rent.INF-ACC he.said
'my lord told PN to collect the shares of barley' (AbB 13: 4: 7')

(278) *ṭēm-am gamr-am šakān-am aqbi-kum-ma*
report-ACC full-ACC place.INF-ACC I.said-to you-P
'I told you to make a full report' (AbB 3: 10: 16)

In the Middle Babylonian period, however, structures corresponding to the examples above, although still found, are much less common. When the object of the infinitive clause is expressed, it is normally found outside the clause, as in the following example:[50]

(279) *uṭṭet-a ša bēl-ī leq-â iqbû*
barley-ACC REL lord-my take.INF-ACC he.said.SUB
'the barley that my lord ordered to take' (PBS 1/2: 50: 56)

When the object of the infinitive does appear in the clause in Middle Babylonian, the construction is nominal rather than verbal. The 'object' is expressed as a genitive argument, as in the examples below:

(280) *mahār uṭṭat-i ištapr-akku*
receive.INF.of barley-GEN he.wrote-to you
'he wrote to you the receiving of barley'
(~ he wrote to you to receive barley) (PBS 1/2: 29: 22)

(281) *ultu mahār-a ša uṭṭat-i lā iqbû*
since receive.INF-ACC of barley-GEN not he.said.SUB
'since he did not order the receiving of barley' (PBS 1/2: 67: 8)

The flexibility of infinitive complements as real verbal clauses is thus already reduced in the Middle Babylonian period. This process anticipates the developments in Neo-Babylonian.

Before we proceed to Neo-Babylonian, however, it is worth mentioning that Akkadian also shows an extremely common cross-linguistic process, by which directional/dative particles (such as English 'to') are grammaticalized as infinitive markers (Hopper and Traugott 1993: 182). We can observe this process with the preposition *ana* ('to'). During the Old Babylonian period, this preposition was extended from its original directional/dative sense, and could be used to introduce infinitive complements even after verbs of manipulation, as in the examples below. (The use of *ana* with verbs such as 'say/tell' and 'write' is discussed in detail by Aro 1961: 124.)

[50] Of course, such structures are also found in Old Babylonian, as in the example below. But in Middle Babylonian they are more common and seem to be used to avoid having the object of the infinitive verb inside the infinitive clause.

aššum bīt-im š[a a]tta šūṣ-âm taqbi'-am . . .
concerning house-GEN REL you rent.INF-ACC you.said-to me
'concerning the house that you told me to rent' (AbB 6: 62: 6)

(282) *ana lā aṣ-êm iqbû-šim-ma*
to not go out.INF-GEN they.said-to her-P
'they told her not to go out' (AbB 11: 125: 10')

(283) *ana immerī šâm-im tašpur-am*
to sheep.GEN buy.INF-GEN you.wrote-to me
'you wrote to me to buy sheep' (AbB 9: 218: 15)

(284) *ṣibût-am ana epēš-im aqbi-šum*
need-ACC to do.INF-GEN I.said-to him
'I told him to do what is necessary' (AbB 11: 115: 4)

8.2.2. *Past manipulation in Neo-Babylonian*

In the Neo-Babylonian period, infinitive complements almost completely disappeared from the FDC in the colloquial language of the letters (but not in poetry). In particular, infinitive complements were no longer employed to express manipulation.[51] Instead of infinitive complements, we now find the quotative construction with *umma*:

(285) *ana muhhi līṭu . . . ša šarru bēl-a išpur-a umma*
concerning sketch REL king lord-my he.wrote-to me *umma*
šūbil-a
send.IMP-to me
'concerning the sketch about which the king my lord wrote to me: "send (it)!"'
(~ concerning the sketch that the king my lord wrote to me to send)
(Cole and Machinist 1998: 175: 5)

(286) *ana PN kī aqabbû umma miris karāni ina pānātūa ṣahat*
to PN when I.said[52] *umma* grape pulp before me press.IMP
'when I said to PN: "press the grape pulp before my arrival"'
(~ when I told PN to press the grape pulp before my arrival) (CT 22: 38: 25)

[51] The reasons for such a drastic decline are not clear. It is sometimes claimed that the disappearance of the infinitive is related to the loss of cases in the later periods. I do not find this convincing. First, the beginning of the decline in the use of the infinitive predates the loss of cases by a good few centuries. Moreover, there is no obvious reason why the loss of cases should result in the loss of infinitive complements. The construction of the infinitive as the direct object of the verb may indeed be affected by the loss of the distinction between nominative and accusative. But infinitive complements in manipulative use could have been introduced by a preposition instead. Indeed such constructions (with *ana* 'to') did develop already in Old Babylonian, as was explained above. Infinitival complements introduced by prepositions such as 'to' can easily survive in languages without case systems, as many modern European languages will attest.

The decline of infinitive complementation is perhaps most famous in the Balkan Sprachbund (for a detailed study cf. Joseph 1983). This may suggest areal influence in the case of Akkadian as well. But the most obvious candidate for contact in the later stages, Aramaic, uses infinitive construction to a much greater extent than Neo-Babylonian. It is thus difficult to find convincing external causes for the Babylonian development.

[52] Cf. Streck (1995: 106), for the use of *iparras* in the past, and this example on p. 107.

(287) *aššu uqnû ša šarru bēl-ī išpur-a umma*
about lapis lazuli REL king lord-my wrote-to me *umma*
uqnû liššûni
lapis lazuli they.should.deliver.to me
'concerning the lapis lazuli about which the king my lord wrote to me: "they should deliver the lapislazuli"' (ABL 1240: 16')

(288) *šarru iqtab-â umma ana šatammu šupur-ma*
king said-to me *umma* to administrator write.IMP-P
lišpur-akkaš-šunūtu
let.him.send-to you-them
'the king said to me: "write to the director, and he should send them to you"' (CT 22: 160: 10)

The use of direct speech to code manipulation was not 'invented' only in the Neo-Babylonian period. We can find it even in Old Babylonian, as in example (289) below. But whereas in Old and Middle Babylonian the quotative construction is a fairly rare variant (compared to infinitive complements), in Neo-Babylonian it seems to be the only option.

(289) *aššum amurrīt-im ša tašpur-am umma atta-ma*
about Amorite-GEN REL you.wrote-to me *umma* you-P
ṭurd-aš-ši
send.IMP-to me-her
'concerning the Amorite woman about whom you wrote to me: "send her to me"'
(~ concerning the Amorite woman whom you wrote to me to send)
(AbB 12: 59: 6)

8.2.3. *Direct and indirect past manipulation*

As was explained in §3.5.4, the infinitive can be used both in a nominal construction (with arguments in the genitive) or in a verbal construction (with arguments in the nominative and accusative). In the Old Babylonian period, the overwhelming tendency is for manipulation to be expressed by a verbal infinitival construction, rather than by a nominal one. Examples of the two constructions can be contrasted with the same verb *qabûm*. In the manipulative meaning of this verb ('tell'), the infinitival clause is usually a verbal one (290), whereas in the non-manipulative meaning ('say'), a nominal construction is used, as in (291):

(290) *bēl-ī ana PN še'-am makās-am iqbi*
lord-my to PN barley-ACC collect rent.INF-ACC he.said
'my lord told PN to collect the shares of barley' (AbB 13: 4: 7')

(291) *wašāb-šu ina āl-im mahrī-ka iqbû-nim*
stay.INF-his in town-GEN presence-your they.said-to me
'they told me (of) his staying in town in your presence' (AbB 9: 62: 18)

Nevertheless, manipulation can also be expressed with a nominal construction, although this occurs much more rarely. A few examples are given below:

(292) *Sippar ili āli-šu Šamaš b[a-l]a-zu iqtabi*
Sippar god.of town-its Šamaš live.INF.its he.said ('its' stands for Akkadian 'his')
'Sippar—its town god Šamaš ordered its living'
(~ ordered that it should live) (AbB 5: 239: 32)

(293) *PN_1 u PN_2 . . . ana mehr-im ša pī nārātim alāk-šunu*
PN_1 and PN_2 to weir-GEN of mouth.of canals.GEN go.INF-their
šarr-um iqtabi
king-NOM he.said
'PN_1 and PN_2—the king has ordered their going to the weir at the mouth of the canals' (RA 53: 29, D 12: r5)

It seems that the verbal infinitive construction implies direct manipulation, whereas the nominal infinitival construction is used only for 'indirect' manipulation. The verbal construction 'the king ordered them to go' implies that the king spoke to them personally and told them to go, but the nominal construction in (293) above ('the king ordered their going') implies the existence of some intermediaries: 'the king ordered someone to make sure that they went'.

A different type of indirect manipulation can be expressed with an infinitival clause introduced by the conjunction *aššum* ('about', 'concerning'). This construction is similar to English 'I wrote to you about sending the man', as in examples (294)–(297) below. The opposition between the construction with *aššum* and the direct manipulation 'I wrote to you to send the man' seems to be that the 'about' clause is a paraphrase of the real command given, rather than the command itself.

(294) *aššum* 10 ŠE.GUR *ana* NUMUN . . . *nadān-im ašpurak-kum*
aššum 10 kor of barley for seed give.INF-GEN I.wrote-to you
'I wrote to you about giving 10 kor of barley for seed' (AbB 11: 66: 12)

(295) *ana PN . . . aššum 2 puhādī nēmetti-šu leq-êm-ma ana Sippar*
to PN *aššum* 2 lambs.GEN payment-his take.INF-GEN-P to Sippar
alāk-im nišpur-šum-ma
go.INF-GEN we.wrote-to him-P
'we wrote to PN concerning taking 2 lambs, his payment, and coming to Sippar' (AbB 2: 72: 10)

(296) *ina ṭuppi šarr-im aššum PN . . . ana Bābili ṭarād-im*
in letter.of king-GEN *aššum* PN to Babylon send.INF-GEN
iššapr-am
it.was written-to me
'in the king's letter it was written to me concerning the sending of PN to Babylon' (AbB 13: 63: 11)

(297) *ana PN+ aššum kasp-im . . . dekêm-ma ana Bābili*
to PN+ *aššum* silver-GEN collect.INF.GEN-P to Babylon
šūbul-im ittašpar
send.INF-GEN it.was.written
'it was written to PN+ concerning the collecting of silver and sending (it) to Babylon' (AbB 2: 68: 19)

8.3. On the distribution of infinitive and coordination

The coordination construction is not always suitable for expressing past manipulation, because it necessarily implies successful manipulation. Thus, if one wants to say 'I told you to go, so why didn't you go?', one cannot say 'I told you and you went, so why didn't you go'. For this reason, it is clear why infinitival clauses (and later direct speech) have to be used for past manipulation. But it is not clear why infinitival complements could not have been used both for past and non-past manipulation. In other words, there does not seem to be an obvious reason why Babylonian should not have used infinitival complements in constructions like 'tell him to go', or 'let my lord tell him to go', as in (298) and (299) below.[53] Nevertheless, such forms are not found, and must have been ungrammatical (hence the asterisks). 'Tell him to go' is always expressed with coordination: 'tell him, and he should go', as in (300):

(298) **alāk-am qibi-šum*
go.INF-ACC say.IMP-to him

(299) **bēl-ī alāk-am liqbi-šum*
lord-my go.INF-ACC he.should.say-to him

(300) *qibi-šum-ma lillik*
say.IMP-to him-P he.should.go
'say to him, and he should go'

It is not in itself surprising that both strategies, coordination and infinitive complements, are used to express manipulation. Noonan (1985: 59) explains that both parataxis and infinitival complements are common cross-linguistic strategies for

[53] Are there Sumerian parallels to this distribution? A cursory glance suggests that non-finite complements in Sumerian are also found mainly in the past (as in the first example below), whereas parataxis is often used in 'non-past' (as in the second example below). This issue, however, requires more careful examination.

é-a-ni dù-da ma-an-dug₄
house-his build(NON-FINITE).PROSPECTIVE.SUBORD (he).told.me
'he told me to build his house' (Gudea A: 4: 20)

sanga hé-na-ab-bé kišib hé-ra-ra di-bé di hé-bé
temple official he.should.say.to him seal he.should.unroll in this case he.should.judge
'he should speak to the temple official, the official should unroll his seal and judge this case' (~ he should tell the temple official to unroll his seal and judge this case) (SAB: Is1: 14)

the expression of manipulation. But what seems to be less common is the very strict complementary distribution on the basis of tense. For example, in a related language to Akkadian, biblical Hebrew, although the same strategies are used to express manipulation, there is no such strict distribution on the basis of tense. Examples (301)–(307) demonstrate the use of coordination, infinitive complements, and direct speech in Hebrew. Coordination could be used for manipulation in both non-past ((301) and (302)) and in the past ((303)), and the same applies to infinitive complements ((304) and (305)), and direct speech ((306) and (307)):

(301) *w-ʿattâ ṣawwēh w-yikrtû lî ărāzîm min ha-lbānôn*
and-now order.IMP and-they.shall.fell to.me cedars from the-Lebanon
'now order, and let them fell cedar trees from the Lebanon for me' (1 Kings 5: 20)

(302) and though they hide from my sight at the bottom of the sea,
mi-šām ăṣawwēh et ha-nāḥāš û-nšāk-ām
from-there I.shall.order ACC the-serpent and-it.shall.bite-them
'from there I shall order the serpent, and it shall bite them' (Amos 9: 3)

(303) *wa-yṣawwēh ha-melek Ṣidqiyyāhû wa-yapqidû et*
and-ordered.3MSG the-king Zedekiah and-they.committed ACC
Yirmyāhû ba-ḥāṣar ha-maṭṭārâ
Jeremiah in-court.of the-guard
'the king Zedekiah ordered, and they committed Jeremiah to the court of the guard' (Jeremiah 37: 21)

(304) *ēllēh ha-dbārîm ăšer ṣiwwâ yhwh la-ʿăsōt ōtām*
these the-things REL ordered.3MSG yhwh to-do.INF them
'these are the things that the Lord has commanded (you) to do' (Exodus 35: 1)

(305) *hen ăṣawwēh ʿal ḥāgāb le'ĕkôl hā-'āreṣ*
if I.order on locust to.eat.INF the-land
'if I order the locust to eat the land' (2 Chronicles 7: 13)

(306) *wa-yṣaw ʿālāyw lē'mōr lō' tiqqaḥ iššâ mi-bnôt*
and-he.ordered on.him QUOT not you.take woman from-daughters.of
knāʿan
Canaan
'and he ordered him: "you shall not take a wife from the daughters of Canaan"' (Genesis 28: 6)

(307) *w-attâ tṣawwēh et ha-kōhănîm lē'mōr ". . ."*
and-you you.shall.order ACC the-priests QUOT
'and you shall order the priests: "when you come to the brink of the river Jordan, you shall stand still in the Jordan"' (Joshua 3: 8)

In §6.4, I mentioned Givón's 'binding hierarchy' as a principle that governs the relation between syntax and semantics in the FDC. According to Givón, the more the events coded by the main and the complement clause are integrated semantically, the more tightly integrated the clauses will be in structure. This claim is in general borne out in Babylonian, and also has overwhelming cross-linguistic support. But the distribution of infinitives and coordination in the expression of manipulation demonstrates that the relation is not always a perfect match. Infinitive complements and coordination are on two different extremes of the integration scale. Infinitive complements are tightly integrated, whereas coordinated clauses are only very loosely integrated. Nevertheless, in Babylonian the two structures are both used to express manipulation, and there is no difference in meaning (and in the degree of semantic integration) between them. Their distribution is determined purely on the basis of tense.

8.4. Modality

Most modal functions are not expressed by periphrastic verbs in Akkadian. They are either implicit in the 'present' form of the verb, or expressed by the precative verbal form.[54] The verb *le'ûm* ('be able to') is one exception. In Old Akkadian, this verb is only attested with parataxis (coordination with *-ma*):

(308) *bēl-ī miššu lā-mi ala''e-**ma** lā allakam*
lord-my why not-P I.can-P not I.come
'my lord, why am I not able, and I will not come?'
(~ my lord, why can I not come?) (SAB: Di 10: 16')

By contrast, in Old Babylonian letters, the verb *le'ûm* appears exclusively with infinitival complements.[55] Thus, compare the Old Akkadian construction with (309) and (310) from Old Babylonian:

(309) *alāk-am ul ele''i-ma*
go.INF-ACC not I.can-P
'I cannot come' (AbB 13: 45: 11')

(310) *ina qāti-šunu elepp-am bu''-âm ul ele''i*
in hand-their boat-ACC check.INF-ACC not I.can
'I cannot check the boat under their control' (AbB 2: 84: 16)

In Old Babylonian, infinitive complements are used also with verbs such as 'let' or 'agree'. As the following parallel examples show, both the verbal infinitive

[54] Some modal functions are also expressed by coordination, e.g. 'start and do' = 'start doing', 'repeat and do' = 'do again', etc. These constructions are discussed in great detail in Kraus (1987).

[55] But there are isolated examples of coordination in Old Babylonian literature; see Veenhof (1986).

construction and the nominal construction can be used in this context, apparently without any difference in meaning:

(311) *ana lā erēb ṣāb-im amgur-šunūti*
to not enter.INF.of troops-GEN I.agreed-them
'I agreed (with) them not to have the troops enter (the town)'
(Falkenstein 1963: 57 ii 12)

(312) *ana ṣāb-im lā erēb-im amgur-šunūti*
to troops-GEN not enter.INF-GEN I.agreed-them
'I agreed (with) them not to have the troops enter (the town)'
(Falkenstein 1963: 56 i 27)

In Middle Babylonian, infinitive complements are still used with verbs such as 'let' (313) or 'agree' (314), but the verb *le'ûm* ('be able to') is no longer attested with infinitive complements.

(313) *āšib pānī-šunu ana petê ul inamdin-šunūti*
neighbour-their to open.INF.GEN not he.lets-them
'their neighbour doesn't let them open (the canal)' (BE 17: 13: 9)

(314) *ana utūn-i ana šakān-i ul imangurū*
to oven-GEN to put.INF-GEN not they.agree
'they do not agree to put (the gold) in the oven' (Bernhardt and Aro 1958: 112: 8)

In Neo-Babylonian, the verb *le'ûm* appears very often, but mainly in constructions such as 'let someone do as he can' (315). Infinitive complements with this verb are not used at all.

(315) *šarru bēl-a kī ša ile''û līpuš*
king lord-my as REL he.can let.him.do
'let the king my lord do whatever he can' (ABL 269: r13)

Instead of the verb *le'ûm*, the 'present' verbal form (*iparras*) is used to express various modal meanings, including 'be able to' (Streck 1995). I quote here two examples from Streck (1995: 97) to demonstrate this use:

(316) *uṭṭatu u kaspu ina pānīja ja'nu*
I have no barley and no silver
mīnu kī ana idi GIŠ.MÁ.MEŠ . . . *anamdin*
what to rent.of boats I.give
'I have no barley and no silver. What *could* I give as rent for the boats?'
(BIN 1: 38: 13)

(317) *kī* *taqabbâ* *umma PN hīṭu ina libbi lihṭû . . .*
how you.say.to me *umma* PN could have made an error in it
'how *could* you say to me: "PN could have made an error in it"?'
(YOS 3: 17: 34)

We have seen that in the oldest period, Old Akkadian, the verb *le'ûm* ('be able to') is only used with parataxis. During the Old Babylonian period, when infinitives are at their height, the verb enjoys an affair with infinitive complements. But the relationship is short-lived, and does not survive beyond Old Babylonian.

9

The *Wh*-Functional Domain, Direct and Indirect Questions

9.1. Overview

This chapter presents a historical survey of the *wh*-functional domain, which is closely related to the FDC. The chapter is concerned with the range of different structures which are used to perform similar functions to that of '*wh*-complements' (or indirect questions). Embedded indirect questions are only a late development in Babylonian. We do not have enough material to draw a picture of the Old Akkadian situation, but even in the Old Babylonian period, only the very beginning of indirect questions is evident. Whereas finite complements became widespread already in the Old Babylonian period (as we have seen), embedded questions only fully developed in the latest period of the language, Neo-Babylonian.

In the Old Babylonian period, two main strategies were used instead of indirect questions. The first strategy is based on direct questions. Instead of saying 'write to me how much work you did', for example, an Old Babylonian speaker would say 'how much work did you do? write (this) to me!'. The second strategy is the nominal strategy of 'concealed questions'. Instead of saying 'write to me how much barley you need', the Old Babylonians would say 'write to me the barley that you need'. The only indirect questions which are (rarely) attested in Old Babylonian are 'whether' questions. In the Middle Babylonian period, these 'whether' questions seem to have gained currency. But only in the Neo-Babylonian period did other indirect questions appear and become widespread. In Neo-Babylonian, interrogative particles could be used regularly to introduce embedded indirect questions, in many contexts in which only direct questions and 'concealed questions' had been available in the older periods.

Before starting the historical survey, one remark on 'concealed questions' should be made. Consider the relation between the two constructions in (318) below. In (318*a*), the verb has a nominal object, and in (318*b*) it has a '*wh*-complement', or indirect question. The nominal construction in (318*a*) is often called a 'concealed question', and it seems that at least in generative literature, this construction is considered to be a derived form, based on the 'underlying' *wh*-complements in (*b*) (cf. Grimshaw 1979).

(318) (*a*) John asked the height of the building.
(*b*) John asked what the height of the building was.

But from a diachronic perspective, it makes little sense to consider (*a*) as a derived form. In Babylonian, *wh*-complements like (*b*) develop only very late, whereas nominal constructions like (*a*) are common from the earliest stage of the language. Such structures also remain common throughout the history of Babylonian, and are often used where English, for example, would have *wh*-complements. The following examples demonstrate the stable use of 'concealed questions' throughout the history of Babylonian. Examples (319)–(322) show the use of the noun *šulmum* ('well-being') from Old Akkadian to Neo-Babylonian, and in examples (323)–(326) we can see another common phrase, with the noun *awātum* ('word', 'matter').

(319) *šulum bīt-im kali-šu in ṭupp-im lišṭurū-nim*
well being.of house-GEN all of-it in tablet-GEN let.them.write-to me
'let them write down on a tablet the well-being of the whole household'
(~ let them write down on a tablet how the whole household is)
(OAkk. SAB: Eš 2: r3')

(320) *šulum-ka šupr-am*
well being-your write.IMP-to me
'write me your well-being' (OB. AbB 9: 208: 21)

(321) *šulm-a ša bēli-ja ištālan-ni*
well being-ACC of lord-my he.asked-me
'he asked me the well-being of my lord' (MB. BE 17: 21: 5)

(322) *PN$_1$ šulum ša PN$_2$ ahī-šu iša''alu*
PN$_1$ well being of PN$_2$ brother-his he.asks
'PN$_1$ asks the well-being of his brother PN$_2$' (NB. CT 22: 6: 16)

(323) *bēl-ī awāt-ī lišme*
lord-my word-my he.should.hear
'let my lord listen to my word'
(~ let my lord listen to what I say) (OAkk. SAB: Ad 3: 17)

(324) *awāt niqabbû-šunūšim ul išemmû*
word.of we.say.SUB-to them not they.hear
'they don't hear the word which we say to them'
(~ they don't listen to what we say to them) (OB. AbB 11: 102: 5')

(325) *amâti mala ibaššû ana PN adabbub*
words.ACC REL there.are to PN I.(will)speak
'I will speak to PN (about) matters whatever there are'
(~ I will speak to PN about whatever matters there are) (MB. BE 17: 81: 14')

(326) *amāt-ka ittī-ja lā tašannâ*
word-your with-me not you.(should)change
'you should not change your word with me'
(~ you should not change what you said to me) (NB. CT 22: 182: 23)

The nominal strategy is a basic form, not a form which is derived from a more complex underlying structure. In the following discussion, I shall use the term 'concealed questions' as a convenient shorthand, but this use should not be taken as an indication that 'concealed questions' are in any way derived from a more basic *wh*-complement.

9.2. Old Babylonian

In the Old Babylonian period, two strategies are used instead of embedded questions: direct questions, and the nominal strategy of 'concealed questions'.

9.2.1. *Direct questions*

Direct questions are used both for 'whether' questions, as in examples (327)–(328) below, and for questions such as 'who', 'what', or 'how much', as in (329)–(332):

(327) *iṣṣū ša innaksū maṣṣarū qišātim ikkisū ina*
trees.NOM REL they.were felled keepers.of forests.GEN they.felled in
qāt-im ahīt-im innaksū warkat-am purus-ma
hand-GEN foreign-GEN they.were felled matter-ACC investigate.IMP-P
ṭēm-am gamr-am šupr-am
report-ACC complete-ACC send.IMP-to me
'The trees which were felled—did the forest keepers fell (them)? Were they felled by a foreign hand? Investigate the matter and send me a complete report.'
(~ investigate whether . . .) (AbB 4: 20: 21)

(328) *qablīt-am ana še'-im u rēš-am ana šamn-im*
middle-ACC for barley-GEN or head-ACC for oil-GEN
inneppeš annīt-am lā annīt-am šupr-am-ma
is cultivated.3MSG this-ACC not this-ACC write.IMP-to me-P
'Should (the field) be cultivated in the middle part for barley and/or in the upper part for oil? This or not this, write to me.' (Kienast 1978: 178: 40)

(329) *adi inanna* A.ŠÀ *šipr-am kī maṣi īpuš*
until now field work-ACC how much he.did
ina ṭuppi-ka pānam šurši'-am-ma šupr-am
in letter-your make clear.IMP-to me-P write.IMP-to me
'How much work has he done in the field until now? Make (it) clear for me and write (it) to me in your letter.' (AbB 10: 182: 7)

(330) *ajjûm abū-šu u eqlētu-šunu ajjûm eqel bīt abī-šu*
who father-his and fields-their which field.of house.of father-his
magana ina kakk-im ša il āl-im birr-am
now then in weapon-GEN of god.of city-GEN establish.IMP-for me
ṭēm-šu gamr-am šupr-am-ma
report-his complete-ACC send.IMP-to me-P
'Who is his father? And (from) their fields—which is the field of his family? Now then, establish (this) with the weapon of the city god, and send me his complete report.' (AbB 4: 118: 28)

(331) *aššum PN$_1$ PN$_2$ ša eql-am ibqur-u-šu kī*
concerning PN$_1$ PN$_2$ REL field-ACC he.claimed-SUB-(from)him how
qās-su ina mīnim ilik-šu . . . eql-am šâti kī ibqur-šu . . .
hand-his in what service-his field-ACC this.ACC how he.claimed-him
magana ṭēm-šu šupr-am
now then report-his send.IMP-to me
'Concerning PN$_1$, PN$_2$ who claimed the field from him, how is his "hand"? In what does his service consist? How did he claim that field from him? Now then, send me a report about him.' (AbB 9: 199: 5)

(332) *awāt-am šuātu bīr-ši*
matter-ACC this.ACC establish.IMP-her (matter is F)
u eql-am mannum ana PN iddin bīr-ma
and field-ACC who to PN he.gave establish.IMP-P
'Establish this matter, and who gave the field to PN? Establish (this).' (AbB 11: 189: 23)

One may wonder why the interrogative particles in (329)–(332) above did not develop into indirect questions in Old Babylonian, given that such developments happen so often and so naturally in many languages (Harris and Campbell 1995: 293–307). In (332) above, it would be particularly tempting to interpret the question ('who gave the field to PN?') as an embedded question, because an embedded question would make this sentence a closer parallel to the previous sentence. But such an interpretation would have no parallels in the corpus. The main barrier for the reinterpretation of interrogatives as embedded indirect questions may have been the distinction between the subordinative and independent forms of the verb. The independent form of the verb (which can be seen in the verb 'gave' in (332) above) could have made it difficult for direct questions to be reinterpreted as embedded indirect questions.

9.2.2. *'Concealed questions'*

The second main strategy in the *wh*-functional domain in Old Babylonian is based on the use of nominal objects as 'concealed questions'. A few examples are given below:

(333) *PN . . . kīam lizkur-u dā'ik PN$_2$ lā īdû*
PN thus he.should.swear-SUB murderer.of PN$_2$ not I.know.SUB
'let PN swear thus: I do not know (~ who is) PN$_2$'s murderer' (CT 29: 42: 13, CAD s.v. *idû* 1b2'a')

(334) *balṭ-ūs-su ul īde-ma*
alive-NOMINALIZATION-his not I.knew-P
'I didn't know his aliveness' (~ whether he was alive) (AbB 13: 21: 7)

(335) *muškēn-ūt-ī atti ul tīde*
poor-NOMINALIZATION-my you(F) not you.know
'don't you know my poverty?' (~ how poor I am) (AbB 6: 1: 40)

(336) *šībū ša mār-ūt PN īdû*
witnesses REL son-NOMINALIZATION.of PN they.know
'witnesses who know the filial status of PN' (Leichty 1989, p. 350: ii.5)

(337) *šumma tarāman-ni u šumma ana kasp-im iššāmū*
if you.love-me and if for silver-GEN they.were bought
u na-di[-na-ni] limad
and sellers find out.IMP
'if you love me and if they were bought for silver, find out the sellers' (AbB 2: 123: 9)

The nominal strategy can involve more than one simple noun as the object of the verb. The object noun can be augmented by a relative clause, in order to form more elaborate 'concealed questions'. The two main relative particles used for this purpose are *ša* and *mala. Ša* is the general relativizer that can stand for 'which' questions, as in (338)–(340), or for 'how much' questions, as in (341)–(342):

(338) *warh-am ša tallakam šupr-am-ma*
month-ACC REL you.(will)come write.IMP-to me-P
'write to me the month that you will come' (~ in which month . . .) (AbB 4: 145: 26)

(339) *kir-âm ša kapd-u u lā*
orchard-ACC REL taken care.STATIVE-SUB and not
kapd-u amur-ma
taken care.STATIVE-SUB see.IMP-P
'find out the orchard that is taken care of and that is not taken care of' (~ find out which orchard is taken care of . . .) (TCL 17: 15: 17)

(340) *āl-am ša wašbāti ina ṭupp-i šuṭrī-ma*
town-ACC REL you(FSG).stay.STATIVE in letter-GEN write.IMP-P
aqerr[ubakkim]
I.(will)approach.you
'write in a letter the town in which you stay and I will approach you' (~ write in which town . . .) (AbB 11: 39: 7)

(341) *kasp-am ša īšû ul tīde*
silver-ACC REL I.have.SUB not you.know
'don't you know the silver that I have?' (~ how much silver I have) (AbB 1: 89: 17)

(342) *še'-am ša amhur-u u ša atta tušābila*
barley-ACC REL I.received-SUB and REL you you.brought
atta-ma tīde
you-P you.know
'you yourself know the barley that I received and that you brought' (~ you yourself know how much barley I received and you brought) (AbB 10: 4: 26)

The second relativizer, *mala*, is used more specifically for quantities:

(343) *še'-am mala ina eqel PN ibbašû libirrū-ma*
barley-ACC REL in field.of PN was available.SUB let.them.determine-P
'let them determine the barley, as much as was available in PN's field' (~ determine how much barley was available (i.e. grew) in PN's field) (AbB 2: 28: 11)

(344) *ṭēm eql-im mala tēriš-u . . . ul tašpur-am*
report.of field-GEN REL you.cultivated-SUB not you.sent-to me
'you have not sent me a report of the field, as much as you cultivated' (~ a report on how much of the field you cultivated) (AbB 12: 137: 13)

(345) *damqa u maska mala imhur-akka ṭēm-ka ul tašpur*
good and bad REL happened-to you report-your not you.sent
'you didn't send a report on the good and bad, as much as happened to you' (AbB 9: 154: 9)

The two relative particles *ša* and *mala* can also introduce a 'headless' relative clause, as in (346)–(349) below. Alternatively, *mala* can serve as a head for *ša*, as in (350):

(346) *ša PN warad-ka īpuš-anni bēl-ī atta ul tīde*
REL PN servant-your did-to me lord-my you not you.know
'my lord, don't you know that which PN your servant did to me?' (~ what PN did to me) (AbB 12: 125: 4)

(347) *ša kasp-am iddin-u lā iddin-u šuṭrā-nim-ma*
REL silver-ACC he.gave-SUB not he.gave-SUB write.IMP(PL)-to me-P
lušme
let.me.hear
'write to me who gave money (and who) didn't, so that I may hear' (AbB 6: 88: 10)

(348) *mala iqabbûni-ku ina ṭuppi-ka šuṭur-ma šupr-am*
REL they.say-to you in letter-your write.IMP-P send.IMP-to me
'whatever they say to you write in your letter and send me' (AbB 13: 66: 24)

(349) concerning the barley . . .
mala ušaddinū-ma ana PN iddinū mala šunu ihbulū
REL they.collected-P to PN they.gave REL they harmed
birr-am-ma šupr-am u PN_2 *ina āli-šu*
establish.IMP-for me-P write.IMP-to me and PN_2 in town-his
mala ilqû birr-am-ma šupr-am
REL he.took.SUB establish.IMP-for me-P write.IMP-to me
'Establish and write to me whatever they collected and gave to PN and whatever they disadvantaged (him). Also establish and write to me whatever PN_2 took in his town.' (AbB 2: 124: 3)

(350) *mala ša ippal-u-ka ṭēm-am šupr-am*
REL REL he.replies-SUB-you report-ACC write.IMP-to me
'send me a report (on) everything which he replies to you' (AbB 2: 92: 32)

In translation, we can easily render these headless relatives as embedded questions, but *mala* and *ša* are not interrogative particles in any sense, so the Babylonian constructions are clearly headless relative clauses rather than embedded questions. Such headless relatives are actually quite common in Babylonian, not only as objects of verbs in the *wh*-functional domain. Examples (351) and (352) demonstrate such uses of headless relatives outside the *wh*-functional domain:

(351) *ša kali'āku ul ihhubti ul ina pilši*
REL imprisoned.1SG.STATIVE not in.robbery not in theft
kašdāku
caught.1SG.STATIVE
'(I) who am imprisoned, was not caught in a robbery or a theft' (AbB 2: 83: 31)

(352) *ša elī-ka ṭābu lūpuš*
REL to-you good let.me.do
'let me do (that) which is pleasing to you' (AbB 3: 79: 26)

There is a special relative particle which is used for 'where' questions. This is the particle *ašar* ('place.of'), which is the construct state of *ašrum* ('place'):

(353) *ašar ašb-u kulliman-ni*
place.of he.lives.STATIVE-SUB show.IMP-me
'show me the place in which (~ where) he lives' (AbB 11: 25: 4')

(354) *PN šāl-ma ašar ihliq-u liqbi-kum-ma*
PN ask.IMP-P place.of it.disappeared-SUB let.him.tell-you-P
'ask PN, and let him tell you where it disappeared' (AbB 1: 122: 26)

(355) *šumma ašar šakn-u idâta*
if place.of it.lies.STATIVE-SUB you.know.STATIVE
šupr-am-ma
write.IMP-to me-P
'if you know where it (the tablet) is, write to me' (AbB 6: 195: 14')

As with the headless relatives above, in translation it is most natural to render *ašar* simply as 'where', but it should be remembered that the Babylonian construction is a relative clause, not an embedded question (*ašar* can never be used as an interrogative particle).[56]

9.2.3. *The beginning of indirect questions*

In the Old Babylonian period, we have evidence only for the very beginning of embedded indirect questions. These are a few examples of 'whether' questions, introduced by the complementizer *kīma*, which we find after the verb 'ask':

(356) *ma-ri-a-ka šāl kīma alp-am lā īšû*
your fattener? ask.IMP *kīma* ox-ACC not I.have.SUB
'ask your fattener? whether I don't have an ox' (AbB 13: 134: 5)

(357) *mārī-ka u Isin kala-šu [š]āl kīma . . .*
sons-your and Isin all of-it ask.IMP *kīma*
'ask your sons and the whole of Isin whether . . .' (AbB 6: 73: 18)

[56] In West Semitic, the locative relativizer *ašar* was bleached of its purely locative meaning, and was used as a general relative particle. This use is also evident in the Mari dialect of Old Babylonian. It is possible that some examples from the 'core' dialect(s) of Old Babylonian also show such bleaching of the locative meaning of *ašar*, but the examples are few and of uncertain status:

šumma balum šībī u rīksātim ana maṣṣarūtim iddinma
if he gives goods for safekeeping without witnesses or contract and
ašar iddin-u ittakrū-šu
ašar he.gave-SUB they.deny-him
'they deny (taking from) him where/what he gave' (CH §123)

U_8.UDU.HÁ-[*j*]*a ša tuterram ašar ana Sippar aṭrudušināti PN+ itbal*
my sheep that you returned to me *ašar* I sent them to Sippar PN+ he.took

Kraus translates 'PN+ took the sheep that you returned to me (in the place) where I sent them to Sippar' (AbB 6: 157: 12).
CAD (s.v. *ašar* 2) translates: '. . . as soon as I sent them to Sippar'.

In addition to *ašar*, there is also another (much rarer) locative particle, *ēma* ('wherever'), which introduces relative constructions in the same way:

we searched for these tablets but didn't find them
ēma ṭuppū šunu šaknū ul nīde
wherever tablets.NOM these.NOM lie.STATIVE.3PL not we.know
'wherever (it may be that) these tablets are deposited, we don't know (this)'
(Schorr 1913, 281: 31)

9.3. Middle Babylonian

There do not appear to be radical changes in the *wh*-functional domain between the Old and Middle Babylonian periods. Both direct questions and concealed questions are still commonly used in Middle Babylonian. Direct questions can appear in the same format as in the Old Babylonian period (as in (358) below), but they seem to appear more commonly in constructions with the quotative particle *ummā*, as in (359) and (360):

(358) *liqta amahhar ana utūn-i ašakkan*
gold nuggets I.(should)get to oven-GEN I.(should)put
bēl-ī lišpur-a
lord-my let.him.write-to me
'Should I get the gold nuggets and put them in the oven? My lord should write to me.' (Bernhardt and Aro 1958, n. 112: 10)

(359) *aššu mê ša PN ša bēl-ī išpur-a ummā*
about water.GEN of PN REL lord-my wrote-to me *ummā*
eqel-šu ammīni mê lā išatti
field-his why water.ACC not it.drinks
'concerning the water of PN about which my lord wrote to me: "why doesn't his field get water?"' (PBS 1/2: 19: 15)

(360) *aššu bīr-i ša bēl-ī išpur-a ummā ammīni kanna*
about calf-GEN REL lord-my he.wrote-to me *ummā* why like this
tēpuš-anni
you.did-to me
'concerning the bull calf about which my lord wrote to me: "why have you done this to me?"' (UM 29–15–380: 6)

'Concealed questions' are used in a similar way to Old Babylonian, as in (361) and (362):

(361) *šum abī-šu ul īde*
name.of father-his not he.knew
'he didn't know the name of his father' (BE 14: 8: 6, CAD s.v. *idû* 1b9'a')

(362) *hīṭa-šu ul īde-ma ana bēli-ja ul aqbi*
crime-his not I.knew-P to lord-my not I.said
'I didn't know his crime, so I didn't tell my lord' (Bernhardt and Aro 1958, n. 109: 14)

The indirect 'whether' questions with *kīma* are used in Middle Babylonian as well. They now appear with the shortened complementizer *kī* instead of *kīma* (cf. note 45, p. 109):

(363) *mār šipri-ka šaʾal kī māt-u rūqat-u-ma*
messenger-your ask.IMP *kī* land-NOM is far.STATIVE(3FSG)-SUB-P
'ask your messenger whether the land (of Egypt) is far away' (EA 7: 28)

9.4. Neo-Babylonian

Direct questions are still used frequently in Neo-Babylonian. As in the Middle Babylonian period, it seems that they are most often introduced by the quotative particle *umma*, as in the examples below. The common use of *umma* before direct questions must be a consequence of the development of *umma* as a bleached and obligatory quotative marker after speech verbs:

(364) *aššu ṣuhārī ša tašpur umma ēkânu*
about agents REL you.wrote *umma* where
'concerning the agents about whom you wrote: "where (are they)?"'
(Cole 1996: 61: 5)

(365) *šarru iltālan-ni umma kīmaʾ* NÍG.GA *ša Bēlti ša Uruk . . .*
king he.asked-me *umma* how much property of Lady of Uruk
ēlâ
it.came up
'the king asked me: "how much property of the Lady of Uruk came up"'
(Beaulieu 1993: 249: 30)

But in the Neo-Babylonian period, we see a marked change from Old and Middle Babylonian, since indirect questions now become widespread. First, the indirect 'whether' questions with *kī* are very common in Neo-Babylonian:

(366) *bēl pīhāti šarru lišāl kī libb-a ana šarri bēli-ja lā*
governor king he.should.ask *kī* heart-my to king lord-my not
gummuru
entire
'let the king ask the governor whether I am not fully devoted to the king my lord' (ABL 846: r19)

(367) *šipirtu kī ana PN taddinu u kī lā taddinu šupr-a*
message *kī* to PN you.gave or *kī* not you.gave write.IMP-to me
'write to me whether you gave the message to PN or you didn't give (it)'
(UET 4: 184: 18)

(368) *šarru bēl-a lišāl-ma līmur kī lā iltēn tilû anāku u šū*
king lord-my let.him.ask-P let.him.see *kī* not one breast I and he
nīkulu
we.sucked
'the king my lord should ask and see whether we didn't both suck the same breast' (ABL 920: r8)

(369) *kī attalâ iškunu u lā iškunu ul nīde*
kī darkness it.made or not it.made not we.know
'we don't know whether (the moon) made the darkness or did not make the darkness' (ABL 895: 6)

More strikingly, other indirect questions now appear. For the first time in the history of Babylonian, in Neo-Babylonian, 'real' interrogative particles can introduce indirect questions, as in examples (370)–(374) below. These are also 'real' indirect questions, because they can involve the shift in personal deixis which is associated with indirect speech, as in (372) and (374).

(370) *anāku īde agâ mannu u agâ mannu*
I know this who and this who
ṭābtu ša gabbikunu kī iltēn ina muhhija
the goodness of all of you is like one to me
'(Can) I know who this one is and who that one is? The goodness of all of you is like one to me.' (ABL 287: r12)

(371) *attunu tīdâ manna ana rabi unqāta iqbi*
you.PL know who to master.of seals he.spoke
'you know who spoke to the official in charge of the seals' (BIN 1: 22: 13)

(372) *šarru lišāl-šu ana muhhi mīni illika*
king he.should.ask-him why he.came
'the king should ask him why he came' (ABL 1255: r14)

(373) *iltēn* LÚ . . . *ṣabtā-nim-ma lušāl-šu mīnamma emūqu*
one man seize.IMP(PL)-for me-P let.me.ask-him why troops
ma'du ša Aššur ana Uruk iphurūni u ana ēkânu harrān-šunu
many of Assyria to Uruk they.assembled and to where way-their
'seize one man for me so that I will ask him why many Assyrian troops assembled in Uruk and where they are heading' (ABL 1028: 13)

(374) *šarru bēl-a lišāl-šu mīnu ṣibûs-su ana Elamti*
king lord-my he.should.ask-him what desire-his from Elam
ana mīni ana Elamti lillik
why to Elam he.should.go
'the king my lord should ask him what his desire from Elam is, (and) why he wants to go to Elam' (ABL 998: 9)

In Neo-Babylonian, we find indirect questions even for 'how much' questions, which were once the traditional stronghold of concealed questions. Thus, compare the Old Babylonian nominal strategy in (343) above, with the indirect questions in (375) and (376) below.

(375) *lē'ē . . . amur akkā'i qīme u gimir . . . taddin*
boards check.IMP how much flour and expenses you.gave
'check (in) the (writing) boards how much flour and expenses you gave' (YOS 3: 106: 19)

(376) *ina īnī-kunu amurā kīma' kī zēru muššuru*
in eyes-your(PL) see.IMP(PL) how much *kī* arable land is.abandoned
'see with your (own) eyes how much arable land is abandoned' (CT 22: 20: 8)

It seems, in fact, that in the Neo-Babylonian period, *kī* has developed the function of turning interrogative particles into *wh*-complements. This use of *kī* can be seen in example (376) above, as well as in the examples (377)–(379) below:

(377) *ina pān mannu kī ašbatu bēlu lišpur-a*
in presence.of who *kī* she.lives lord let.him.write-to me
'the lord should write to me with whom she lives' (UET 4: 177: 9)

(378) *mīnu kī PN iqabbâkkinūšu ana muhhi šugarrû epšā*
what *kī* PN he.says-to you(PL) concerning payment do.IMP(PL)
'do whatever PN will tell you concerning the payment' (CT 22: 9: 14)

(379) *šāl-šunūtu akkā'i kī dullu akanna inneppuš*
ask.IMP-them how *kī* work here is.done
'ask them how the work here is being done' (BIN 1: 40: 32)

The older structures with *ašar* are still used for 'where' questions in Neo-Babylonian, as in (380), but indirect questions can now be used as well, as in (381):

(380) *ašar ašbatu PN īde*
place.of she.lives PN knows
'PN knows where she lives' (Ebeling 1949, n. 287: 10, Streck 1995: 147)

(381) *ul īdû ēkâme šū*
not I.know where he
'I don't know where he is' (Cole 1996: 17: 19)

To summarize then, indirect questions become widespread in Neo-Babylonian. It seems that most interrogative particles can now be embedded as indirect questions, either on their own, or with the help of the conjunction *kī*. These indirect questions replace many of the direct questions and 'concealed questions' of earlier periods.

Part IV

The Development of Complementation as an Adaptive Process

10

Functional Parallels for the Babylonian Development

The previous chapters demonstrated that there was a general historical development in Babylonian, in which finite complements and finite embedded questions replaced alternative strategies in the FDC. This chapter presents a brief survey of some parallels from other languages for this functional development. I aim to show that neither the late emergence of finite complements nor the extension in their use during the historical period is unique to Babylonian. Rather, the changes in Babylonian seem to be an instance of a general trend. Before surveying the history of some ancient languages, two modern languages are mentioned: Dyirbal and Tok-Pisin.

10.1. Dyirbal

In previous chapters, I claimed that Old Akkadian had no finite complementation, and outlined the alternative structures which were used instead of finite complements. The assertion that a language can 'survive' without finite sentential complementation may be met with scepticism on theoretical grounds. It is therefore useful to mention that one does not need to go four thousand years back in history to find languages without finite complementation. Such languages exist today. In fact, according to Dixon (1995: 199), Dyirbal has no sentential complementation at all:

> People have occasionally asked me why my grammar of Dyirbal . . . has no mention of complement clauses. The grammar was based on an analysis of Dyirbal texts and describes every grammatical pattern that occurs. Quite simply, there are no complement-clause constructions.

According to Dixon, Dyirbal has two alternative 'strategies of complementation'. (In the terminology used in this book, we have called these strategies 'alternative structures in the FDC'.) The first is a nominal strategy of relativization, and the second is based on a purpose construction. The relative strategy is used in Dyirbal with verbs such as 'see', 'watch', 'hear', 'dream', and 'imagine'. It can be demonstrated by (382) below. (For comparison, we have seen that in Babylonian, the relative strategy is regularly used in the *wh*-functional domain, as in examples (341)–(345) in chapter 9.)

(382) *ŋaja ŋamban ŋinu-na milga-ŋu*
I.NOM heard you-ACC chastise.TRANSITIVE-REL+ABSOLUTIVE
'I heard you, who were being chastised'
(~ I heard you being chastised) (Dixon 1995: 208)

The second strategy in the Dyirbal FDC is based on parataxis and purposive clauses. This strategy is used with the verbs 'tell to do', 'ask', 'like', and can be demonstrated by (383) and (384) below.

(383) [*bayi yara*] *walŋgarranyu* [*baŋgun yibiŋgu*]
[the man].ABSOLUTIVE wanted [the woman].ERGATIVE
bura-li
see-PURPOSIVE
'the man wanted, so that the woman should see him'
(~ the man wanted the woman to see him) (Dixon 1995: 205)

(384) [*balan yibi*] [*baŋgul yaraŋgu*] *ŋanban*
[the woman].ABSOLUTIVE [the man].ERGATIVE asked
yanu-li
go-PURPOSIVE
'the man asked the woman, so that she should go'
(~ the man asked the woman to go) (Dixon 1995: 205)

Purposive inflection on verbs in Dyirbal is not a mark of structural subordination, since it appears on verbs in independent clauses. For example, the addition of the purposive inflection to the verb 'go' in the Dyirbal equivalent of 'the man goes', would result in a sentence meaning 'the man has to go' (Dixon 1995: 202). In fact, the use of the purposive inflection in Dyirbal is very similar to the use of the precative form in Akkadian (§3.5.5). The construction in the examples above is an exact parallel to the Akkadian coordination construction which we have seen especially with manipulative verbs in §8.1. Thus, compare for example (384) above to (385) from Old Babylonian:

(385) *Pajakum eris-su lirdi'ak-kum-ma*
Pajakum ask.IMP-him he.should.lead-to you-P
'ask him (for) Pajakum, he should lead him to you'
(~ ask him to lead Pajakum to you) (AbB 13: 7: 16)

There is no indirect speech in Dyirbal. The verb 'speak/say' is simply followed by the quoted direct speech. There is also no verb for 'be able to'. Instead of 'I can swim', speakers might say, 'I habitually swim', or 'I have swum'. There is also no verb corresponding to English 'know' (Dixon 1995: 211). The Dyirbal system shows that a language can have a viable system of clausal cohesion without any embedded sentential complements, either finite or non-finite. The FDC in Dyirbal consists of two alternative strategies, a nominal relative strategy, and a clausal paratactic strategy.

10.2. Tok-Pisin

A different perspective for comparison can be offered by the study of Creole languages. Since the rate of change in these languages is very high, they can provide parallels for historical developments which may be observed over a relatively short period of time. In a recent grammar of Tok-Pisin (New Guinea Creole), Mühlhäusler (1985: 408) explains:

> Very little has been said about complementation in Tok-Pisin in the available grammatical description. This may well reflect a genuine lack of such constructions until very recently, together with the absence of formal devices to indicate the subordinate status of complement sentences. Thus as late as 1971, Wurm . . . writes: 'Noun clauses have no distinguishing characteristics, and precede (as subject) or follow (as object) other clauses without a conjunction'.

However, in the data he collected between 1972 and 1978, Mühlhäusler found that 'formal signalling of complementation in both subject and object sentences is often found' (1985: 408). The emergence of finite complementation in Tok-Pisin thus seems to be a recent process.

Tok-Pisin also uses coordination with the morpheme *na*, as in (386)–(388) below. These again are very similar to the Babylonian manipulative construction with coordination. Interestingly, the coordination constructions are receding in Tok-Pisin. According to Mühlhäusler (1985: 410), they are used mainly by older speakers. Younger speakers replace them with complement clauses and complementizers such as *olsem*, *long*, and *bilong*.

(386) *Ol papamama na ol hetman i mas tok na ol i marit*
the parents and elders must say and they marry
'the parents and elders must tell them to get married' (Woolford 1979: 120)

(387) *Husat tokim yo na yu kam?*
who told you and you come?
'who told you to come?' (Woolford 1979: 120)

(388) *Gutpela na yu kam*
good and you come
'it's good that you come' (Woolford 1979: 120)

10.3. Sumerian

Although the Sumerian language is attested during a long period, a historical study of Sumerian presents very serious problems, because of the special nature of the development of its writing system. We often cannot tell to what extent the changes observed in the documents represent changes in the language, or only in writing. Nevertheless, a cursory glance suggests that Sumerian moves in a similar direction to the one I sketched for Akkadian, but in an earlier period. In

Old Sumerian (the early letters and legal texts from the period before 2200 BC), parataxis rather than subordination is used with perception and knowledge verbs, as in the examples below:

(389) beer and bread [. . .] ⌜*é*⌝*-gal-šè* ⌜*šu*⌝ *im-mi-nu-*[*ús*]
[someone] sent beer and bread to the palace
lugal-mu géštu-ga-ni hé-zu
lord-my he should take notice
'someone sent beer and bread to the palace, my lord should take notice' (SAB: Gir 12: 4)

(390) *é-ba-zi-zi-ka* *1* ^{giš}*gígir-é-*UMBINXLU-2 *al-gál*
in Bazizi's house 'two-wheeled box cart' there is
lú-mu *igi im-mi-du*$_8$*-àm*
man-my looked-COPULA
'there is a "two-wheeled box cart" in Bazizi's house, my man really$^?$ saw (this)' (SAB: Ad 8: 9)

(391) $^2/_3$ *kù ša-na-bì-ta mu-*20 LÁ 3*-šè PN*$_1$ ^{giš}*dusu-šè ì-lá* *PN*$_2$*+ ab-gi-ì*
PN_1 weighed $^2/_3$ (mina) silver (for) 17 years for the . . . PN_2+ proved
'PN_1 weighed $^2/_3$ (mina) silver (for) 17 years for the . . ., PN_2+ proved (this)' (Edzard 1968, p. 123)

But in the later period (Neo-Sumerian, from around 2200 BC), although parataxis is still used,[57] we also find many examples of subordinate complements, such as (392)–(394), which use the nominalization/subordination morpheme *-a*, glossed here as SUBORD.[58] Example (394) is particularly complex. It contains three subordinate clauses: a relative clause embedded within a complement clause, which is itself embedded within an adverbial clause. [SUBORD^1] marks the 'adverbial' clause: 'on account of . . .', [SUBORD^2] marks the 'complement'

[57] For example:

2 (*bur*) *iku a-šà am-rí-ma PN*$_1$*+ .ra lugal-e* *in-na-ba*
2 bur field in Amrima PN_1+ -to king-ERGATIVE gave to him
PN$_1$*+ PN*$_2$ *dumu-ni-ir in-na-ba* *PN*$_4$ *PN*$_5$ *lú-inim-ma-bi-me*
PN_1+ PN_2 son-his-to gave to him PN_4 PN_5 were the witnesses for this
'The king gave to PN_1 2 bur of field in Amrima. PN_1 gave it to his son PN_2.
PN_4 and PN_5 were the witnesses for this.' (NG 110: 1)

[58] The morpheme *-a* is not used only for complementation, but is the general subordination/nominalization morpheme in Sumerian, used to nominalize clauses in any position, relatives, adverbials, and complements. On the role of *-a* cf. Limet (1975). For other languages which do not distinguish between complementation and relativization, cf. Comrie and Horie (1995). The precise status of the morpheme *-a* in Sumerian, and especially the scope of its operation, are not entirely clear. Some uses of this morpheme in Sumerian are incompatible with a particle which nominalizes a whole clause, but rather suggest that its scope is only the verb. For example, it is possible to retain a direct speech quotation in a clause 'governed' by *-a*, as in the first example below. Also, when several verbs are subordinate to a main predicate, the morpheme *-a* is repeated with each of them, as in the second example below:

clause: 'that he was a king . . .', and [SUBORD^3] marks the 'relative' (or 'participial') clause: 'to whom Enlil has given strength'.

(392) *mu-lugal* *PN+ dam-šè ha-tuku* *bí-in-dug$_4$-ga* *PN$_2$ PN$_3$*
[name of king PN+ wife-as I shall take he said].SUBORD PN$_2$, PN$_3$
nam.érim-àm
testimony-COPULA
'it is the testimony of PN$_2$ and PN$_3$ that he said "(by) the name of the king, I shall take PN+ as a wife"' (NG 15: 4)

(393) *PN+.e* *PN$_2$ ìr* *PN$_3$.a(k) ì-me-a-aš*
PN+.ERGATIVE PN$_2$ slave PN$_3$.GEN he is-SUBORD-DIRECTIONAL
in-gi-in
he proved
'PN+ proved that PN$_2$ was the slave of PN$_3$' (NG 60: 1)

(394) *lú* *Dabrum.ak.e* *^{d}Utu-hegal*
people Dabrum.GEN.ERGATIVE Utu-hegal
bar *lugal* *^{d}Enlil.e* *á* *šúm.a*
account [^{1}[^{2}king [^{3}Enlil.ERGATIVE strength give].SUBORD^3
ì-me.a *ì-zu.a.ak.eš*
(he)is].SUBORD^2 (they)knew].SUBORD^1.GEN.on
Tirigan-ra šu nu-niba
(they) did not let Tirigan escape.
'The people of Dabrum, on account of their knowing that Utu-hegal was a king to whom Enlil has given strength, did not let Tirigan escape' (Royal inscription of Utu-hegal (2019–2013 BC), (attested only from OB copies) Frayne 1993, p. 285)

10.3.1. *Contact and borrowing*

We know that there was a prolonged and intimate contact between Sumerian and Akkadian, which resulted in borrowing and convergence on all levels (cf. §3.2). For this reason, if the development of complementation in Sumerian preceded that of Akkadian, it is natural to ask to what extent the Akkadian development was influenced by Sumerian. There are two distinct issues involved in this question. First, we can ask whether finite complements in Akkadian were

PN ama-ar-gi$_4$-mu in-gar-ra *bí-in-du$_{11}$*
PN freedom-my placed.SUBORD he.declared
'he declared that "PN granted my freedom"' (NG 186: 17')

é kù-šu-na-ta-àm in-sa$_{10}$-a
she bought the building plot with her own money-SUBORD
nì-ga PN la-ba-ši-lá-a *PN$_2$ nam-erím-àm*
it was not paid for by property of PN-SUBORD is the testimony of PN$_2$
'it is the testimony of PN$_2$ that she bought the building plot with her own money (and) that it was not paid for by property of PN' (NG 99: 11)

structurally modelled on Sumerian ones. Then, we can ask whether the structural possibilities of the Sumerian system could have given functional impetus for the development of finite complementation in Akkadian.

It is unlikely that Akkadian finite complements were structurally modelled on Sumerian, because the strategies for forming finite complements in Akkadian and Sumerian are incompatible. The Sumerian structure is based on nominalization, whereas the Akkadian complements developed from adverbial clauses. Had Akkadian modelled its finite complements on Sumerian, we would have expected it to use the relative particle *ša* to introduce complements, since this would have been the nearest equivalent to the use of the nominalizing/subordinating particle *-a* in Sumerian.[59] But as we have seen, finite complements in Akkadian developed by semantic bleaching of the causal adverbial conjunction *kīma*. Such a process has no obvious parallel in Sumerian, and is best understood as a development which stems from the internal configuration of the Akkadian system. (This process was explained in detail in chapter 4.)

Nevertheless, contact on a functional level may indeed have been an important factor in the development of finite complements in Akkadian. The existence of elaborate constructions in Sumerian such as (394) above may well have given a functional impetus for the development of structures in Akkadian which perform a similar function. In Old Akkadian, there are no structures attested even remotely on this level of complexity. In Old Akkadian, the same scenario would probably be described using parataxis: 'Utu-hegal is a king to whom Enlil has given strength. The people of Dabrum knew (this), and did not let Tirigan escape.' Sumerian may well have widened the functional horizon for the Akkadians, and thereby encouraged the development of new structures.

10.3.2. *Contact in legal terminology*

As explained in the previous section, the structural configuration of finite complements in Akkadian is not parallel to that of Sumerian. The situation with the 'proving' verbs (*kunnum* and *burrum*), however, is more complex. The domain of legal terminology is a prototypical arena for cultural borrowing, and indeed there are clear signs of structural and semantic convergence between Sumerian and Akkadian in this area.[60] There are obvious structural parallels between formulae used with the proving verbs in the two languages. One example is the simple Akkadian formula in (395) below, which is structurally equivalent to the Sumerian formula in (396):

(395) *kir-âm* *u* *bīt-am* *ana PN ubirrū*
orchard-ACC and house-ACC to PN they.established
'they established the orchard and the house to PN' (Schorr 1913: 259: 29)

[59] Of course, the relative particle *ša* was eventually used as a complementizer in Babylonian, but only in the Neo-Babylonian period, more than a millennium after the death of Sumerian.

[60] For a recent study of possible convergence in a specific legal construction (with the verb *baqārum* 'make a claim', 'contest') see Dombradi (1997).

(396) *é* *PN-ra ba-na-gi-in*
house PN-to is.established.to him
'the house is established to PN' (NG 106: 14)

Moreover, although there is no parallel in Sumerian to the use of *kīma* with speech, perception, and knowledge verbs, there are clear parallels between the use of *kīma* and the use of the Sumerian postposition *-šè* with the proving verbs. The use of *kīma* with the proving verbs derives from its comparative or 'equative' role, which is not limited to the proving verbs, as can be seen for example in (397) below.[61] The postposition *-šè* can be used in Sumerian for a similar purpose, as in (398) below.

(397) *abī* Ì[R *š*]*uāti kīma qīšti ana jâši liddina*
'my father should give me this slave as a present' (AbB 11: 60: 29)

(398) *níg.ba-aš ha-ma-an-ba-e*
'let her give it to me as a present' (OB Sumerian. Thomsen 1984, n. 206.)

The parallel between the use of *kīma* and the use of *-šè* extends to many (but not all) of the constructions with the proving verbs. In §11.3.4, all the structures used with the proving verbs will be discussed in detail. Here, only a few examples are given to demonstrate the parallel with the Sumerian constructions. Akkadian uses *kīma* with verbless clauses ((399) and (400)), and with finite verbal clauses (401), but it uses *ina* with infinitival clauses. Sumerian uses *-šè* in all cases: for verbless clauses ((402) and (403)), non-finite verbal clauses ((404)), and finite verbal clauses ((393) above).

(399) *kīma warassu ukānšuma*
'he proves him as his slave' (CH §282)

(400) *kīma mār Nippuri šū ubtirrūšu*
'they proved him that he is a citizen of Nippur' (BE 6/2: 62, CAD s.v. *bâru* A3b)

(401) *kīma PN . . . eqlam šuāti lā iṣbatu . . . ubirrūnimma*
'they proved for me that PN did not take this field' (AbB 4: 40: 12)

(402) *PN_1 nam-ìr-šè PN_2-ra ba-na-gi-in*
'PN_1 was proved as a slave to PN_2' (NG 34: 14)

(403) *nam-dumu-nibru^{ki}-šè PN mu-ši-gin-na*
'(when) PN proved him as a citizen of Nippur' (Edzard 1968, n. 54, 'Akkadezeit')

(404) *PN má šúm-ma-aš ba-gi-in*
'PN is convicted of giving the boat' (NG 62: 11)

[61] However, in Akkadian not only *kīma* is used in such contexts: the preposition *ana* can also be used for the same function, as in *ana qīštim taddinaššu*, 'you gave it to me as a gift' (AbB 11: 16: 18).

The parallels between the constructions above are clear, but it is less obvious whether a simple borrowing scenario can be drawn for the use of *kīma* with the proving verbs. To start with, even when convergence is evident, it is not always clear in which direction borrowing proceeds. The usual assumption is that borrowing is from Sumerian to Akkadian, but there are cases where influence in the other direction has been suggested, even in the legal domain. For example, Edzard (1967: 49) sees the unusual word order of Old Sumerian oath formulae such as *mu-PN-šè lú lú nu-ba-gi$_4$-gi$_4$-da* as borrowing or translation from Akkadian structures (*na'āš PN itma*).

The use of *kīma* in constructions such as 'he proved X *kīma* Y' (where I called X the 'criminal' and Y the 'crime') seems entirely native for Akkadian. (In fact, particles such as English 'as', German *als*, or French *comme*, which were mentioned in §4.1, and which have semantic range similar to that of *kīma*, can be used in a very similar way.) Moreover, the distribution between *ina* and *kīma* has no parallel in Sumerian, and seems to follow very naturally from the internal syntactic configuration of Akkadian. Nevertheless, Sumerian could easily have encouraged the extension from nominal to clausal structures with the proving verbs in Akkadian. (This process was described in §4.4, and will be discussed in more detail in §11.3.) Sumerian, which has a more fluid distinction between nominalization, non-finite subordination, and finite subordination, could have encouraged the expansion of the 'criminal' argument from a noun phrase ('he proved X *kīma* murderer') to a clause ('he proved X *kīma* he murdered').

It is well known that in situations of contact, influence is most effective when it reinforces developments which are already underway in the language (or at least for which the conditions in the language are ripe). For this reason, it is often difficult to determine the direct role of borrowing in diachronic developments. It seems to me that the constructions used with the proving verbs are a good case in point. Section 11.3 will demonstrate, using the proving verbs, the motivation for the expansion of nominal arguments to clausal ones. The discussion there does not explicitly consider external influence on this development, but encouragement from Sumerian may well have played a role. The internal motivation for the expansion of nominal arguments to clausal arguments is valid both for Akkadian and for Sumerian (as well as for other languages, as I argue in §11.3). For this reason, the precise role of borrowing in this case is not only difficult to establish, but also less crucial for the understanding of the process.

10.4. Biblical Hebrew

Givón (1991) studied subordination patterns in biblical Hebrew, and showed how in earlier biblical Hebrew, non-finite subordination and parataxis were more widespread, whereas in later stages, finite subordinate clauses gained more ground. Givón examined subordination in general, but the developments he sketches are evident also in the Functional Domain of Complementation in particular. Although finite complements are present already in early biblical Hebrew (as well as Ugaritic and early Aramaic, cf. §4.5.4 above), the distribution within the FDC in the early stages still leans more heavily towards parataxis and non-finite complements. In later stages, finite complements gain more ground at the expense of the other strategies. For example, paratactic constructions with the particle *hinnēh*, as in (405) below, are very common with the verbs 'see' and 'dream' in early biblical Hebrew,[62] but seem to be drastically reduced in later biblical Hebrew, and disappear entirely in Mishnaic Hebrew. There is a similar reduction in the use of infinitive complements with knowledge and perception verbs, which is attested in early biblical Hebrew (and Ugaritic), as in examples (406)–(410) below.

(405) *wa-yar' w-hinnēh ḥārbû pnê hā-'ădāmâ*
and-he.saw and-P dried.3MPL face.of the-earth
'and he saw and 'behold' the surface of the earth dried up'
(~ and he saw that . . .) (Genesis 8: 13)

(406) *hlk aḥt-h b'l y'n*
go.INF.of sister-his Baal he.saw
'Baal saw the coming of his sister' (Ugaritic. Parker 1997: 9.IV. 39, p. 114)

(407) *hlk kṯr k y'n*
go.INF.of Kothar verily he.sees
'he verily sees the coming of Kothar' (Ugaritic. Sivan 1997: 125)

(408) *lō' ēda' ṣē't wā-bō'*
not I.know go out.INF and-come in.INF
'I do not know going out or coming in' (~ how to go out or come in) (1 Kings 3: 7)

(409) *w-šibt-kā w-ṣēt-kā û-bō'ă-kā*
and-sit down.INF-your and-go out.INF-your and-come.INF-your
yādā'tî w-'ēt hitraggez-kā ēlāy
I.know and-ACC rage.INF-your on.me
'but I know your sitting down and your going out and coming in, and your raging against me' (2 Kings 19: 27)

(410) *zkōr 'āmd-î l-pānê-kā*
remember.IMP(MSG) stand.INF-my to-face-your
'remember my standing before you' (~ how I stood . . .) (Jeremiah 18: 20)

62 Cf. the use of *inūma* as a complementizer in Canaanite Akkadian, e.g. in CAD s.v. *inūma*, p. 161

In later stages, finite complements gain ground at the expense of these alternative strategies. They are also extended to verbs of manipulation in later biblical Hebrew. We saw in §8.3 above how manipulation in Hebrew is expressed by various strategies: coordination (411), infinitive complements (412), and direct speech (413). But in late biblical Hebrew, finite complements start being used to express manipulation as well, as in (414):

(411) *w-'attâ ṣawwēh w-yikrtû lî ărāzîm min ha-lbānôn*
and-now order.IMP and-they.shall.fell to.me cedars from the-Lebanon
'now order, and let them fell cedar trees from the Lebanon for me' (1 Kings 5: 20)

(412) *ēllēh ha-dbārîm ăšer ṣiwwâ yhwh la-'ăsōt ōtām*
these the-things REL ordered.3MSG yhwh to-do.INF them
'these are the things that the Lord has commanded (you) to do' (Exodus 35: 1)

(413) *wa-yṣaw 'ālāyw lē'mōr lō' tiqqaḥ iššâ mi-bnôt*
and-he.ordered on.him QUOT not you.take woman from-daughters.of
knā'an
Canaan
'and he ordered him: "you shall not take a wife from the daughters of Canaan"' (Genesis 28: 6)

(414) *kî Mordŏkay ṣiwwâ 'ālê-hā ăšer lō' taggîd*
because Mordechai he.ordered on-her COMP not she.says
'because Mordechai ordered her that she should not say' (Esther 2: 10)

10.5. Indo-European

10.5.1. *Hittite*

The developments in the FDC in Babylonian are also mirrored in the history of Indo-European languages. The closest parallel is offered by the earliest attested Indo-European language, Hittite. The system of complementation in Hittite was studied by Justus (1979, 1980*a*, 1980*b*), Luraghi (1990, 1997), and Cotticelli-Kurras (1995). As in Old Akkadian, Old Hittite had no finite complementation. The only available structures in the FDC were parataxis and non-finite complements. The verb 'know' appeared with parataxis, as in (415), whereas the verb 'hear' appeared with non-finite complements, as in (416) (a participle), and in (417) (a verbal noun):

(415) KUR *uru alasya-wa ammel nu-war-at* QATAMMA *šak*
country Alasya-P 1SG.GEN P-QUOT-3SG likewise know.2SG.IMP
'the country of Alasya belongs to me, you likewise must know this' (Justus 1980*a*: 100)

(416) *mahhan-ma* KUR.KUR^{meš} ^{lú}KÚR ^{m}*Arnuwandan* ŠEŠ-*JA* *irman*
when-P lands enemy PN.ACC brother-my sick.ACC
ištamaššir
heard.3PL
'when the enemy lands heard my brother PN being sick'
(~ that my brother PN was sick) (Justus 1980*b*: 197)

(417) LÚ^{meš} KUR ^{uru}*Mizra-ma mahhan* *ŠA* KUR ^{uru}*Amka* GUL*ahhuwar*
men land Egypt-P when of land Amka defeat.VERBAL NOUN
ištamaššanzi
they.hear
'when the men of Egypt hear the defeat of the land of Amka'
(~ when they hear that the land of Amka has been defeated) (Justus 1979: 103)

Finite complements, with the complementizer *kuit*, appear only in later stages of Hittite:

(418) [GI]M-*ya IDI* *kuit-za*
[as?]-P I.know COMP-P
KUR ^{uru}*Mizri* KUR ^{uru}*Hatti-ya* 1^{EN} KUR^{TIM} *kišari*
the land of Egypt and the land of Hatti are becoming one land (Justus 1980*b*: 195)

(419) *nu mahhan austa anda-kan kuit*
P when I.saw into-P COMP
hatkesnuwantes nu-smas halki$^{\text{hi.a}}$*-us tepaueszi*
they were oppressed and their food was diminishing
'when I saw that they were being oppressed and their food was diminishing' (Luraghi 1997: 59)

10.5.2. *Other Indo-European languages*

It is well known that the older Indo-European languages relied more heavily on parataxis and non-finite subordination than their modern descendants. Moreover, of the three major categories of subordinate clauses, W. P. Lehmann (1980: 12) explains that in the ancient Indo-European languages, finite complements are used the least. A detailed survey of the historical developments will not be given here, because most of the facts are well known.

The early stages of the older dialects use non-finite complementation and parataxis in the FDC. In later stages of Latin and Greek, finite clauses replace various participial and infinitival constructions in the FDC (Cuzzolin 1994*a*). This is the case in Sanskrit as well. According to W. P. Lehmann (1980: 128), whereas early Sanskrit used verbal nouns for complementation, these verbal nouns are generally lost in post-Vedic Sanskrit, and in later Sanskrit, finite complements are found. The general picture in the Indo-European FDC is very similar to what

I described for Babylonian. The earliest attested stage (early Hittite) does not have finite complements at all. The earliest stages of other ancient Indo-European languages also show a predominance of parataxis and non-finite complements in the FDC. Later, the FDC moved in the direction of finite complements.

10.5.3. *Developments in Indo-European: OV to VO?*

The absence of finite complements, and scarcity of other subordinate structures in Hittite, and in early Indo-European languages, have caused unease to some Indo-Europeanists, such as W. P. Lehmann and C. Justus.[63] To try to explain the situation in the early Indo-European dialects, Lehmann (1980) and Justus (1980*a*, 1980*b*) advanced a theory which is based on changing patterns of word order. They maintain that the use of parataxis and non-finite complementation in early Indo-European does not present a stage in which subordination was 'less developed', but rather should be explained by the strict verb-final (OV) word order patterns of early Indo-European. According to them, the subsequent development of finite subordinate complements is due to the loosening of the strict word-order patterns and consequently the gradual shift towards VO word order.

I suggest that their explanation cannot be correct. First, there is no convincing reason why verb-final languages should not have finite complements or other finite subordinate clauses. Many languages (including Babylonian) demonstrate this point very clearly. Moreover, the developments in Indo-European and in Akkadian run in parallel, although the word-order situation in these languages is very different. Akkadian is verb final (SOV), but this word order is actually a borrowed innovation. The early Semitic languages are very consistent VSO languages, with all the expected 'VO' characteristics. Akkadian, however, borrowed strict verb-final word order, because of intimate cohabitation with verb-final Sumerian. So the lack of finite complements in early Akkadian cannot be claimed to be a result of the history of the language as an 'OV type'. Furthermore, once the verb-final order was borrowed, the word-order situation remained quite stable throughout the history of the language, and the development of complements did not coincide with any change in word-order 'type'. The language remained generally verb-final until its death around 500 BC.[64] Moreover,

[63] W. P. Lehmann (1980: 116), for example, says: 'We cannot agree that there was a primitive stage in the development of language when humans knew only simple clauses, that is no subordination. Such a view lacks credibility, certainly in a period as late as the PIE community. Accordingly we must seek a more credible explanation for a PIE with no apparent indicators for subordination.'

Justus (1980: 183) shares the same unease: 'But one important consideration makes the Indo-Europeanist hesitate: is it possible that the oldest data could represent a stage of language different in kind from human language today, a stage in which some of our universal categories and functions were not yet developed? In reality the proto-language of ca. 3000 BC or even 5000 BC is not early enough in the history of our species to have been different in kind from human language today.'

[64] The only major change in word order was in fact the migration of finite complements to post-verbal position, which we have already seen in chapter 4. Finite complements were the only constituent which migrated. The explanation for the change in the position of finite complements has little

as I indicated in §10.3, similar developments in the FDC can also be observed in languages like Hebrew, which have had VO word order throughout their recorded history.

In the next chapter, I suggest what seems to me a more plausible explanation for the emergence of finite complements, both in Babylonian and in Indo-European. Regardless of word-order patterns, finite complementation is better at handling more complex propositions than both parataxis and non-finite complementation. I therefore suggest that the emergence of finite complementation can be seen as an adaptive process, linked to the development of more complex communicative needs.

to do with a general drift in the language from OV to VO. As I mentioned in chapter 4, there is a general tendency for sentential complements to be post-verbal, even in otherwise strict verb-final languages (Dryer 1980).

11

The Development of Complementation as an Adaptive Process

Chapter 4 followed the emergence of finite complements in Babylonian. In Part III, we saw that during the history of Babylonian, finite complements (and embedded indirect questions) gradually took over some of the functions which were performed earlier by parataxis and by non-finite complements. In the previous chapter, I argued that this development is not unique to Babylonian, but in fact seems to be part of a general trend. This chapter suggests a motivation for this trend. I claim that finite complementation is a more powerful linguistic tool than the alternative constructions, because it is better at dealing with more complex communicative contents. The expansion in the use of finite complements may therefore be seen as an adaptation to the development of more complex communicative needs.

Section 11.1 asks first what areas in language can be adaptive. Section 11.2 suggests that subordination is an area of language structure which can be adaptive. Section 11.3 discusses complementation in particular. Using the 'proving verbs' as a test case, I show why finite complements are more effective in expressing more detailed and complex propositions than both parataxis and non-finite complementation. Section 11.4 suggests that the development of finite complementation is an instance of a more general change in the mechanisms of cohesion, from greater reliance on time iconicity to more explicit marking of dependence between clauses using subordination. Finally, section 11.5 discusses briefly the role of writing and literacy in this development.

11.1. What in language can be adaptive?

It is not controversial that some areas in language adapt to the communicative environment. The adaptive nature of language change is most obvious with vocabulary, which evolves constantly and adapts to the communicative needs of speakers. Nevertheless, when one considers the structure of language, the issue becomes controversial. Can the structure of language be adaptive, in a similar way to vocabulary? The matter is controversial for two reasons: the question of the autonomy of syntax, and the contentious issue of complexity.

Some formalist theories do not accept that functional factors can play a major role in shaping the structure of language. If one maintains that structure is autonomous (that is, independent of function), it necessarily follows that structure cannot adapt to functional or communicative forces. Nevertheless, the core assumption of functionalist linguistics is that structure is shaped by function, and to Functionalists it should therefore be evident that the structure of language can undergo adaptive changes. A well-known dictum, for example, is that 'grammar codes best what it does most frequently'.

Moreover, the mechanisms by which the adaptation of structure occurs are relatively well understood. For example, the range of processes which have been considered under the umbrella of grammaticalization are responsible for the emergence of many grammatical structures. One of the basic conditions for grammaticalization is the *repeated use* of a certain lexical (or less grammatical) expression in a certain context. Expressions which are more relevant to communication, those which make more relevant distinctions or denote relevant concepts, are more likely to be used more often, and are therefore more likely to grammaticalize. The consequence is that the grammatical distinctions expressed by a language are likely to be affected by the communicative needs of its speakers. More relevant and useful structures are more likely to emerge than less relevant structures.

11.2. Complexity and subordination

Nevertheless, even in functionalist linguistics, the adaptability of structure becomes more controversial when one approaches the emotive issue of subordination in particular, and 'complexity' in general. Alongside the well-known dictum that 'grammar codes best what it does most frequently', there are even better known slogans, such as 'all languages are of equal complexity', or 'all languages are created equal'. Such beliefs seem to be dominant in current linguistics, in spite of (or perhaps just because of?) the fact that they carry very little meaning. In particular, as Comrie (1992) has pointed out, no one has suggested a scale to measure the 'overall complexity' of a language in a way which would weigh different areas in language against one another in a non-arbitrary way.

Linguists are particularly suspicious of attempts to relate any features of language structure to the complexity of society. Nevertheless, there have recently been some attempts to examine whether the complexity of society can influence aspects of the structure of language. The most interesting example is a study by Perkins (1992), which tries to establish specific areas in the structure of language as adaptive. Perkins claims that there is strong statistical evidence for a link between the complexity of society and the number of grammaticalized deictic markers in a language. He conducted a survey of forty-nine languages, and tested the number of grammaticalized deictic markers in each of them. On the basis of this survey, he claims that there is a significant inverse correlation between the level of complexity of a society (or 'cultural complexity')[65] and the complexity of the deictic system of the language spoken in the society. The less complex the society, the more elaborate the deictic system of the language is likely to be (that is, there are likely to be more grammaticalized deictic distinctions). In more complex societies, there will be fewer grammaticalized deictic distinctions.

Perkins explains this correlation by the different patterns of communication in societies with different levels of complexity. In less complex societies, the context-dependence for interpreting statements can be higher, because communication is more often with intimates than strangers. There is thus more shared background of pragmatic presuppositions, and the topic of conversation is more often visible or at hand. Such a communicative environment makes more deictic distinctions relevant, and these distinctions are then more likely to be grammaticalized. In more complex societies, on the other hand, 'communication in general involves a requirement for decreasing dependence on context for the interpretation of messages' (Perkins 1992: 92). In such societies, finer deictic distinctions are less relevant and therefore less likely to be grammaticalized, or more likely to be eroded.

Similar inverse correlations between the complexity of society and some grammatical distinctions have also been noted by other linguists, although, as far as I am aware, not quantitatively. Dixon (1997: 120), for example, says that 'detailed systems of evidentials tend to be found only among non-industrialised people'. He also states (117):

> Small political groups generally have an intricate social structure with an articulated system of classificatory relationships and communal obligations. (In contrast, the social networks of city dwellers are rudimentary, and could appropriately be described as primitive.) Associated with this social structure tend to go complex systems of pronouns, with several numbers of distinctions.

The sentiments expressed by Dixon may not be very controversial. But when the issue of subordination is examined in a similar way, it seems that sensitivities are heightened. Subordination is seen as the prototypical bearer of complexity in language, and attempts to establish subordination as an adaptive area in language may appear as a direct assault on the doctrine of equality. The sensitivity

[65] Perkins measures the level of 'cultural complexity' according to scales which are apparently established in anthropology. He bases himself on Hayes, and uses a list of criteria from Murdock's Ethnographic Atlas to establish the level of cultural complexity. Among these criteria are subsistence economy, estimated relative dependence on animal husbandry and agriculture, type and intensity of agriculture, settlement patterns, mean size of local communities, craft specialization, class stratification, inheritance of real property, inheritance of movable property, regional organization (Perkins 1992: 140). Of course, none of these features measures patterns of communication themselves, so the categories listed above are only surrogate measures.

of this issue can be glimpsed in an article by Mithun (1984), which starts in the following way (493):

> We all know that all languages are created equal. We also know that they are equally adaptable to the needs of their speakers, so that different languages will develop vocabulary in different areas . . . Languages even develop different grammatical distinctions, such as highly individual repertoires of pronouns marking various categories of animacy, gender, and social relationships. Are grammatical constructions like subordination amenable to the same type of adaptation, fluctuating according to the conceptual needs of their speakers, or do they represent fundamental human intellectual constants?

Mithun observes that subordination is rarely used in various Native American languages, and consequently, she asks whether subordination is indeed an adaptive property, or whether it is a 'universal constant of language'. She concludes that subordination is not a universal constant. According to her, subordination is rare in the languages she examined partly because they are polysynthetic, and mainly because they lack a written tradition. (The issue of literacy will be discussed in §11.5 below.)

In the following section, I argue that finite complements are better at handling more complex propositions than the alternative strategies in the FDC (parataxis and non-finite complementation). I then suggest that the development which we have followed in the previous chapters may be seen as an adaptive change, related to the development of more complex patterns of communication. Such a suggestion may arouse suspicion, especially because many linguists are wary of arguments which imply that subordination was 'less developed' in earlier languages (cf. §2.4). For this reason, the precise nature of the argument presented here should be stressed again. I do not accuse older languages of lacking a basis for inter-clausal cohesion. The emergence of finite complementation is not the emergence of inter-clausal cohesion, but rather the emergence of one particular strategy for achieving such cohesion. In the older stages, the alternatives to finite complementation were more prominent, as we have seen in the previous chapters. The adaptive nature of the emergence and extension in the use of finite complements lies in the fact that finite complements are better than the alternatives at dealing with more complex contents, and therefore better adapted to more complex communicative patterns.

11.3. Anything you can do, I can do better

Finite complementation is a more powerful mechanism because it combines the two essential qualities of its rival strategies. Like parataxis, finite complementation can link sentence-like clauses. It thus retains the flexibility and range of expression that sentence-like clauses can afford (as opposed to noun phrases, or reduced clauses). But finite complementation, unlike parataxis, also expresses explicitly the dependence between the clauses. In this respect, finite complementation is similar to the embedding of noun phrases or of non-finite clauses. Finite complementation is therefore more 'powerful', because it can express explicitly the relation between clauses, but at the same time retain the flexibility of sentence-like clauses.

11.3.1. *The 'proving' verbs*

It should not be difficult to see the advantages of both explicitness and flexibility in describing more complex situations. One good test case for the advantages of finite complementation is the language used in legal proceedings. Legal circumstances provide a very good demonstration of the more complex communicative patterns of a more complex society. In trials and other judicial proceedings, one has to make a case before strangers, and the reliance on context must be substantially more restricted than in simple everyday speech. One also has to describe complex situations as accurately and explicitly as possible, and in as much detail as possible.

I shall try to demonstrate the advantages of finite complementation in dealing with more complex contents, using the Babylonian verbs *kunnum* and *burrum*, which we have already met in §4.4 and §7.5. As was explained in §4.4, these two verbs can be translated as 'prove', 'establish', or 'convict', and for our purposes can be treated indiscriminately. If there are any differences in meaning between them, these only involve fine points of legal terminology (examined in Dombradi 1996). In terms of structure, the two verbs behave identically.

The proving verbs have complex and varied patterns of use, and they are sometimes regarded by Assyriologists as difficult, if not erratic. It seems to me, however, that their apparent complexity can be unravelled by the realization that what we observe are various coexisting stages of a diachronic development, in which parataxis and simpler nominal strategies were expanded and replaced by more flexible clausal strategies. The range of variation in the structures used with the proving verbs stems initially from the fact that they are used to describe complex situations, with different types of participants and semantic relations. Thus, when the verb 'prove' is used in the sense of 'convict', it should have a human being as an argument, as in (420*a*). But when it is used as 'establish' it should have a proposition as an argument, as in (420*b*):

(420) (*a*) The prosecutor proved ('convicted') the defendant.
(*b*) The prosecutor proved ('established') the murder.

For the sake of convenience, let us call the human argument the 'criminal', and the proposition argument the 'crime'. The reason why a range of different structures is used with these verbs should not be difficult to see. First, even if the 'crime' argument can sometimes be expressed with a simple noun phrase like 'murder', this 'crime' is by nature a propositional argument rather than a nominal one. This type of argument therefore naturally 'aspires' to be expressed with a clausal strategy. Second, the two types of argument, 'crime' and 'criminal', are often participants in the same event (or 'notional unit'), and there is thus a natural tendency to combine these two arguments into one clause. In English, the two types of argument can be combined and expanded in various ways, as can be seen in (421) below. They can be retained as two distinct arguments of the verb (421*a*, *b*), or the two arguments can be merged into one complement clause (421*c*):

(421) (*a*) The prosecutor convicted the defendant of the murder.
(*b*) The prosecutor convicted the defendant of having committed the murder.
(*c*) The prosecutor proved/established that the defendant had committed the murder.

The story of the 'proving' verbs in Babylonian consists of the various strategies by which the nominal 'crime' argument was expanded to a clause, and the ways by which the two arguments, 'crime' and 'criminal', could be combined as arguments of one verb. We shall see that at least with more complex contents, the strategy which does this most efficiently is finite complementation.

11.3.2. *Nominal arguments*

The embedding of noun phrases makes the dependence of the argument on the predicate explicit, but it places strict limitations on the flexibility of the 'crime' itself. These limitations may not pose problems when simple situations need to be described, for example in 'I proved(=established) the murder'. We can see such simple examples in (422) and (423) below, where the 'crime' appears as the object of the verb, and the 'criminal' is not expressed at all:

(422) *awīl-um habt-um mimmâ-šu halq-am mahar*
man-NOM robbed-NOM property.ACC-his lost-ACC in front.of
il-im ubār-ma
god-GEN he.proves-P
'the man who has been robbed will prove his lost property before the god' (~ will prove the extent of his lost property . . .) (OB. CH §23)

(423) *ištu ina bīt Jablija dabāb-a anni'-a ukinnū*
after in house.of Jablija statement-ACC this-ACC they.proved
'after they proved/established this statement in the temple of Jablija' (OB. AbB 13: 60: 23)

But for more complex situations, a simple noun phrase is not detailed or flexible enough. One obvious expansion strategy is to use a relative clause to augment the 'crime' noun phrase, as in (424):

(424) *še'-am ša . . . ina eql-im šuāti PN ilteq-û . . .*
barley-ACC REL from field-GEN this.GEN PN he.took-SUB
birrā-ma
establish.IMP(PL)-P
'establish the barley that PN has been taking from this field'
(~ establish how much barley . . .) (OB. AbB 4: 79: 27)

The following two examples show further elaboration, in that not only the 'crime' is augmented by a relative clause, but the two nominal arguments, 'crime' and 'criminal', are now both expressed in the same sentence, and appear as two arguments of the verb. In (425), the two arguments both appear as accusative objects of the verb. In (426), however, a different strategy is used. The 'criminal' is the direct object, whereas the 'crime' is governed by the preposition *ina* 'in' (cf. English 'convict him *of* the murder').

(425) *še'-am mala taddin-u-šum-ma ikkir-u-ka*
barley-ACC REL you.gave-SUB-to him-P he.denies-SUB-you
bīr-šu
prove.IMP-him
'prove him the barley, as much as you gave him and he denies you'
(~ prove against him how much barley you gave him and he denies'
(OB. TCL 1: 34: 12)

(426) *bēl šēbult-im awīl-am šuāti ina mimma ša*
owner.of consignment-GEN man-ACC this.ACC in whatever REL
šūbul-u-ma lā iddin-u ukān-šu-ma
consigned-SUB-P not he.delivered-SUB he.(will)prove-him-P
'the owner of the consignment will convict this man of whatever was consigned and he failed to deliver' (OB. CH §112)

Another strategy for expanding the simple nominal 'crime' argument is to augment it by a prepositional phrase, as in (427).

(427) *kir-âm u bīt-am ana PN ubirrū*
orchard-ACC and house-ACC to PN they.proved
'they proved the orchard and the house to PN'
(~ they proved that the orchard and the house belong to PN)
(OB. Schorr 1913, n. 259: 29)

Nevertheless, even if the nominal 'crime' argument can be expanded in different ways, the flexibility of these nominal strategies is still fairly limited compared to that of real verbal clauses.

11.3.3. *Parataxis*

When the 'crime' proposition is more complex or elaborate, it has to be expressed by a full clause. The older strategy for expressing a clausal 'crime' with the proving verbs was based on parataxis. In example (428), only the 'crime' argument is expressed. In (429), the 'criminal' is the direct object of the verb, and the 'crime' is a clause in parataxis:

(428) *X u Y šūt ramānija-ma ukīn*
X and Y they my own-P I.proved
'X and Y are my own, I proved' (OB. Whiting 1987: 26: 5)

(429) *šumma awīl-um awīl-am ubbir-ma nērt-am elī-šu*
if man-NOM man-ACC he.accused-P murder-ACC on-him
iddī-ma lā uktīn-šu
he.cast-P not he.proved-him
'if a man accused a man, and cast murder on him, and did not prove him (i.e. did not establish the accusation) . . .' (OB. CH §1)

Parataxis does not restrict the inner-clausal flexibility, but it fails to make the logical dependence between the clauses explicit. For simpler situations this may not be a problem, but if the situations to be described are more complex, parataxis can be less satisfactory, as the Old Akkadian example below demonstrates:

(430) *ana PN_2 PN_1 eqel PN_3 šūlu'-am iqbi . . .*
to PN_2 PN_1 field.of PN_3 dispossess.INF-ACC he.said
'PN_1 told PN_2 to dispossess the field of PN_3'

eqel PN_4 . . . uštēli PN_1 ula īde
field.of PN_4 he.dispossessed PN_1 not he.knew
'he (PN_2) dispossessed the field of PN_4, PN_1 didn't know (about this)'

mahar laputtî ukīn-šu
in.front.of inspectors.GEN he.proved-him
'he (PN_1) proved him (PN_2) in front of the inspectors.'
(~ PN_1 proved in front of the inspectors that he told PN_2 to dispossess the field of PN_3, but without his knowledge, PN_2 dispossessed the field of PN_4) (OAkk. Foster 1990: 2: 1)

The translation above seems the most plausible from the context. But one could also translate differently, for example: 'PN_1 told PN_2 to dispossess the field of PN_3; PN_1 then proved (against PN_2) in front of the inspectors that he didn't know that PN_2 dispossessed the field of PN_4'. So in this example, where more than two clauses are involved, parataxis does not make explicit which clauses are dependent on which other clauses. In more complex situations in general, the lack of explicit marking of the scope of dependence can be problematic.

11.3.4. *Infinitive complements*

We have seen the deficiencies of both parataxis (lack of explicit marking of dependence) and of nominal arguments (lack of flexibility in expressing more complex propositions). The embedding of infinitival clauses to express the 'crime' naturally allows for more flexibility, since the 'crime' can now be expressed by a verbal clause. The most common strategy for combining the infinitive 'crime' clause with a nominal 'criminal' is to retain the 'criminal' as the direct object of the verb, and to use the preposition *ina* to govern the infinitival complement.[66] (This pattern is similar to the nominal construction with *ina* in (426) above.) The structure of these examples is demonstrated in (431), and some examples follow (all the following examples are from OB):

(431) he stole barley → they proved/convicted him *ina* steal.INF barley
'they convicted him of stealing barley'

(432) *ina še'-im zabāl-im āl-um ukīn-šunūti*
in barley-GEN carry.INF-GEN town-NOM convicted.3SG-them
'the town convicted them of carrying (= stealing) barley' (AbB 3: 70: 9)

(433) *ina . . . še'-im leq-êm ubarrūnik-kunūti-ma*
in barley-GEN take.INF-GEN they.(will)prove-you(PL)-P
pānī-kunu ul ubbal
face-your(PL) not I.(shall)bring
'if they convict you of taking barley, I shall not be lenient with you' (AbB 9: 183: 11)

(434) *tamkār-um šū . . . ina kasp-im leq-êm*
merchant-NOM this.NOM in silver-GEN take.INF-GEN
šamall-âm ukān-ma
trading agent-ACC he.proves-P
'this merchant shall convict the trading agent of having taken the silver' (CH §106)

(435) *ina amt-im . . . ana bīti-ka šūrub-im ukannūnin-ni-ma*
in slave girl-GEN to house-your put in.INF-GEN they.prove-me-P
'(if) they convict me of making the slave girl enter your house' (AbB 9: 49: 9)

(436) *dajān-am šuāti ina dīn idīn-u en-êm*
judge-ACC this.ACC in judgement.of he.judged-SUB change.INF-GEN
ukannū-šu-ma
they.(will)convict-him-P
'they will convict this judge of changing the judgement that he gave' (CH §5)

[66] A much less common way is to retain both the infinitival clause and the 'criminal' argument as two accusative objects:

maggirt-am ša PN_1 ana PN_2 qab-âm ul ubirrā-ši
slander-ACC of PN_1 to PN_2 say.inf-ACC not they(F).convicted-her
'they did not convict PN_1 (female) of speaking slander against PN_2'.
(UET 5: 256: 8 (= BE 6/2: 58); CAD s.v. *bâru*, p. 128)

The infinitival clauses clearly allow for much more flexibility than a 'crime' expressed only by a noun phrase. The infinitival construction functions well when the 'crime' can be expressed as a verbal clause, and when the 'criminal' object is identical to the subject of the 'crime' complement. In this case, just as in English 'I convict him of stealing the barley', the 'criminal' is expressed only once, as the direct object ('him') of the main verb. The subject of the 'crime' clause is not expressed overtly, but is 'controlled' by the direct object of the main verb.

In other contexts, however, the infinitive clauses are less adequate. For example, if the subject of the 'crime' clause is not the same as the 'criminal', infinitive complements cannot easily cope. The expression of the subject in an infinitival clause is in general quite problematic, and it is difficult to include both the subject and the object of the verb in the infinitival clause.[67] Thus, if a judge wants to pronounce his verdict on Mr X, and if he wants to use an infinitive complement to do so, he could easily say 'I convict X of stealing the barley'. But he would find it more difficult to say 'I establish (against X) that X's brother stole the barley for him'. Infinitives, as reduced clauses, are in general better at coping with simpler propositions. They are less effective with more complex propositions, especially those with more elaborate argument structure.

11.3.5. *Finite complements*

We saw in chapter 4 that finite complements with the proving verbs developed by the merging of the two arguments, 'crime' and 'criminal'. The use of *kīma* with the proving verbs derives from its role as an equating particle, as demonstrated in example (437). We also saw that *kīma* was extended from this role to be used with full clauses, as in (438) below.

(437) *kīma waras-su ukān-šu-ma*
kīma slave-his he.proves-him-P
'he proves him as his slave' (CH §282)

(438) *kīma šum PN ušapšiṭ-u-ma šum-šu*
kīma name.of PN he.caused to erase-SUB-P name-his
ušašṭer-u . . . PN+ ubtirrū
he.caused to write-SUB PN+ they.proved
'they proved PN+ that he had PN's name erased and his name written down' (AbB 4: 15: 14)

[67] Such examples are found in Babylonian, but extremely rarely, and apparently only in stylized literary contexts. A famous example is from the prologue of the Code of Hammurabi:

dann-um enš-am ana lā habāl-im
strong-NOM weak-ACC to not oppress.INF-GEN
'in order for the strong not to oppress the weak' (CH: Prologue: i. 37)

Finally, because the subject of a finite complement clause is expressed in the clause itself (and need not be controlled by the object of the main verb), the object of the main verb could be dropped, giving 'true' finite complements, as in (440):

(439) *kīma ištu* MU.3.KAM *ina bīt PN wašb-u*
COMP since 3 years in house.of PN he.lives.STATIVE-SUB
ubirrū-ma
they.proved-P
'they proved that he has been living in the house of PN for 3 years' (AbB 6: 181: 19')

With finite complements, the restrictions on the structure of the clause are minimal. The construction now allows one to express the statement 'I prove the fact that . . .', where 'the fact' is not constrained by any structural or semantic factors. For example, the subject of the complement clause can now be different from the 'criminal' object of the verb 'prove', and the clause can be either verbal or non-verbal. The following examples demonstrate some statements which would be difficult to express with infinitive complements:

(440) *PN ina pī ramāni-šu kīma dūr-šu*
PN in mouth.of own-his COMP permanent status-his
iššakk-um pagar-šu ubīr
privileged farmer-NOM self-his he.proved
'PN proved with his own mouth that his permanent position is (that of a) privileged farmer' (AbB 2: 43: 15)

(441) *kīma PN . . . eql-am šuāti lā iṣbat-u*
COMP PN field-ACC this.ACC not he.took-SUB
eql-um šū ṣibit-ni-ma ubirrū-nim-ma
field-NOM this.NOM property-our-P they.proved-for me-P
'they proved for me that PN did not take this field, and (that) this field is our property' (AbB 4: 40: 12)

Using the proving verbs, I have argued in this section that finite complements can cope better with more complex contents. Finite complements can mark the dependence between clauses explicitly (like nominal and non-finite arguments), but they also retain the flexibility of finite clauses. The legal contexts that we examined served well to demonstrate the advantages of both explicitness and flexibility. But the general principle is not limited to legal circumstances, and applies to other contexts as well. To demonstrate this, I conclude this section with one example which does not belong to the legal sphere, but which demonstrates another obvious quality of finite complementation: recursion in subordination. Some reduced clauses (such as infinitives) may have recursive constructions, as for example in 'Sarah told John to tell Mary to come'. But recursive behaviour with reduced clauses is restricted to a few particular constructions. True recursive subordination is only possible with the flexibility of finite (or sentence-like) clauses. Example (442) below shows recursive subordination with finite complements. This example (which seems to be from the late Old Babylonian period) is the only example I have found in the Old Babylonian corpus of a complement clause embedded within another complement clause. But its existence shows that this was a possible strategy in the language. Again, it would be difficult to paraphrase this example with infinitive complements or nominal strategies.

(442) *kīma ina lā wašābi-ja*
COMP in not be present.INF-my
kīma še'-um ina bīt PN+ lā ibaššû
COMP barley-NOM in house.of PN+ not there.is.SUB
ana šarr-im taqbû
to king-GEN you.said.SUB
ešme-ma
I.heard-P
'I heard that in my absence you told the king that there is no barley in the house of PN, your servant' (AbB 12: 172: 12')

Finite complements, therefore, are more effective 'tools' for expressing more elaborate propositions, not only in judicial language, but with more complex contexts in general. For this reason, finite complements are more likely to be used, and to be used more often, when more complex situations and events need to be communicated. I suggest that the expansion in the use of finite complements during the historical period can be seen as an adaptation to the increasing complexity of communicative needs. We shall return to this issue in the conclusion of this chapter.

11.4. Different strategies of cohesion: iconicity and subordination

The previous section described the advantages of finite complementation over all the alternative strategies (parataxis, nominal structures, and non-finite complementation), but it concentrated on the differences between finite and non-finite complementation. This section concentrates on the difference between finite complementation and parataxis. I attempt to put this difference in the more general perspective of the relation between two strategies of inter-clausal cohesion: subordination and time iconicity.[68]

11.4.1. *Time iconicity in Hittite and Akkadian*

A long line of research into the structure of narrative discourse has identified the essence of the distinction between 'narrative' and 'non-narrative' discourse in the

[68] The term 'iconicity' has been applied to a wide range of phenomena. In this discussion, I use only a very restricted sense of 'time iconicity': the appearance of clauses in the order of their appearance in reality. A different aspect of iconicity is used by Koewenberg (1997) in his important study of gemination in the verbal system of Akkadian.

adherence to time iconicity. 'Narrative clauses' have to appear according to the temporal order in which they occur in reality (*veni vidi vici*). 'Non-narrative clauses', on the other hand, may be, but do not *have to* be, temporally ordered (Labov 1972, chapter 9; Thompson 1987). To demonstrate the relevance of time iconicity, I want to start with an example not from Akkadian, but from another ancient language, Hittite. Justus (1981) tries to define the basis of inter-clausal cohesion in Hittite. She discusses examples such as (443) below, and compares the Hittite order of clauses with what would be a more idiomatic order of clauses in modern European languages, as in (444).

(443) *UMMA ŠAMŠI Muršili* LUGAL.GAL
this is what the Sun King Muršili the great king said
INA ^{uru}*Til-Kunnu nannahhun nu haršiharši udaš namma* ^{d}*U-aš*
to Til-Kunnu I.marched P bad storm brought further Stormgod
hatuga tethiškit nu nahun nu-mu-kan memiaš iššī anda
terribly kept.thundering P I.feared P-me-P speech mouth in
tepwešta
became small
'This is what the Sun King Muršili the great king said: I marched to Til-Kunnu, there came a *haršiharši* [big storm], the Stormgod further kept thundering terribly, I feared, the speech in my mouth became small.' (Justus 1981: 380)

(444) The speech in my mouth became small because, when I marched to Til-Kunnu, there came a *haršiharši* in which the Stormgod kept thundering so terribly that I feared.

Justus tries to explain the difference in the order of clauses between Hittite and modern European languages by relying on the distinction between 'ascending' word order (Hittite) and 'descending' word order (modern European languages).[69] She claims that the order of clauses in Hittite is related to the clause-internal word order of the language. According to her, the 'ascending' order of clauses derives from the verb final (OV) nature of Hittite.

But a much simpler explanation for the order of clauses in Hittite is to be gained from time iconicity. In the Hittite text in (443), the clauses simply follow the temporal order of events in reality. All the clauses are paratactic, and time iconicity is crucial for maintaining inter-clausal cohesion. In the English para-

[69] The terms 'ascending' and 'descending' were coined by Henri Weil (1978) [1869]. In modern terminology, these terms would correspond to the distinction between 'left-branching' (where the modifier precedes the modified) and 'right-branching' (where the modifier appears after the modified). But the terms 'ascending' and 'descending' were used by Weil to denote not only the word order of the constituents within the clause, but also the order of whole clauses in the sentence or period. Justus claims that Hittite (a left-branching, verb-final language) shows ascending order both inside the clause, and between clauses, and that the ascending order between clauses derives from the ascending order within the clause.

phrase in (444), on the other hand, the clauses do not follow the temporal sequence of reality. They do not have to follow the real order of events, because the subordinating words ('because', 'when', 'so that') explicitly mark the nature of the dependence between the clauses. Thus, for example, we could easily paraphrase the Hittite text in English with a different ordering of the clauses:

(445) When I marched to Til-Kunnu, I feared so much that the speech in my mouth became small, because there came a *haršiharši* in which the Stormgod kept thundering so terribly.

The same requirement of time iconicity also applies to Akkadian paratactic clauses. The Old Akkadian legal example that we saw above (repeated here as (446)) can serve to demonstrate this point. In this example, the order of the paratactic clauses follows their temporal order in reality (but cf. §11.4.3 below for the situation with the verb 'know'). In the English paraphrase, however, the temporal order is less important, because of the explicit marking of subordination.

(446) *ana* PN_2 PN_1 *eqel* PN_3 *šūlu'-am* *iqbi* . . .
to PN_2 PN_1 field.of PN_3 dispossess.INF-ACC he.said
eqel PN_4 . . . *uštēli* PN_1 *ula īde*
field.of PN_4 he.dispossessed PN_1 not he.knew
mahar *laputtî* *ukīn-šu*
in.front.of inspectors.GEN he.proved-him
'PN_1 told PN_2 to dispossess the field of PN_3, he (PN_2) dispossessed the field of PN_4, PN_1 didn't know (about this), he (PN_1) proved (it against) him (PN_2) in front of the inspectors.'
(~ PN_1 proved in front of the inspectors that he told PN_2 to dispossess the field of PN_3, but without his knowledge, PN_2 dispossessed the field of PN_4) (Foster 1990: 2: 1)

We can demonstrate the difference between subordinate and paratactic clauses not only with English paraphrases, but in Akkadian itself. Consider first example (447) from Old Babylonian. The clauses are in paratactic relation, and their order follows their occurrence in time: '(first) he broke the tablets, (and then) they told me about it'. Using parataxis, this is the only order in which these clauses can appear.

(447) *balumma šaptija . . . išmû ina bīt napṭari-šu ṭuppātī-ja ihpi-ma*
without hearing my lips in warehouse-his tablets-my he.broke-P
iqbû-nim
they.said-to me
'without hearing me he broke my tablets in his warehouse, and they told me (about it)'
(~ I was told that without hearing me he broke my tablets in his warehouse) (Finkelstein 1965: 37)

When subordinate clauses are used, however, the order of the clauses does not depend on time iconicity. The order may still be time iconic, as in (448) below, but the opposite order may occur as well, as in (449). In fact, time iconicity with finite complements does not play any role. The change in the position of the complement clause between (448) and (449) is a result of purely structural factors (mainly heaviness, as was explained in §4.3.1).

(448) *kīma bīti napṭari-ja buzzû PN ahū-ka*
COMP warehouse-my pressed.STATIVE.3SG PN brother-your
iqbi'-am
he.said-to me
'PN your brother told me that my warehouse was pressed (for payment)' (AbB 2: 97: 6)

(449) *ú-li iqbûnik-ki kīma ištu ūm-im ša ana āli-ja*
not they.said-to you(F) COMP since day-GEN REL to town-my
allik-u ina šubt-im ṭābt-im lā ušb-u . . .
I.came-SUB in dwelling-GEN good(F)-GEN not I.lived-SUB
'did they not tell you that since I came to my town I have not lived in pleasant dwellings?' (AbB 1: 134: 25)

11.4.2. *Iconicity and manipulation*

The difference in the ordering of clauses between paratactic and subordinate clauses is especially clear with verbs of manipulation. In chapter 8, we saw that two different strategies are used in Babylonian for manipulation. Past manipulation is expressed by infinitive complements, and non-past manipulation is expressed by coordination. The embedded infinitive complements are preverbal in Akkadian, and so in examples like (450), the sequence of clauses is not time iconic. But with coordination, as in (451), the sequence of clauses has to be time iconic: 'speak to him, so that he will then return my canal'.

(450) *bēl-ī ana PN še'-am makās-am iqbi*
lord-my to PN barley-ACC collect rent.INF-ACC he.said
'my lord told PN to collect the shares of barley' (OB. AbB 13: 4: 7')

(451) *qibi-šum-ma nār-ī literr-am*
say-to him-P canal-my he.should.return-to me
'speak to him and he should return my canal to me' (OB. AbB 9: 252: 20)

The same time iconic order must be observed with manipulative verbs in other languages, whenever coordination is used. A few examples make this clear:

(452) *w-'attâ ṣawwēh w-yikrtû lî ărāzîm min ha-lbānôn*
and-now order.IMP and-they.shall.fell to.me cedars from the-Lebanon
'now order, and let them fell cedar trees from the Lebanon for me' (Biblical Hebrew. 1 Kings 5: 20)

(453) *sanga* *hé-na-ab-bé* *kišib hé-ra-ra*
temple official he should say to him seal he should unroll
di-bé *di hé-bé*
this case he should judge
'he should speak to the temple official, (the temple official) should unroll his seal and judge this case'
(~ he should tell the official to unroll his seal and judge this case)
(Sumerian. SAB: Is1: 14)

(454) *Wahori'wanòn:tonhse' ne rón:kwe ahoié:nawa'se'*
he asked him the man he would help him
tahaià:ia'ke'
he would cross there
'he asked the man, he would help him, he would cross there'
(~ he asked the man to help him get across) (Mohawk. Mithun 1984: 497)

(455) *Ol papamama na ol hetman i mas tok na ol i marit*
the parents and elders must say and they marry
(~ the parents and elders must tell them to get married)
(Tok-Pisin. Woolford 1979: 120)

(456) *n-as* UL *tarnahhun n-an-kan* UL *kuennir*
CONNECTIVE-them not I.left CONNECTIVE-him-P not they.killed
'I did not allow them they did not kill him'
(~ I did not allow them to kill him) (Hittite. Luraghi 1990: 76)

11.4.3. *Iconicity and perception verbs*

With the verb 'know', the order of clauses is fairly free even in parataxis. We commonly find both structures of the type 'I know, something is the case', and 'something is the case, I know' (examples are given in §7.2). This freedom can be explained by the fact that 'know' describes a state rather than an action, and there is no obvious temporal ordering of the fact being known and the state of knowing. But it seems that 'know' is the only verb in Babylonian which allows such freedom.

We can observe a more subtle manifestation of time iconicity with verbs of perception such as 'hear' and 'see'. One could claim that simple time iconicity with these verbs is irrelevant, just like with the verb 'know', since the act of perception and the perceived event take place at the same time. But a distinction is nevertheless observed with verbs of perception. To demonstrate the difference between the two possible orders, consider the examples below. In (457) and (458), the act of perception appears before the perceived event ('they saw, and something was the case'). In (459), the order is reversed; the perceived event comes before the act of perception ('something is the case, we saw this').

(457) *šumma tattaplasī-ma tulû-ša lā damiq*
if you(FSG)inspect-P breast-her not good
'if you inspect and her breast is not good' (OB. AbB 1: 31: 17)

(458) *kī ša īmurū-ma ṣābē šaplānu-šunu ma'du*
when they.saw-P soldiers beneath-them many
'when they looked and there were many soldiers beneath them' (NB. ABL 520: 25)

(459) *20 ṣābum nīnu ana hāmī kamās-im nillik-ma*
20 people we to chaff.GEN gather.INF-GEN we.went-P
GIŠ.GIGIR.HI.A u ERIM.GÌR *mādam-ma . . . ana GN*
chariots and foot soldiers many-P to GN
illakū-ma nīmur
they.marched-P we.saw
'20 of us went to gather chaff and many chariots and foot-soldiers were marching towards GN, and we saw (this)' (OB. AbB 10: 150: 9)

The variation is not random, and the orders are not interchangeable. When the perception verb comes before the perceived event, the volitional nature of the perception is emphasized. We should accordingly translate the examples as 'look' or 'watch', not just 'see'. But where the order is reversed, it is precisely the lack of intent or volition that is emphasized: 'we went to gather chaff and we happened to see that . . .'.

The same distinction applies with the verb 'hear'. In (460) below, the verb 'hear' comes before the statement which was heard, and this emphasizes the intent ('I made inquiries and heard that'). In (461) the order is reversed, and the meaning accordingly emphasizes the lack of intent: 'the field will be abandoned, and you will come to hear about it'.

(460) *ina ahīt-im ešme-ma* ÉNSI.MEŠ *ina* ERIM.MEŠ . . .
in neighbourhood-GEN I.heard-P managers in workers
šutemṭû
be short of.STATIVE.PL
'I heard in my neighbourhood and the managers were underprovided with workers' (OB. AbB 13: 78: 1)

(461) *eql-um imaqqut-ma tešemme-ma libba-ka imarraṣ*
field-NOM (will)fall.3SG-P you.(will)hear-P heart-your (will)worry.3SG
'the field will be abandoned and you will hear about it and will become worried' (OB. AbB 10: 193: 16)

11.4.4. *From iconicity to subordination*

As we have seen, the ordering of clauses in a time iconic way is an important strategy of inter-clausal cohesion, which can sometimes be employed to achieve intricate nuances (for example, with verbs of perception). But we have also seen that when subordination is used, the ordering of clauses in a time iconic way is no longer necessary, because the nature of the relation between the clauses is explicitly marked by the subordinating conjunction (or by the subordinating construction as a whole). Some subordinate structures thus allow greater freedom in the ordering of clauses, and this freedom may be used to achieve additional idiomatic goals.

In a study of English narrative discourse, Thompson (1987) shows that even if subordinate clauses do not have to follow time iconic order, some subordinate clauses do so nonetheless. She claims that in each case when subordinate clauses are used in time iconic order, 'the use of a subordinate clause allows the writer to accomplish a text-creation goal *in addition* to the obvious one of maintaining a temporal line' (1987: 451).

In fact, the difference in the relative prominence of linear-ordering and subordination between the ancient and modern languages may explain why the ancient texts often appear to us 'unidiomatic'. Thompson explains that when only linear (time iconic) ordering is used, the result is unidiomatic. She says that 'a strictly linearly organized written narrative text would not only be boring, but hard to attend to' (1987: 451). But the appeal of non-linear (non-iconic) ordering is an acquired taste! Babylonian and Hittite (as well as other ancient Semitic and Indo-European languages) used linear ordering much more extensively, because they lacked some of the mechanisms of subordination that are used by modern European languages. The sparser use of subordination meant greater reliance on time iconicity. It is for this reason that the narrative structure of these ancient languages often seems to us unidiomatic, and indeed sometimes 'boring' and 'hard to attend to'.[70]

11.5. The role of writing and literacy

I suggested in this chapter that the development of finite complementation and the extension in its use may be seen as an adaptation to the increasing complexity of communicative patterns. The relation of this development to writing and literacy is an obvious and important question which has so far not been mentioned at all. This section argues very briefly that although the significance of writing is unquestionable, the developments which we have followed cannot simply be dismissed as a result of the difference between spoken and written language.

First, it is important to stress that the developments which were examined in the previous chapters represent real changes in the spoken idiom. One

[70] I am not expressing a very original sentiment here. In 1892, in an article entitled 'The order of the sentence in the Assyrian historical inscriptions', a certain Lester Bradner, Jr., Ph.D. had the following to say about the subject: 'And one cannot fail to note that the spirit of Assyrian cares little for subordinate ideas. Coördination is the rule, to an extent which grows rather tiresome to modern ears.' (*Hebraica*, vol. 8, p. 5)

sometimes hears claims that the paucity of subordinate structures in ancient texts is not a feature of the language itself, but rather stems from the stylized nature of the texts that have been preserved. While this claim may have some validity for the classical Indo-European languages, it is absurd in the case of Babylonian. This study was based mainly on a large corpus of letters, whose style was explained in detail in §3.1. The letters were written in a colloquial style, as close to the spoken language as we can hope to reach in any type of text. More importantly, they form a stable genre across two millennia of history. The developments which were outlined for Babylonian thus represent real changes in the language, not changes between styles or genres.

To what extent are these historical developments influenced by writing and literacy? In order to tackle this question, I think it is helpful to differentiate between 'direct' and 'indirect' correlates of writing. The indirect correlates are the pressures that writing exerts on language through its influence on the structure of society, and thus on communication patterns. The direct correlates are the intrinsic linguistic features of written communication, which distinguish it from spoken communication. I suggest that whereas the vital indirect influence of writing on language is unquestionable, the role of direct influence is less obvious, especially in ancient Mesopotamia.

The advent of writing was probably the most significant factor in the evolution of civilization in the past five thousand years. The vital role of writing in the development of complex societies has been demonstrated, perhaps most famously, in the works of Goody (1977, 1986, 1987). It was only through the possibilities of organization afforded by writing that societies like the one that emerged in Mesopotamia could attain (and maintain) their level of complexity. The 'increasing complexity of communicative needs', which I mentioned in previous sections, thus crucially depends on writing. But this type of dependence is indirect. Writing enables the development of more complex societies, and the increasing complexity of communicative needs in such societies can influence language itself.

When we consider the direct influence of writing on the developments outlined in this study, the situation appears less clear. To what extent is the development of subordinate structures a direct result of the characteristics of written communication? It is well known that spoken and written languages differ in their use of subordination. Written English texts use subordination much more frequently than spoken registers, as has been documented quantitatively by Chafe (1982, 1985) and Biber (1995).[71] Some scholars have even viewed the advent of literacy as the sole reason for the appearance of subordination in a language (Kalmár 1985).

[71] For discussion of the linguistic differences between written and spoken language in general, see for example Olson et al. (1985), Tannen (1982, 1984), Harris and Campbell (1995: 308–10), Perkins (1992: 81–90).

Nevertheless, it seems far from clear that the direct influence of written communication should be seen as the only reason, or even the main reason, for the changes outlined in previous chapters. To start with, we know that subordination exists also in languages which have never been written. It should also be remembered that the developments examined in this study do not describe the 'emergence of subordination'. They relate to the emergence of one particular strategy of subordination (finite complementation), and its expansion at the expense of other strategies of inter-clausal cohesion. Moreover, recent research has come to see the difference between spoken and written communication not as a simple dichotomy, but rather as a cluster of differences between registers. Biber (1995: 7) sums up this view as follows:

> The existence of . . . linguistic characteristics particular to written exposition can be attributed to the cumulative influence of three major communicative factors: . . .
>
> (1) Communicative purpose. Written expository registers have communicative purposes different from those found in most other registers: to convey information about non-immediate (often abstract) referents with little overt acknowledgement of the thoughts or feelings of the addressor or the addressee . . . Most spoken registers (and many written registers) are more personal and immediately situated in purpose.
>
> (2) Physical relation between addressor and addressee. Spoken language is commonly produced in face-to-face situations that permit extensive interaction, opportunity for clarification, and reliance on paralinguistic channels to communicate meaning. Written language is typically produced by writers who are separated in space (and time) from their readers, resulting in a greater reliance on the linguistic channel by itself to communicate meaning.
>
> (3) Production circumstances. The written mode provides extensive opportunity for careful, deliberate production; it can be revised and edited repeatedly before the text is considered complete. Spoken language is typically produced on-line, with speakers formulating words and expressions as they think of ideas.

On the extreme ends of the scale, some written registers are abstract, separated in space and time from the addressee, and the result of careful deliberation, whereas some spoken registers are spontaneous, informal, personal, and deal with simple everyday topics. Nevertheless, as Biber (1995: 7) stresses, other spoken registers may display many of the characteristic features of written registers, whereas some written registers may be hardly different from particular spoken registers. The Babylonian letters are a good example of such a written register. The letters mostly deal with everyday situations, in simple informal language. They do not deal with abstract ideas. In terms of production circumstances, the letters are generally dictated to quick and able scribes, and they often display very obvious spontaneity.

On the other hand, the legal situations which I used to exemplify the advantages of finite complementation are essentially oral in Mesopotamia. Literacy in Mesopotamia was restricted to a small set of scribes, and writing was used for specific local functions. Although there are scribes in judicial proceedings who make records for future reference, the judges and the participants are normally illiterate. When written evidence has to be presented to the judges (for example, if previous contracts have to be consulted) this evidence is read aloud. The phrase 'the judges heard the tablet' is normally used. (On the restricted role of writing in legal procedures see Kienast 1996.) Nevertheless, these legal situations are very formal. Production is probably much more deliberately planned than in normal conversation. More complex statements have to be made, with a high degree of detail, and with less reliance on context. This is why these oral situations were useful in demonstrating the motivation for the development of a more 'powerful' linguistic mechanism.

The legal language shows that the motivation for the development and expansion of finite complementation is not restricted to written communication. The advantages of finite complementation over the alternative strategies can be manifested just as well in some spoken registers. When we also consider that only a fraction of the population in Mesopotamia was literate, it becomes difficult to maintain that the developments in Babylonian depended directly on the use of written communication. Of course, this does not mean that written communication played no direct role in the linguistic developments at all. Written communication may have been a factor, but not necessarily a crucial one.

11.6. Conclusion

I have claimed that finite complementation is a more powerful structural mechanism than parataxis and infinitive complementation, because it is better at dealing with more complex contexts. I have also suggested that this fact may explain the developments that we have followed in Babylonian in the previous chapters. Before elaborating this point further, perhaps a few caveats are required.

First, finite complementation is not necessarily the most effective strategy in all circumstances. In some contexts (especially in 'control' constructions, and with simpler propositions), infinitive complementation is clearly more efficient. Moreover, I do not wish to imply a fanatic type of linguistic determinism, which views the development of language as the relentless weeding out of less efficient constructions, and the unfailing ascent of more powerful and efficient structures. The complexity of the language system, and the diversity of the functional pressures which propel it in different directions, ensure that such crude causality is bound to fail. Indeed, language change has defied all attempts to tie it to the straitjacket of any single overriding principle.

Even some elements of the development we have followed in Babylonian can in fact demonstrate the weakness of a simplistic principle of efficiency. We saw that in the Neo-Babylonian period, the use of infinitive complementation declined drastically, even with manipulative verbs. Infinitive complements (like

'I told you to go') seem by all accounts to be the most effective strategy for manipulation. Yet in Neo-Babylonian, these structures almost entirely disappeared, and were replaced by a construction which seems much more unwieldy (the quotative construction). Thus, although the general direction of the development that we have followed in Babylonian is mirrored in many other languages, I do not want to imply that every detail of this development stems from universal principles, and that no changes in different directions are ever possible. In the history of English, for example, infinitival complements have gained some ground at the expense of finite complements (Rohdenburg 1995).

Bearing all these caveats in mind, I suggest nevertheless that the developments in Babylonian, and their parallels in many other languages, are unlikely to be entirely coincidental. I believe that the late emergence of finite complementation and the steady expansion in its use during the historical time are related to the increased complexity of communicative patterns.

Some languages (such as Old Akkadian and Old Hittite, but also languages spoken today, such as Dyirbal) seem to manage fairly happily without finite complementation. Before finite complements had emerged in Old Akkadian and Old Hittite, the alternative strategies in the FDC (parataxis and non-finite complementation) provided a coherent system of inter-clausal cohesion. This system relied more heavily than that of modern European languages on time iconicity to achieve inter-clausal cohesion, and this is the reason why the narrative structure of these languages may often sound to us unidiomatic.

Although languages can manage without finite complementation, I argued nevertheless that the alternative strategies are less effective than finite complementation in expressing more elaborate propositions. It is of course simplistic to claim that *just because* a construction is useful, it will emerge. The structural changes that gave birth to finite complements in Akkadian may occur at any given time, but may also never occur at all. Nevertheless, such changes are surely more likely to occur (and to be carried through to completion) in certain communicative environments than in others. (One obvious reason for this is that the source constructions may be used in the 'bridging contexts' more frequently in one environment than in another.) The development of more complex patterns of communication provided an environment in which the emergence of finite complements was more probable. Moreover, once finite complements did emerge, the more complex communicative environment encouraged the extension of their use into more areas in which only the alternative constructions had been available before.

In this light, the developments that we have followed may be seen as an adaptation to the emergence of more complex communicative patterns, which must have accompanied the growth of complex societies in the Near East and elsewhere. We may perhaps use the metaphor of technology to think about these developments. Structures such as finite complementation may be likened to linguistic 'tools' or 'technology'. The cognitive ability to handle finite complementation must have already been a feature of the human brain in the more distant past. But in the development of human society, tools and technological practice lag behind cognitive potential (Renfrew 1996). The appearance of the actual mechanisms of finite complementation, the linguistic 'technology', seems to be a recent feature in the history of many languages. I suggest that the most likely reason why this 'tool' did not develop before was that the simpler communicative environment was less favourable for such a development in earlier times.

Glossary of a few linguistic terms

(Based on the *Oxford Concise Dictionary of Linguistics*, by P. H. Matthews (1997), by kind permission of the author.)

Note: For the terms '(sentential) complement' and 'complementation', see detailed discussion in §2.1.

bleaching Change by which the meaning of a word becomes increasingly unspecific. Typically, therefore, in instances of grammaticalization: e.g. the meaning of French *pas* (from Latin *passus*, 'step, pace') was 'bleached' as it developed into a mark of negation: (*ne* . . .) *pas* 'not'.

cline (gradience.) A series of instances intermediate between two categories or constructions.

control Relation or principle by which, in a language like English, an element in a larger clause supplies the subject of a non-finite verb subordinate to it. E.g. in *I promised* [*to leave*], the subject of [*to leave*] is supplied by *I* as the subject of the main clause; in *I asked Mary* [*to leave*], by its object *Mary*.

embedding The inclusion of one clause or sentence in another.

factive (Verb etc.) whose use commits a speaker to the truth of a subordinate proposition. E.g. *know*: to say *She doesn't know that it has stopped raining* is to commit oneself to the truth of 'It has stopped raining'. *Think*, by contrast, is non-factive: one makes no such commitment if one says *She thinks it has stopped raining*.

grammaticalization The process by which, in the history of a language, a unit with lexical meaning changes into one with grammatical meaning. E.g. in Italian *ho mangiato* 'I-have eaten', a form that was in Latin a full verb ('to have, possess') has been grammaticalized as an auxiliary (*ho*). In *mangerò* 'I-will-eat', the same form, first combined as an auxiliary with an infinitive (lit. 'to-eat I-have), has further changed to an inflectional ending (*-ò*).

iconicity Principle by which semantic relations are reflected in the formal patterns by which they are realized. [In this book, used only in the specific sense of 'time iconicity': the ordering of clauses according to the order of their occurrence in reality (e.g. in *veni, vidi, vici*).]

raising A syntactic process by which a noun phrase or other element is moved from a subordinate clause into the structure of the larger clause that includes it.

semantic role Usually of the roles of nouns, etc. in relation to a verb: e.g. in *I can feel it in my chest* the semantic roles of *I*, *it*, and *in my chest* might be those of experiencer, theme, and locative.

References

Al-A'dami, K. (1967), 'Old Babylonian Letters from ed-Der', *Sumer*, 23: 151–65.

Aro, J. (1955), *Studien zur mittelbabylonischen Grammatik* (Studia Orientalia 20; Helsinki).

—— (1961), *Die akkadischen Infinitivkonstruktionen* (Studia Orientalia 26; Helsinki).

Baumgartner, W. (1974), *Hebräisches und aramäisches Lexicon zum Alten Testament* (Leiden: E. J. Brill).

Beaulieu, P. A. (1993), 'An Episode in the Fall of Babylon to the Persians', *Journal of Near Eastern Studies*, 52/4: 241–61.

Behrens, H., et al. (eds.) (1989), *Dumu-e$_2$-dub-ba-a: Studies in Honor of Åke W. Sjöberg* (Occasional Publications of the Samuel Noah Kramer Fund 11; Philadelphia: University Museum).

Bernhardt, I., and Aro, J. (1958), 'Mittelbabylonische Briefe in der Hilprecht-Sammlung', *Wissenschaftliche Zeitschrift der Friedrich-Schiller Universität Jena*, 8–4/5: 565–74.

Biber, D. (1995), 'Cross-Linguistic Evidence Concerning the Linguistic Correlates of Literacy', in B. Wårvik, S. K. Tanskanen, and R. Hiltunen (eds.), *Organization in Discourse* (Anglicana Turkuensia 14; Turku: University of Turku), 1–13.

Biggs, R. (1965), 'A Letter from Kassite Nippur', *Journal of Cuneiform Studies*, 19: 95–102.

Buccellati, G. (1996), *A Structural Grammar of Babylonian* (Wiesbaden: Harrassowitz).

Chafe, W. L. (1982), 'Integration and Involvement in Speaking, Writing and Oral Literature', in Tannen (1982), 35–53.

—— (1985), 'Linguistic Differences Produced by Differences between Speaking and Writing', in Olson et al. (1985), 105–23.

Charpin, D., et al. (1988), *Archives épistolaires de Mari* 1/2 (Archives royales de Mari 26/2; Paris: Éditions Recherche sur les Civilisations).

Christol, A. (1989), 'Prolepse et syntax indo-européenne', in G. Calboli (ed.), *Subordination and Other Topics in Latin* (Amsterdam: John Benjamins), 65–89.

Cocquerillat, D. (1968), *Palmeraies et cultures de l'Eanna d'Uruk* (559–520) (Ausgrabungen der deutschen Forschungsgemeinschaft in Uruk-Warka, Band 8; Berlin: Gebr. Mann).

Cole, S. W. (1996), *Nippur IV, The Early Neo-Babylonian Governor's Archive from Nippur* (Oriental Institute of Chicago Publications 114).

—— and Machinist, P. (1998), *Letters from Priests to the Kings Esarhaddon and Assurbanipal* (State Archives of Assyria 13; Helsinki: Helsinki University Press).

Comrie, B. (1992), 'Before Complexity', in Hawkins and Gell-Mann (1992), 193–212.

—— and Horie, K. (1995), 'Complement Clauses Versus Relative Clauses: Some Khmer Evidence', in W. Abraham, T. Givón, and S. Thompson (eds.), *Discourse Grammar and Typology* (Amsterdam: John Benjamins), 65–75.

Cornwall, W. (1952), 'Two Letters from Dilmun', *Journal of Cuneiform Studies*, 6: 137–45.

Cotticelli-Kurras, P. (1995), 'Hethitische Konstruktionen mit *verba dicendi* und *sentiendi*', *Studia Mediterranea* (Pavia: Gianni Iuculano Editore), 9: 87–100.

Cristofaro, S. (1998*a*), 'Grammaticalization and Clause Linkage Strategies', in A. G. Ramat and P. J. Hopper (eds.), *The Limits of Grammaticalization* (Amsterdam: John Benjamins), 59–88.

—— (1998*b*), 'Deranking and Balancing in Different Subordination Relations: A Typological Study', *Sprachtypologie und Universalienforschung*, 51: 3–42.

Croft, W. (1998), 'Syntax in Perspective: Typology and Cognition', unpublished MS (*Deutsche Gesellschaft für Sprachwissenschaft* Summerschool, Mainz, September 1998).

Cuzzolin, P. (1994*a*), *Sull'origine della construzione* dicere quod: *Aspetti sintattici e semantici* (Firenze: La Nuova Italia).

—— (1994*b*), 'On Sentential Complementation after *verba affectuum*', in J. Herman (ed.), *Linguistic Studies on Latin* (Amsterdam: John Benjamins), 201–10.

Dalley, S. (ed.) (1998), *The Legacy of Mesopotamia* (Oxford: Oxford University Press).

de Vaan, J. M. C. T. (1995), *»Ich bin eine Schwertklinge des Königs« Die Sprache des Bēlibni* (Alter Orient und Altes Testament 242; Kevelaer: Butzon & Bercker).

Dietrich, M. (1969), 'Untersuchungen zur Grammatik des Neubabylonischen: Die neubabylonischen Subjunktionen', in *Lišān mithurti: Festschrift Wolfram Freiherr von Soden zum 19. VI. 1968 gewidmet von Schülern und Mitarbeitern* (Alter Orient und Altes Testament 1; Kevelaer: Butzon & Bercker), 65–99.

—— (1970), *Die Aramäer Südbabyloniens in der Sargonidenzeit* (Alter Orient und Altes Testament 7; Kevelaer: Butzon & Bercker).

——, Loretz, O., and Sanmartín, J. (eds.) (1976), *Die keilalphabetischen Texte aus Ugarit. Teil 1 Transkription* (Alter Orient und Altes Testament 24/1; Kevelaer: Butzon & Bercker).

Dixon, R. M. W. (1995), 'Complement Clauses and Complementation Strategies', in F. Palmer (ed.), *Grammar and Meaning* (Cambridge: Cambridge University Press), 175–220.

—— (1997), *The Rise and Fall of Languages* (Cambridge: Cambridge University Press).

Dombradi, E. (1996), *Die Darstellung des Rechtaustrags in den altbabylonischen Prozessurkunden* (2 vols.) (Freiburger Altorientalischen Studien 20; Stuttgart: Franz Steiner).

—— (1997), '*baqāru*: Ein Fall von lexikalischem Transfer infolge von Plurilingualismus?', *Die Welt des Orients*, 28: 31–57.

Dryer, M. S. (1980), 'The Positional Tendencies of Sentential Noun Phrases in Universal Grammar', *Canadian Journal of Linguistics*, 25: 123–95.

Ebeling, E. (1930–4), *Neubabylonische Briefe aus Uruk* (vols. I–IV) (Berlin: im Verlage des Herausgebers).

—— (1949), *Neubabylonische Briefe* (Munich: Bayerische Akademie der Wissenschaften).

Edzard, D. O. (1967), 'Das sumerische Verbalmorphem /ed/ in den alt- und neusumerischen Texten', in *Heidelberger Studien zum Alten Orient, Adam Falkenstein Festschrift* (Wiesbaden: Harrassowitz), 29–62.

—— (1968), *Sumerische Rechtsurkunden des III. Jahrtausends, aus der Zeit vor der III. Dynastie von Ur* (Munich: Bayerische Akademie der Wissenschaften).

—— (1970), *Altbabylonische Rechts- und Wirtschaftsurkunden aus Tell ed-Der im Iraq Museum, Baghdad* (Munich: Bayerische Akademie der Wissenschaften).

—— (1977), 'Der gegenwärtige Stand der Akkadistik und ihre Aufgaben', *Zeitschrift der Deutschen Morgenländischen Gesellschaft*, Supplement III. 1: 47–51.

EDZARD, D. O. (1990), 'Überblick über die sumerische Literatur', in D. O. Edzard et al. (ed.), *Reallexikon der Assyriologie und vorderasiatischen Archäologie* (Berlin: de Gruyter), VII: 36–48.

FALKENSTEIN, A. (1956–7), *Die neusumerischen Gerichtsurkunden* (parts I–III) (Munich: Bayerische Akademie der Wissenschaften).

—— (1963), 'Zu den Inschriftfunden der Grabung in Uruk-Warka 1960–1961', *Baghdader Mitteilungen*, 2: 1–82.

FINET, A. (1956), *L'Accadien des lettres de Mari* (Mémoires de l'Académie Royale de Belgique 51; Brussels).

FINKELSTEIN, J. (1965), 'Some New Misharum Material and its Implications', in *Studies in Honor of B. Landsberger on his Seventy-Fifth Birthday, April 21, 1965* (Assyriological Studies 16; Chicago: Oriental Institute of the University of Chicago), 235–8.

FISHER, O. (1992), 'Syntax', in N. Blake (ed.), *The Cambridge History of the English Language* (Cambridge: Cambridge University Press), II: 207–408.

FOLEY, W. A. (1997), *Anthropological Linguistics: An Introduction* (Oxford: Blackwell).

FORSTON, B. W. (1998), 'A New Study of Hittite *-wa(r)*', *Journal of Cuneiform Studies*, 50: 21–33.

FOSTER, B. R. (1990), 'Two Old Akkadian Documents', *Acta Sumerologica*, 12: 51–6.

FRAJZYNGIER, Z. (1991), 'The *de dicto* Domain in Language', in Traugott and Heine (1991), I: 219–51.

—— (1996), *Grammaticalization of the Complex Sentence, a Case Study in Chadic* (Amsterdam: John Benjamins).

FRAYNE, D. R. (1993), *The Royal Inscriptions of Mesopotamia: Sargonic and Gutian Periods* (Toronto: University of Toronto Press).

GARDINER, A. H. (1957), *Egyptian Grammar* (Oxford: Oxford University Press).

GELB, I. J. (1969), *Sequential Reconstruction of Proto-Akkadian* (Chicago: Oriental Institute of the University of Chicago).

—— (1984), '*šibût kušurrā'im*, Witnesses of the Indemnity', *Journal of Near Eastern Studies*, 43: 263–76.

—— and KIENAST, B. (1990), *Die altakkadischen Königsinschriften des Dritten Jahrtausends v. Chr.* (Stuttgart: Franz Steiner).

GENEE, I. (1998), *Sentential Complementation in a Functional Grammar of Irish* (The Hague: Holland Academic Graphics).

GIVÓN, T. (1980), 'The Binding Hierarchy and the Typology of Complements', *Studies in Language*, 4. 3: 333–77.

—— (1990), *Syntax: A Functional-Typological Introduction* (vol. II) (Amsterdam: John Benjamins).

—— (1991), 'The Evolution of Dependent Clause Morpho-Syntax in Biblical Hebrew', in Traugott and Heine (1991), II: 257–310.

GOETZE, A. (1958), 'Fifty Old Babylonian Letters from Harmal', *Sumer*, 14: 3–78.

GOLDENBERG, G. (1991), 'On Direct Speech and the Hebrew Bible', in K. Jongeling et al. (eds.), *Studies in Hebrew and Aramaic Syntax* (Leiden: E. J. Brill), 79–96.

GOODY, J. (1977), *The Domestication of the Savage Mind* (Cambridge: Cambridge University Press).

—— (1986), *The Logic of Writing and the Organization of Society* (Cambridge: Cambridge University Press).

—— (1987), *The Interface between the Written and the Oral* (Cambridge: Cambridge University Press).

Grimshaw, J. (1979), 'Complement Selection and the Lexicon', *Linguistic Inquiry*, 10. 2: 279–326.

Gurney, O. R. (1949), 'Texts from Dur-Kurigalzu', *Iraq*, 11: 131–42.

Haiman, J., and Thompson, S. A. (eds.) (1988), *Clause Combining in Grammar and Discourse* (Amsterdam: John Benjamins).

Harris, A. C., and Campbell, L. (1995), *Historical Syntax in Cross-Linguistic Perspective* (Cambridge: Cambridge University Press).

Haspelmath, M. (1989), 'From Purposive to Infinitive – A Universal Path of Grammaticalization', *Folia Linguistica Historica*, 10: 287–310.

Hawkins, J., and Gell-Mann, M. (eds.) (1992), *The Evolution of Human Languages* (Redwood City: Addison-Wesley Publishing Company).

Heine, B., Claudi, U., and Hünnemeyer, F. (1991*a*), *Grammaticalization, a Conceptual Framework* (Chicago: University of Chicago Press).

—— —— —— (1991*b*), 'From Cognition to Grammar – Evidence from African Languages', in Traugott and Heine (1991), I: 149–87.

—— and Reh, M. (1988), 'On the Use of the Nominal Strategy for Coding Complex Complements in some African Languages', in M. Jazayeri and W. Winter (eds.), *Languages and Cultures* (Berlin: Mouton de Gruyter), 245–57.

Hetzron, R. (ed.) (1997), *The Semitic Languages* (London: Routledge).

Hewitt, B. G., and Crisp, S. R. (1986), 'Speech Reporting in the Caucasus', in F. Coulmas (ed.), *Direct and Indirect Speech* (Berlin: Mouton de Gruyter), 121–43.

Hoftijzer, J., and Jongeling, K. (1995), *Dictionary of the North-West Semitic Inscriptions* (Leiden: E. J. Brill).

Holland, G. B. (1984), 'Subordination and Relativization in Early Indo-European', in C. Brugman and M. Macaulay (eds.), *Proceedings of the Tenth Annual Meeting of the Berkeley Linguistics Society*, 609–22.

Hopper, P. J. (1991), 'On some Principles of Grammaticization', in Traugott and Heine (1991), I: 17–35.

—— and Thompson, S. A. (1980), 'Transitivity in Grammar and Discourse', *Language*, 56: 251–99.

—— and Traugott, E. C. (1993), *Grammaticalization* (Cambridge: Cambridge University Press).

Horn, G. M. (1985), 'Raising and Complementation', *Linguistics*, 23: 813–50.

Huehnergard, J. (1997), *A Grammar of Akkadian* (Atlanta: Scholars Press).

Hueter, G. (1996), 'Grammatical Studies in the Akkadian Dialects of Babylon and Uruk 556–500 bc', D.Phil. dissertation (University of Oxford).

Hug, V. (1993), *Altaramäische Grammatik der Texte des 7. und 6 Jh.s v. Chr.* (Heidelberg: Heidelberger Orientverlag).

Joseph, B. D. (1983), *The Synchrony and Diachrony of the Balkan Infinitive: A Study in Areal, General, and Historical Linguistics* (Cambridge: Cambridge University Press).

—— (1992), 'Diachronic Perspectives on Control', in R. K. Larson et al. (eds.), *Control and Grammar* (Studies in Linguistics and Philosophy 48; Dordrecht: Kluwer), 195–234.

Justus, C. F. (1979), 'Hittite *ištamaš* – "hear": Some Syntactic Implications', *Münchener Studien zur Sprachwissenschaft*, 38: 93–115.

Justus, C. F. (1980*a*), 'Implications of Pre-Complementizers with Hittite *šak-/šek-* "know"', in E. Traugott (ed.), *Papers from the 4th International Conference on Historical Linguistics* (Amsterdam: John Benjamins), 97–106.

—— (1980*b*), 'Typological Symmetries and Asymmetries in Hittite and IE Complementation', in Ramat (1980), 183–206.

—— (1981), 'Visible Sentences in Cuneiform Hittite', *Visible Language*, 15. 4: 373–408.

Kalmár, I. (1985), 'Are There Really No Primitive Languages?', in Olson et al. (1985), 148–66.

Khan, G. (1988), *Studies in Semitic Syntax* (Oxford: Oxford University Press).

Kienast, B. (1978), *Die altbabylonischen Briefe und Urkunden aus Kisurra* (Freiburger Altorientalische Studien 2; Wiesbaden: Franz Steiner).

—— (1996), 'Mündlichkeit und Schriftlichkeit im keilschriftlichen Rechtswesen', *Zeitschrift für altorientalische und biblische Rechtsgeschichte*, 2: 114–30.

—— and Volk, K. (1995), *Die sumerischen und akkadischen Briefe des III. Jahrtausends* (Freiburger Altorientalische Studien 19; Stuttgart: Franz Steiner).

Klein, E. (1987), *A Comprehensive Etymological Dictionary of the Hebrew Language* (Jerusalem: Carta).

Knudtzon, J. (1915 (1964)), *Die El-Amarna Tafeln* (Aalen: Otto Zeller Verlagbuchhandlung).

Koewenberg, N. J. C. (1997), *Gemination in the Akkadian Verb* (Studia Semitica Neerlandica; Assen: Van Gorcum).

Kogan, L., and Korotayev, A. (1997), 'Sayhadic (Epigraphic South Arabian)', in Hetzron (1997), 220–41.

Kortmann, B. (1997), *Adverbial Subordination* (Berlin: Mouton de Gruyter).

—— (1998), 'The Evolution of Adverbial Subordinators in Europe', in M. S. Schmid et al. (eds.), *Historical Linguistics 1997* (Amsterdam: John Benjamins), 213–28.

Kraus, F. R. (ed.) (1964–94), *Altbabylonische Briefe in Umschrift und Übersetzung*, I–XIII (from vol. XIII under the editorship of K. R. Veenhof) (Leiden: E. J. Brill).

—— (1975), 'Einführung in die Briefe in altakkadischer Sprache', *Ex Oriente Lux*, 24: 74–104.

—— (1987), *Sonderformen akkadischer Parataxe: Die Koppelungen* (Amsterdam: North-Holland).

Labov, W. (1972), *Language in the Inner City* (Oxford: Blackwell).

Langacker, R. W. (1987), *Foundations of Cognitive Grammar, Vol. I: Theoretical Prerequisites* (Stanford: Stanford University Press).

Lass, R. (1997), *Historical Linguistics and Language Change* (Cambridge: Cambridge University Press).

Leemans, W. F. (1960), *Foreign Trade in the Old Babylonian Period* (Leiden: E. J. Brill).

Lehmann, C. (1988), 'Towards a Typology of Clause Linkage', in Haiman and Thompson (1988), 181–225.

Lehmann, W. P. (1980), 'The Reconstruction of Non-Simple Sentences in PIE', in Ramat (1980), 113–44.

Leichty, E. (1989), 'Feet of Clay', in Behrens et al. (1989), 349–55.

Limet, H. (1975), 'Le Morphème suffixe /-a/ en sumérien', *Revue d'assyriologie*, 69: 5–18.

Lipinski, E. (1997), *Semitic Languages. Outline of a Comparative Grammar* (Orientalia Lovaniensia Analecta 80; Leuven: Uitgeverij Peeters).

Lord, C. (1993), *Historical Change in Serial Verb Constructions* (Amsterdam: John Benjamins).

Luraghi, S. (1990), *Old Hittite Sentence Structure* (London: Routledge).

—— (1997), *Hittite* (Languages of the World Series; Munich: Lincom Europa).

Lutz, H. (1919), *Selected Sumerian and Babylonian Texts* (Publications of the Babylonian section 1/2; Philadelphia: University of Pennsylvania Museum).

Matisoff, J. A. (1991), 'Areal and Universal Dimensions of Grammatization in Lahu', in Traugott and Heine (1991), II: 383–453.

Matras, Y. (1998), 'Utterance Modifiers and Universals of Grammatical Borrowing', *Linguistics*, 36 (2): 281–332.

Matthews, P. H. (1981), *Syntax* (Cambridge: Cambridge University Press).

—— (1997), *Oxford Concise Dictionary of Linguistics* (Oxford: Oxford University Press).

Matthiessen, C., and Thompson, S. A. (1988), 'The Structure of Discourse and "Subordination"', in Haiman and Thompson (1988), 275–329.

Michalowski, P. (1993), *Letters from Early Mesopotamia* (Atlanta: Scholars Press).

Miller, C. (1995), 'Discourse Functions of the Quotative Frames in Biblical Hebrew Narrative', in W. Bodine (ed.), *Discourse Analysis of Biblical Literature* (Atlanta: Scholars Press), 155–82.

Milner, J. C. (1980), 'La Prolepse en grec ancien', *Lalies*, 1: 39–52.

Mithun, M. (1984), 'How to Avoid Subordination', *Proceedings of the Tenth Annual Meeting of the Berkeley Linguistics Society*, 493–509.

Moore, E. W. (1935), *Neo-Babylonian Business and Administrative Documents* (Ann Arbor: University of Michigan Press).

Moran, W. L. (1992), *The Amarna Letters* (Baltimore: Johns Hopkins University Press).

Moscati, S., Spitaler, A., Ullendorff, E., and von Soden, W. (1964), *An Introduction to the Comparative Grammar of the Semitic Languages* (Wiesbaden: Harrassowitz).

Mühlhäusler, P. (1985), *Handbook of Tok Pisin (New Guinea Pidgin)* (Pacific Linguistics, Series C, no. 70; Canberra: The Australian National University).

Munro, P. (1982), 'On the Transitivity of "say" Verbs', in P. J. Hopper and S. A. Thompson (eds.), *Studies in Transitivity* (Syntax and Semantics 15; New York: Academic Press), 301–18.

Noonan, M. (1985), 'Complementation', in T. Shopen (ed.), *Language Typology and Syntactic Description* (Cambridge: Cambridge University Press), II: 42–140.

Oates, J. (1986), *Babylon* (revised edition) (London: Thames and Hudson).

Olson, D. R., Torrance, N., and Hildyard, A. (eds.) (1985), *Literacy, Language, and Learning: The Nature and Consequences of Reading and Writing* (Cambridge: Cambridge University Press).

Oppenheim, A. L. (1964), *Ancient Mesopotamia: Portrait of a Dead Civilization* (Chicago: University of Chicago Press).

Panhuis, D. (1984), 'Prolepsis in Greek as a Discourse Strategy', *Glotta*, 62: 26–39.

Parker, S. B. (ed.) (1997), *Ugaritic Narrative Poetry* (Atlanta: Scholars Press).

Parpola, S. (1993), *Letters from Assyrian and Babylonian Scholars* (State Archives of Assyria 10; Helsinki: Helsinki University Press).

PEDERSÉN, O. (1989), 'Some Morphological Aspects of Sumerian and Akkadian Linguistic Areas', in Behrens et al. (1989), 429–38.

PERKINS, R. D. (1992), *Deixis, Grammar and Culture* (Amsterdam: John Benjamins).

PUSTET, R. (1999), 'Echo Pronominalization and Complementation in Lakota', paper delivered at the International Symposium on Grammaticalisation, Potsdam.

RADAU, H. (1908), *Letters to Cassite Kings* (The Babylonian Expedition, Series A: Cuneiform Texts, vol. XVII, part 1; Philadelphia: Dept. of Archaeology, University of Pennsylvania).

RAMAT, P. (ed.) (1980), *Linguistic Reconstruction and Indo-European Syntax* (Amsterdam: John Benjamins).

RENFREW, C. (1996), 'The Sapient Behaviour Paradox: How to Test for Potential', in P. Mellars and K. Gibson, *Modelling the Early Human Mind* (Cambridge: McDonald Institute), 11–14.

ROAF, M. (1990), *Cultural Atlas of Mesopotamia and the Ancient Near East* (New York: Facts On File).

ROBERT (1992), *Dictionnaire historique de la langue française* (ed. A. Rey) (Paris: Dictionnaires Le Robert).

ROHDENBURG, G. (1995), 'On the Replacement of Finite Complement Clauses by Infinitives in English', *English Studies*, 4: 367–88.

ROMAINE, S., and LANGE, D. (1991), 'The Use of *like* as a Marker of Reported Speech: A Case of Grammaticalization in Progress', *American Speech*, 66. 3: 227–79.

RÖMER, W. H. P. (1994), *Die Sumerologie* (Alter Orient und Altes Testament 238; Kevelaer: Butzon & Bercker).

ROTH, M. T. (1997), *Law Collections from Mesopotamia and Asia Minor* (2nd edition) (Atlanta: Scholars Press).

SASSON, J. M. (ed.) (1995), *Civilizations of the Ancient Near East*, I–IV (New York: Scribners).

SAUZET, P. (1989), 'Topicalisation et prolepse en occitan', *Revue des langues romanes*, 93: 235–73.

SCHORR, M. (1913), *Urkunden des altbabylonischen Zivil- und Prozessrechts* (Vorderasiatische Bibliothek 5; Leipzig: J. C. Hinrichs).

SIVAN, D. (1997), *A Grammar of the Ugaritic Language* (Leiden: E. J. Brill).

SODEN, W. VON (1952), 'Zu den Amarnabriefen aus Babylon und Assur', *Orientalia*, 21: 426–34.

—— (1965–81), *Akkadisches Handwörterbuch* (Wiesbaden: Harrassowitz).

—— (1995), *Grundriss der akkadischen Grammatik* (3rd edition) (Rome: Pontificium Institutum Biblicum).

STEINKELLER, P. (1989), *Sale Documents of the Ur-III-Period* (Freiburger Altorientalische Studien 17; Stuttgart: Franz Steiner).

STOLA, R. (1972), 'Zur Subjunktion *kīma* im Altbabylonischen und Altassyrischen', *Wiener Zeitschrift für die Kunde des Morgenlandes*, 63–4: 69–104.

STOLZ, C., and STOLZ T. (1996), 'Funktionswortentlehnung in Mesoamerika', *Sprachtypologie und Universalienforschung*, 49: 86–123.

STRECK, M. P. (1995), *Zahl und Zeit: Grammatik der Numeralia und des Verbalsystems im Spätbabylonischen* (Groningen: STYX Publications).

—— (1998), Review of Buccellati (1996), *Archiv für Orientforschung*, 44/45: 314–25.

SWEENEY, D. (1986), 'The Nominal Object Clause of Verbs of Perception in Non-Literary Late Egyptian', in G. Englund and P. J. Frandsen (eds.), *Crossroad* (Copenhagen: Carsten Niebuhr Institute of Ancient Near East Studies), 337–73.

TANNEN, D. (1982), *Spoken and Written Language: Exploring Orality and Literacy* (Norwood: Ablex).

—— (ed.) (1984), *Coherence in Spoken and Written Discourse* (Norwood: Ablex).

—— (ed.) (1986), 'Introducing Constructed Dialogue in Greek and American Conversational and Literary Narrative', in F. Coulmas (ed.), *Direct and Indirect Speech* (Berlin: Mouton de Gruyter), 311–32.

TESTEN, D. D. (1998), *Parallels in Semitic Linguistics* (Leiden: E. J. Brill).

THOMASON, S. G., and KAUFMAN, T. (1988), *Language Contact, Creolization, and Genetic Linguistics* (Berkeley: University of California Press).

THOMPSON, S. A. (1987), '"Subordination" and Narrative Event Structure', in R. S. Tomlin (ed.), *Coherence and Grounding in Discourse* (Amsterdam: John Benjamins), 435–54.

THOMSEN, M. L. (1984), *The Sumerian Language* (Copenhagen: Akademisk Forlag).

TOURATIER, C. (1980), 'L'Accusatif proleptique en latin', *Lalies*, 1: 53–6.

TRAUGOTT, E. C., and HEINE, B. (eds.) (1991), *Approaches to Grammaticalization* (2 vols.) (Amsterdam: John Benjamins).

VEENHOF, K. R. (1986), 'Two Akkadian Auxiliary Verbs', in H. Vanstiphout (ed.), *Scripta Signa Vocis* (Groningen: Forsten), 235–51.

WALKER, C. B. F. (1987), *Cuneiform* (Reading the Past; London: British Museum).

WALTERS, S. D. (1970), *Water for Larsa* (Yale Near Eastern Researches 4; New Haven: Yale University Press).

WASCHOW, H. (1936), *Babylonische Briefe aus der Kassitenzeit* (Mitteilungen der Altorientalischen Gesellschaft 10, no. 1; Leipzig: Harrassowitz).

WATERMAN, L. (1930), *Royal Correspondence of the Assyrian Empire* (Ann Arbor: University of Michigan Press).

WEIL, H. (1978) [1869], *The Order of Words in the Ancient Languages Compared with that of the Modern Languages* (Amsterdam: John Benjamins).

WESTENHOLZ, A. (1988), 'Personal Names in Ebla and in Pre-Sargonic Babylonia', in A. Archi (ed.), *Eblaite Personal Names and Semitic Name-Giving* (Archivi Reali di Ebla, Studi 1; Rome: Missione archeologica italiana in Siria), 99–118.

—— (1999), 'The Old Akkadian Period: History and Culture', in W. Sallaberger and A. Westenholz (eds.), *Mesopotamien: Akkade-Zeit und Ur III-Zeit* (Orbis Biblicus et Orientalis 160/3; Freiburg (Schweiz): Universitätsverlag), 17–120.

WHITING, R. M. (1987), *Old Babylonian Letters from Tell Asmar* (Chicago: Oriental Institute of the University of Chicago).

WOODINGTON, N. (1982), 'A Grammar of the Neo-Babylonian Letters of the Kuyunjik Collection', Ph.D. dissertation (Yale University).

WOOLFORD, E. (1979), 'The Developing Complementizer System of Tok Pisin: Syntactic Change in Progress', in K. Hill (ed.), *The Genesis of Language* (Ann Arbor: Karoma), 108–24.

ZEWI, T. (1996), 'Subordinate Nominal Sentences Involving Prolepsis in Biblical Hebrew', *Journal of Semitic Studies*, 41: 1–15.

Index of Subjects

Index of Quoted Texts

Note: line numbers denote the first quoted line, not the whole range.